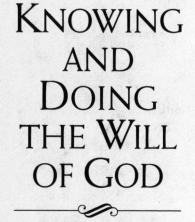

Experiencing God

Knowing and Doing the Will of God

Henry T. Blackaby & Claude V. King

LIFEWAY PRESS
NASHVILLE, TENNESSEE

LifeWay Press
127 Ninth Avenue, North
Nashville, Tennessee 37234

ABOUT THE COVER

Mike Wimmer has been described as "Norman's own Norman Rockwell." Mike has become one of the nation's leading illustrators. He has done numerous book covers, movie posters, and images used in major national advertising campaigns. When he was asked to paint the portrait of Moses for Experiencing God, *Mike's extensive research, talent and commitment led to a classic rendition of the prophet's experience with God at the burning bush.*

(Prints of Mike Wimmer's painting, Experiencing God *are available for $29.95. Write Customer Service Center, 127 Ninth Avenue North, Nashville, Tennessee 37234 or call 1-800-458-2772 and ask for item # 7700-37.)*

PREFACE

When I first met and heard Henry Blackaby teach in 1986, I had no idea how God was going to use him to reorient my life and ministry. Yet, in the past four years, I have experienced some of the most radical changes of my life. Henry directed me to the Scriptures. He pointed me to biblical examples of people who experienced a powerful, loving, and personal God at work through them. He showed me how they came to know and do God's will. I felt as though scales fell from my eyes. God's plan to work through His people was so clear and simple. Why had I not seen it so clearly before?

Too often I had tried a method or formula for knowing God's will. I had tried to follow a set of steps to find God's will. My success record indicated that something was wrong. I felt empty, somewhat confused, frustrated, and unfulfilled in my ministry.

Henry's teaching caught my attention. He said that we do not find God's will; it is revealed. God always takes the initiative. He gave contemporary illustrations of how ordinary people and churches have experienced God work in personal, dramatic, and even miraculous ways. I thought about Paul's statement: "My message and my preaching were not with wise and persuasive words, but with a demonstration of the Spirit's power, so that your faith might not rest on men's wisdom, but on God's power" (1 Cor. 2:4-5). That is what I saw in Henry's teaching—a simple, biblical message coupled with a life through which God demonstrated His power. Henry always pointed me to my relationship to God. That was the key to my experience of God's power at work through me.

I studied the Scriptures. I prayed that God would teach me about Himself and His ways through experience not just theory. My life turned into an exciting adventure. My path of ministry has not always been so thrilling.

Following seminary in 1984, my wife and I resigned our jobs and moved to Gwinnett County, Georgia (near Atlanta). I sensed very strongly that God had called me to be a "tentmaking" church planter—one who provides his own financial support through a secular job and helps start new churches "free of charge." I had studied all the "right" books on church planting and church growth. I dreamed great dreams of what I was going to do for God. I spent 18 months developing my plans. Step-by-step I began to carry them out.

Six months later our furniture was still in storage. In the middle of a 2 1/2 percent unemployment rate, we had no jobs. Our savings were depleted, our checking account empty, and debts were mounting. There was not even the nucleus of a new church. Devastated, we moved back home to live with parents. Until recently, I did not know what was wrong.

I was still confident of my call to be a tentmaking church planter. The only job that I was offered was at the Sunday School Board as an editor. I could not imagine why God put me here behind a desk when so many new churches are needed.

Then I met Henry. He led me to a fresh understanding of knowing God and following Him. My local church association got a new director, James Powers. He had a burden for starting eight new churches by the year 2000. After prayer, I realized this was my opportunity to volunteer as a tentmaking church planter. The association extended a call for me to serve in that way as a volunteer. This time I would not try to work my own plans. I refused to dream my own dreams of what I would do for God.

We decided simply to share with churches the need to reach all people in our county with the gospel. We shared how new churches could be used of God to reach groups and areas that existing churches were not reaching. We talked about the wide variety of ways God might work to start a new church. Then we watched to see where God was at work so we could join Him.

After three months, I had a list of 14 places or people groups that might need a new church. Where did the list come from? A person would stop me after a meeting or church service and say, "God has given me a burden for a new church in . . . " or "Several people in our area feel like we need a new church for . . . " After two years, we have six new churches with full-time pastors and another group meeting in a home Bible study with plans to start the seventh new church. Our churches found out that God had far greater plans for us than we could dream.

God called people to serve and gave them a burden. God called churches to be the sponsors of the new missions. We did not have to find ways to motivate them. They were calling on us to equip them to do what God had called them to do. No individual was the key to the growth. No one church was the key. God did it through His people! We have come to know God more intimately in the past two years. We believe the best days are yet to come!

A Lesson Learned

God allowed me to follow my *own* plans in Georgia, and I failed miserably. He had an important lesson to teach me, and I chose to learn the hard way. I found that I could not plan or even dream how God might want to do His work. I found that my relationship to God was of supreme importance. I learned to love Him more dearly, to pray more faithfully, to trust Him fully, and to wait on Him with anticipation. When He was ready to use me, He would let me know. Then I would have to make the necessary adjustments and obey Him. Until then, I would watch and pray. His timing and His ways ALWAYS would be best and right.

I am praying that God will use this course to radically touch your life for the Kingdom's sake. His work in your life will far surpass all your plans and dreams. He will bring purpose and fulfillment to your life and ministry with overflowing joy. May the grace, joy, and peace of God be yours through Jesus Christ our living Lord. To Him be glory, now and forever.

Claude V. King

CONTENTS

THE AUTHORS

HENRY T. BLACKABY is Director of the Office of Prayer and Spiritual Awakening at the Home Mission Board of the Southern Baptist Convention. He traces his spiritual heritage back to four ministers in his family who attended Spurgeon's College during the Nineteenth Century. His father was a deacon and helped start churches in Canada.

Henry is a graduate of the University of British Columbia, Vancouver, Canada and Golden Gate Baptist Theological Seminary. He pastored a church in the Los Angeles area after seminary. Then he accepted a call to Faith Baptist Church in Saskatoon, Saskatchewan. He authored a book entitled *What the Spirit is Saying to the Churches* in which he recounts the moving activity of God in the midst of His people at Faith Baptist Church. During Henry's 12 years in Saskatoon this church helped to start 38 new churches and missions of the new churches.

Before coming to the Home Mission Board Henry served as Director of Missions in Vancouver, British Columbia. He has written for numerous publications and serves on the Bold Mission PRAYER Thrust committee of the Southern Baptist Convention. He has led conferences throughout the United States, Canada, and in Zambia and Austria. He provides consultative leadership for the development of prayer and spiritual awakening in the life of the Southern Baptist Convention in conjunction with SBC agencies and state, associational, and local church leadership.

His wife is the former Marilynn Sue Wells. They have five children: Richard, Thomas, Melvin, Norman, and Carrie. All five children have responded to God's call to church related ministry or missions.

CLAUDE V. KING is a design editor in the Adult Discipleship Training Section of the Discipleship Training Department, Baptist Sunday School Board. He is active in discipleship training and is becoming recognized as a writer of interactive learning activities. Claude coauthored another LIFE course with John Drakeford entitled *WiseCounsel: Skills for Lay Counseling*. He has served as a volunteer church planter for the Concord Baptist Association of middle Tennessee. A native of Tennessee, he is a graduate of Belmont College and New Orleans Baptist Theological Seminary. He lives in Murfreesboro, Tennessee with his wife Reta and daughters Julie and Jenny.

EDITOR'S NOTE. In the following materials Henry Blackaby is the primary author of content materials. As your personal tutor, he will speak to you just as if he were sitting at your side as you study. Claude King has written the learning activities to assist you in your study.

The personal illustrations of the authors are written solely from their personal viewpoints. Others who were involved, if given the opportunity, could write a different and more complete account. The point of agreement, however, would center on God's activity as He accomplished things that only can be explained in terms of His divine presence and activity.

GOD'S WILL AND YOUR LIFE

When the World's Fair was coming to Vancouver, our association of churches was convinced that God wanted us to try to reach the 22 million people that would come to the fair. We had about 2,000 members in our association's churches in greater Vancouver. How in the world could 2,000 people make a great impact on such a mass of tourists from all over the world?

Two years before the fair we began to set our plans in motion. The total income for our whole association was $9,000. The following year our income was about $16,000. The year of the World's Fair we set a budget for $202,000. We had commitments that would probably provide 35 percent of that budget. Sixty-five percent of that budget was dependent on prayer. Can you operate a budget on prayer? Yes. But when you do that you are attempting something only God can do. What do most of us do? We set the practical budget, which is the total of what we can do. Then we set a hope or faith budget. The budget we really trust and use, however, is the one we can reach by ourselves. We do not really trust God to do anything.

As an association of churches, we decided that God had definitely led us to the work that would cost $202,000. That became our operating budget. All of our people began praying for God to provide and do everything we believed He had led us to do during the World's Fair. At the end of the year, I asked our treasurer how much money we had received. From Canada, the United States, and other parts of the world we had received $264,000. People from all over came to assist us. During the course of the fair, we became a catalyst to see almost 20 thousand people come to know Jesus Christ. You cannot explain that except in terms of God's intervention. Only God could have done that. God did it with a people who had determined to be servants who were moldable and remained available for the Master's use.

I am the vine; you are the branches. If a man remains in me and I in him, he will bear much fruit; apart from me you can do nothing.   —JOHN 15:5

Verse to Memorize this Week

UNIT

1

As you follow Jesus one day at a time, He will keep you right in the center of God's will.

Not a program
Not a method

A love relationship with God

INTRODUCTION

Jesus said, "This is eternal life: that they may know you, the only true God, and Jesus Christ, whom you have sent" (John 17:3). The heart of eternal life and the heart of this study is for you to KNOW GOD and to KNOW JESUS CHRIST whom He has sent. Knowing God does not come through a program or a method. It is a relationship with a Person. It is an intimate love relationship with God. Through this relationship, God reveals His will and invites you to join Him where He is already at work. When you obey, God accomplishes through you something only He can do. Then you come to KNOW GOD in a more intimate way by EXPERIENCING GOD at work through you.

I want to help you move into the kind of relationship to God through which you will truly experience eternal life to the fullest degree possible. Jesus said, "I have come that they may have life, and have it to the full" (John 10:10). Would you like to experience life to the full? You may, if you are willing to respond to God's invitation to an intimate love relationship with Him.

Relationship to Jesus Christ—a Prerequisite

In this course I assume you have already trusted Jesus Christ as Savior and you acknowledge Him to be Lord of your life. If you have not made this most important decision in your life, the rest of the course will have little meaning for you because spiritual matters can only be understood by those who have the indwelling Spirit of Christ (1 Cor. 2:14).

"The man without the Spirit does not accept the things that come from the Spirit of God, for they are foolishness to him, and he cannot understand them, because they are spiritually discerned."
—1 Corinthians 2:14

If you sense a need to accept Jesus as your Savior and Lord, now is the time to settle this matter with God. Ask God to speak to you as you read the following Scriptures:
❏ Romans 3:23—All have sinned.
❏ Romans 6:23—Eternal life is a free gift of God.
❏ Romans 5:8—Because of love, Jesus paid the death penalty for your sins.
❏ Romans 10:9-10—Confess Jesus as Lord and believe God raised Him from the dead.
❏ Romans 10:13—Ask God to save you and He will.

To place your faith in Jesus and receive His gift of eternal life you must:
• Recognize that you are a sinner and that you need a saving relationship with Jesus Christ.
• Confess (agree with God about) your sins.
• Repent of your sins (turn from sin to God).
• Ask Jesus to save you by His grace.
• Turn over the rule in your life to Jesus. Let Him be your Lord.

If you need help, call on your pastor, a deacon, or a Christian friend for help. If you have just made this important decision, call someone and share the good news of what God has done in your life. Then share your decision with your church.

Looking for More in Your Experience of God?

You may have been frustrated in your Christian experience because you know God has a more abundant life for you than you have experienced. Or you may be earnestly desiring God's directions for your life and ministry. You may have experienced tragedy in your life. Standing bewildered in the middle of a broken life, you don't know what to do. Whatever your present circumstances may be, my earnest prayer is that somehow in this time together you will be able to:

• hear when God is speaking to you
• clearly identify the activity of God in your life
• believe Him to be and do everything He promises
• adjust your beliefs, character, and behavior to Him and His ways
• see a direction that He is taking in your life and what He wants to do through your life
• clearly know what you need to do in response to His activity in your life and
• experience God doing through you what only God can do!

That is an impossible task for this course. These are things only God can do in your life. I will try to serve as your guide, encourager, and as a catalyst (one that assists in bringing about an action or reaction) for your deeper walk with God. I will share with you the biblical principles by which God has been guiding my life and ministry. I will be sharing with you some of the "wonderful works" the Lord has done as God's people have applied biblical principles to following God. In the activities I will invite you to interact with God, so He can reveal to you the ways He wants you to apply these principles in your own life, ministry, and church.

Your Study Guide

The Holy Spirit of God will be your personal Teacher (John 14:26). He is the One who will guide you to apply these principles according to God's will. He will be at work revealing God, His purposes, and His ways to you. Jesus said, "If anyone chooses to do God's will, he will find out whether my teaching comes from God or whether I speak on my own" (John 7:17). This will be true of this course as well. The Holy Spirit at work in you will confirm in your own heart the truth of Scripture. When I present what I see as a biblical principle, you can depend on the Holy Spirit to confirm whether that teaching comes from God. Therefore, your intimate relationship with God in prayer, meditation, and Bible study will be an indispensable part of this course.

Your Teacher

"The Counselor, the Holy Spirit, whom the Father will send in my name, will teach you all things." —John 14:26

The Bible is God's Word to you. The Holy Spirit honors and uses God's Word in speaking to you. The Scriptures will be your source of authority for faith and practice. You cannot depend on traditions, your experience, or the experience of others to be accurate authorities on God's will and ways. Experience and tradition must always be examined against the teaching of Scripture.

Your Source of Authority

Anything significant that happens in your life will be a result of God's activity in your life. He is infinitely more interested in your life than you or I could possibly be. Let the Spirit of God bring you into an intimate relationship with the God of the Universe "who is able to do immeasurably more than all we ask or imagine, according to his power that is at work within us" (Eph. 3:20).

The Lay Institute For Equipping

Experiencing God: Knowing and Doing the Will of God is a course in the Lay Institute For Equipping or LIFE. LIFE is an educational system designed to provide quality education to laypersons in the areas of discipleship, leadership, and ministry. All LIFE courses have some common characteristics. These also apply to *Experiencing God*.

- Participants interact with a self-paced workbook (this is your workbook) for 30 to 60 minutes each day and do life related learning activities.
- Participants meet for a one- and one-half to two-hour small-group learning session each week.
- The course leader (or facilitator) guides group members to reflect on and discuss what they have studied during the week and then make practical application of the study to everyday life. This small group becomes a support group for participants as they help each other come to understand and apply the Scriptures to life.
- Optional videotapes provide additional content and learning experiences for the groups that want additional help. *Experiencing God* videotapes allow you to sit in on a conference where Henry Blackaby and Claude King lead participants to understand and apply these principles in their own lives. They answer many questions that may arise as you try to practice this way of knowing and doing God's will.
- An attractive diploma from the Church Study Course system is awarded for those who complete a LIFE course in a small-group study. (See p. 223 for complete details.)

Studying *Experiencing God*

This book is different from most books with which you may be familiar. Its design is not for you to sit down and read it from cover to cover. I want you to study, understand, and apply biblical principles to your life. This challenging goal takes time. To get the most out of this course you must take your time by studying only one day's lesson at a time. Do not try to study through several lessons in a single day. You need time to let these thoughts "sink in" to your understanding and practice. You are wanting to experience a Person—Jesus Christ. Time and meditation are necessary to allow the Holy Spirit to make Christ real in your life.

Do not skip any of the learning activities. These are designed to help you learn and apply the truths to life. They will help you establish a personal daily walk with God Himself.

Do not skip learning activities.

Many of the activities are designed to lead you to interaction with God through prayer, meditation, and Bible study. If you leave out these activities, you may miss an encounter with God that could radically change your life. You will learn that your relationship with God is the most important part of knowing and doing the will of God. Without an intimate relationship with Him, you will miss what He wants to do in and through your life.

The activities will begin (like this paragraph) with ⚹ pointing you to indented type. Follow the instructions given. After you have completed the activity you will return to the content.

Normally you will be given answers following the activity, so you can check your own work. Write your own answer before reading mine. Sometimes your response to the activity will be your own response or opinion, and no right or wrong answer can be given. If you have difficulty with an activity or you question the answers given, write a note about your concern in the margin. Discuss it with your leader or small group.

Once each week you should attend a small-group session designed to help you discuss the content you studied the previous week, share insights and testimonies, encourage each other, and pray together. Small groups should not have more than 10 members for maximum effectiveness. Larger groups will experience less closeness, less intimate sharing, more absenteeism, and more drop-outs. If more than 10 people want to study the course, enlist additional leaders for each group of six to ten.

If you have started studying *Experiencing God* and you are not involved in a small group, enlist a few friends to study through the course with you. You will discover that other members of the body of Christ can help you more fully know and understand God's will. You will miss much of the intended learning from this course apart from a small-group study.

Resources for *Experiencing God* include:
• Member's book: *Experiencing God: Knowing and Doing the Will of God* (Item 7203-00)
• Leader's guide: *Experiencing God Leader's Guide* (Item 7225-00)
• Optional Videotapes: *Experiencing God* (Item 8483-80)
• Optional Audio Cassette Album (Item 5160-43)
• *Experiencing God Print* (Item 7700-37)

Orders or order inquiries may be sent to Customer Service Center, 127 Ninth Avenue North, Nashville, TN 37234, or call 1-800-458-2772. The books also are available at your local Baptist Book Store or Lifeway Christian Book Store.

JESUS IS YOUR WAY

For 12 years I pastored in Saskatoon, Saskatchewan, Canada. One day a farmer said to me, "Henry, come out and visit with me at my farm." His directions went something like this: "Go a quarter mile past the edge of the city and you will see a big red barn on your left. Go to the next road and turn to your left. Take that road for three-quarters of a mile. You'll see a tree. Go right for about four miles, and then you will see a big rock . . ." I wrote all of this down, and one day I got there!

The next time I went to the farmer's house, the farmer was with me. Since there was more than one way to get to his house, he could have taken me any way he wanted to. You see, he was my "map." What did I have to do? I simply had to listen to him and obey him. Every time he said, "turn" I did just what he said. He took me a way I had never been. I could never retrace that route on my own. The farmer was my "map;" he knew the way.

When you come to the Lord Jesus to seek His will for your life, which of the following requests is most like what you ask? Check your response.
  ❑ 1. Lord, what do you want me to do? When do you want me to do it? How shall I do it? Where shall I do it? Who do you want me to involve along the way? And please tell me what the outcome will be.
  ❑ 2. Lord, just tell me what to do one step at a time, and I will do it.

Isn't the first response most typical of us? We are always asking God for a detailed "road map." We say, "Lord, if You could just tell me where I am heading, then I will be able to set my course and go."

He says, "You don't need to. What you need to do is follow Me one day at a time." We need to come to the place where the second response is ours.

Who is it that really knows the way for you to go to fulfill God's purpose for your life? God is. Jesus said, "I am the way."

"I am the way and the truth and the life." —John 14:6

- He did not say, "I will show you the way."
- He did not say, "I will give you a road map."
- He did not say, "I will tell you which direction to head."
- He said, "I am **the** way." Jesus knows the way; He is your way.

If you were to do everything that Jesus tells you one day at a time, do you suppose that you always would be right in the center of where God wants you to be? Check your response.
- ❏ 1. No, Jesus does not really know God's will for my life.
- ❏ 2. No, Jesus might mislead me and take me the wrong way.
- ❏ 3. Well, Jesus would rather I wait until He tells me all the details before I start to follow Him.
- ❏ 4. Yes, If I follow Jesus one day at a time, I will be right in the center of God's will for my life.

When you get to the place where you trust Jesus to guide you one step at a time you experience a new freedom. If you don't trust Jesus to guide you this way, what happens if you don't know the way you are to go? You worry every time you must make a turn. You often freeze up and cannot make a decision. This is not the way God intends for you to live your life.

I have found in my own life that I can release the way to Him. Then I take care of everything He tells me one day at a time. He gives me plenty to do to fill each day with meaning and purpose. If I do everything He says, I will be in the center of His will when He wants to use me for a special assignment.

Abram Followed One Day at a Time

Abram (later, God changed his name to Abraham) is a good example of this principle at work in a Bible character. He walked by faith and not by sight.

Abram

Read about the call of Abram to do God's will. Watch to see how much detail he was given before he was asked to follow. Underline where he was to go and what he was to do.

> The Lord had said to Abram, "Leave your country, your people and your father's household and go to the land I will show you."
>
> "I will make you into a great nation and I will bless you; I will make your name great, and you will be a blessing. I will bless those who bless you, and whoever curses you I will curse; and all peoples on earth will be blessed through you."
>
> So Abram left, as the Lord had told him; and Lot went with him. Abram was seventy-five years old when he set out from Haran. He took his wife Sarai, his nephew Lot, all the possessions they had accumulated and the people they had acquired in Haran, and they set out for the land of Canaan, and they arrived there (Gen. 12:1-5).

What did God say? How specific was He? "Leave" and "go." Go where? "To a land I will show you."

Are you ready to follow God's will that way? Check your response.
- ❏ NO, I don't think God will ever ask me to go anywhere that He doesn't show me ahead of time where I am going.
- ❏ I'm not sure.
- ❏ YES, I am willing to follow Him by faith and not by sight.
- ❏ OTHER: _____

Many times, as with Abram, God called people just to follow Him. (Tomorrow you will read about several.) He is more likely to call you to follow one day at a time than He is to spell out all the details before you begin to obey Him. As we continue our study together, you will find this truth active in the lives of many biblical characters.

Read Matthew 6:33-34 at the left, then pause and pray.

- Agree that God is absolutely trustworthy.
- Agree with God that you will follow Him one day at a time.
- Agree that you will follow Him even when He does not spell out all the details.
- Agree that you will let Him be your Way.

If you cannot agree to these right now, openly confess your struggles to Him. Ask Him to help you want to do His will in His way. Claim the promise: "It is God who works in you to will and to act according to his good purpose" (Phil. 2:13).

Daily Review

At the end of each day's lesson, I will ask you to review the lesson and pray. Ask God to identify for you one or more statements or Scriptures from the lesson that He wants you to understand, learn, or practice. This is a personal application question that has no wrong answer. If God causes a statement or Scripture to be meaningful to you, that is the correct response. I will also ask you to reword that statement or Scripture into a prayer of response. Pray about what God may want you to do in response to that truth. This should become a time of prayer and meditation each day as you ask God what He wants you to do in response to the truths in the lesson. You may want to take notes in the margin each day as you study. God may reveal several responses He wants you to make to a particular lesson. Don't let those thoughts get away from you. Write them down so you can review them. When God speaks, it is important to write it down. You may even want to keep a notebook for recording your spiritual journey. I will talk to you more about a journal in a later unit.

After today's lesson a person might have responded like this:

What was the most meaningful statement or Scripture you read today?

Jesus is my way. I don't need a complete road map to stay in the center of God's will.

Reword the statement or Scripture into a prayer of response to God.

Lord, I will follow you even if I don't know the way.

What does God want you to do in response to today's study?

I need to quit worrying about tomorrow and trust Jesus to guide me one day at a time.

Review today's lesson. Pray and ask God to identify one or more statements or Scriptures that He wants you to understand, learn, or practice. Then respond to the following:

What was the most meaningful statement or Scripture you read today?

_____

_____

Reword the statement or Scripture into a prayer of response to God.

_____

_____

What does God want you to do in response to today's study?

_____

_____

Write out your memory verse for this unit. You may use a different translation for your memory verses if you prefer. Practice your memory verses daily.

_____

_____

_____

_____

JESUS IS YOUR MODEL

Interpret Experience by Scripture

During this course and during your life you will have times when you want to respond based on your own experiences or your own wisdom. Such an approach will get you in trouble. This should be your guideline: Always go back to the Bible for truth (or, for the Holy Spirit to reveal Truth).

Jesus watched to see where the Father was at work and joined Him.

> Look to see what God says and how He works in the Scriptures. Make your decisions and evaluate your experiences based on biblical principles.

When you study the Scriptures, do not base your decision on one isolated case. Look to see how God works throughout the Scriptures. When you learn how God has worked throughout history, you can depend on His working in a similar way with you. Your experience is valid only as it is confirmed in the Scriptures. I never deny any experience that a person has had. I always reserve the right, however, to interpret it according to what I understand in the Scripture. At times individuals get upset with me and say, "Well, I don't care what you say, I've experienced this."

I respond as kindly as I know by saying, "I do not deny your experience. I do question your interpretation of what you experienced, because it is contrary to what I see in the Word of God." Our experiences cannot be our guide. Every experience must be controlled and understood by the Scriptures. The God revealed in Scripture does not change.

To see if you have grasped this idea, mark the following statements as T (true) or F (false).

_____1. Human interpretations of my experiences are an effective way to know and follow God.

_____2. I should always evaluate my experiences based on the truths I find in the Word of God.

_____3. I may get a distorted understanding of God if I do not check my experiences against the truths of Scripture.

_____4. I can trust God to work in my life in similar ways that I see Him working throughout the Scriptures.

Number 1 is false; 2, 3, and 4 are true. In #1 your experiences must be interpreted in light of the Scriptures. Experience alone is not a sound guide. You must be cautious about isolating a single experience from the context of Scripture. You will want to see how God works throughout Scripture. You will never go wrong if, under the Holy Spirit's instruction, you let the Bible be your guide.

The Bible Is Your Guide

Christians are becoming more and more disoriented to the Bible as a guide for faith and practice. Because Christians have become disoriented to the Bible, they turn to worldly solutions, programs, and methods that appear to be the answer to spiritual problems. I use the Word of God as a guide to what we should be doing. Some people say, "Henry, that is not practical." They want to move me away from the Bible and rely on the world's ways or on personal experience. As a Christian disciple, I cannot abandon the guidance I find in the Bible. The Bible is my guide for faith and practice.

How do you let the Word of God become your guide? When I seek God's direction, I insist on following the directives that I see in the Word of God. Yesterday's lesson is an example. Does God call people to follow Him without giving them all the details up front? We know that He called Abram to follow that way. Is that pattern consistent in the Scriptures?

Read the following Scriptures about God's (Jesus') call for people to follow Him. Write the names of those who were called to follow without being given much detail about what the future would hold for them.

1. Matthew 4:18-20 _____
2. Matthew 4:21-22 _____
3. Matthew 9:9 _____
4. Acts 9:1-20 _____

In some cases God gave more details than in others. We will look at Moses' call and discover that God gave him a bigger picture of the assignment than He usually gave. In every case, however, the individuals had to stay close to God for daily guidance. For Moses and the children of Israel, God provided daily guidance through the cloud by day and the fire by night. For Peter, Andrew, James, John, Matthew, and Paul, (answers to the above activity) God gave very little detail about their assignment. He basically said, "Just follow me, and I will show you."

What Is God's Will for My Life?

When people seek to know and do the will of God, many ask the question, What is God's will for my life? A seminary professor of mine, Dr. Gaines S. Dobbins, used to say, "If you ask the wrong question, you are going to get the wrong answer." Sometimes we assume that every question is a legitimate question. When we pursue an answer and always come up wrong, we cannot figure out what is happening. Always check to see if you have asked the right question before you pursue the answer.

The right question is: What is God's will?

What is God's will for my life? - is *not* the right question. I think the right question is, What is God's will? Once I know God's will, then I can adjust my life to Him. In other words, what is it that God is purposing where I am. Once I know what God is doing, then I know what I need to do. The focus needs to be on *God*, not *my life!*

Jesus' Example

When I want to learn how to know and do the will of God, I can find no better model than Jesus. During His 33 years on earth, He perfectly completed every assignment God gave Him to do. He never failed to do the will of the Father. He never sinned. Would you like to understand how Jesus came to know and do the will of God?

17"My Father is always at his work to this very day, and I, too, am working.

"19I tell you the truth, the Son can do nothing by himself; he can do only what he sees his Father doing, because whatever the Father does the Son also does. 20For the Father loves the Son and shows him all he does. Yes, to your amazement he will show him even greater things than these."

—John 5:17, 19-20

Read John 5:17, 19-20 (left) and answer the following questions.

1. Who is always at work? _____
2. How much can the Son do by Himself? _____
3. What does the Son do? _____
   _____
4. Why does the Father show the Son what He is doing? _____
   _____

This is one of the clearest statements of how Jesus knew what to do. I would outline Jesus' approach to knowing and doing God's will like this:

Jesus' Example

- The Father has been working right up until now.
- Now God has Me working.
- I do nothing on My own initiative.
- I watch to see what the Father is doing.
- I do what I see the Father already is doing.
- You see, the Father loves Me.
- He shows Me everything that He, Himself, is doing.

This model is for your life personally and for your church. It is not just a step-by-step approach for knowing and doing the will of God. It describes a love relationship through which God accomplishes His purposes. I would sum it up this way: Watch to see where God is working and join Him!

Watch to see where God is working and join Him!

God Is Always at Work Around You

Right now God is working all around you and in your life. One of the greatest tragedies among God's people is that, while they have a deep longing to experience God, they are experiencing God day after day but do not know how to recognize Him. By the end of this course, you will have learned many ways to recognize clearly the activity of God in and around your life. The Holy Spirit and the Word of God will instruct you and help you know when and where God is working. Once you know where He is working, you will adjust your life to join Him where He is working.

You will experience His accomplishing His activity through your life. When you enter this kind of intimate love relationship with God, you will know and do the will of God and experience Him in ways you have never known Him before. I cannot accomplish that goal in your life. Only God can bring you into that kind of relationship.

☀ **Turn to the diagram inside the back cover of this book. Read all seven of the realities of experiencing God. Personalize the *first* statement and write it below using *me* instead of *you*.**

_____

Later this week, we will take a closer look at the these seven truths.

☀ **Review today's lesson. Pray and ask God to identify one or more statements or Scriptures that He wants you to understand, learn, or practice. Then respond to the following:**

What was the most meaningful statement or Scripture you read today?

_____

_____

Reword the statement or Scripture into a prayer of response to God.

_____

_____

What does God want you to do in response to today's study?

_____

_____

SUMMARY STATEMENTS

- I will look to see what God says and how He works in the Scriptures. I will make my decisions and evaluate my experiences based on biblical principles.
- The Bible is my guide for faith and practice.
- The right question is, What is God's will?
- Watch to see where God is working and join Him.
- God is always at work around me.

To be a servant of God you must be moldable and remain in the hand of the Master.

Many Scripture passages describe Jesus as God's Servant. He came as a servant to accomplish God's will in the redemption of humanity. Here is what Paul said about Him:

> Your attitude should be the same as that of Christ Jesus: Who, being in very nature God, did not consider equality with God something to be grasped, but made himself nothing, taking the very nature of a **servant,** being made in human likeness. And being found in appearance as a man, he humbled himself and became obedient to death—even death on a cross! (Phil. 2:5-8).

In His instructions to His disciples about servanthood, Jesus (the Son of man) described His own role of service:

> Whoever wants to become great among you must be your servant, and whoever wants to be first must be your slave—just as the Son of Man did not come to be served, but **to serve,** and to give his life as a ransom for many (Matt. 20:26-28).

Jesus also told us about our relationship to Him; "As the Father has sent me, I am sending you" (John 20:21).

Based on these Scriptures and others you may be familiar with, do you believe you should be God's servant? Yes ❑   No ❑

Have you ever given your very best effort in trying to serve God and felt frustrated when nothing lasting resulted from your work? Yes ❑   No ❑

What is a servant? In your own words write a definition of a servant.

_____

_____

What is a servant?

Did your definition sound something like this: "A servant is one who finds out what his master wants him to do, and then he does it"? The world's concept of a servant is that a servant goes to the master and says, "Master, what do you want me to do?" The master tells him, and the servant goes off *by himself* and does it. That is not a biblical concept of a servant. You cannot take your definition for biblical truth from the world. You must take your definition of terms from the Scripture.

Like the potter and the clay

"This is the word that came to Jeremiah from the Lord: 'Go down to the potter's house, and there I will give you my message.' So I went down to the potter's house, and I saw him working at the wheel. But the pot he was shaping from the clay was marred in his hands; so the potter formed it into another pot, shaping it as seemed best to him.

"Then the word of the Lord came to me: 'O house of Israel, can I not do with you as this potter does?' declares the Lord. 'Like clay in the hand of the potter, so are you in my hand, O house of Israel.'"

—*Jeremiah 18:1-6*

My understanding of a servant is more like the potter and the clay. (See Jer. 18:1-6.) The clay has to do two things. First of all, the clay has to be molded. The clay has to be responsive to the potter, so the potter can make any instrument of his choosing. Then the clay has to do a second thing — it has to remain in the potter's hand. When the potter has finished making the instrument of his choosing, that instrument has no ability to do anything whatsoever. It now has to remain in the potter's hand. Suppose the potter molds the clay into a cup. The cup has to remain in the potter's hands, so the potter can use that cup in any way he chooses.

That is very different from the world's view of a servant. When you come to God as His servant, He first wants you to allow Him to mold and shape you into the instrument of His choosing. Then He can take your life and put it where He wills and work through it to accomplish His purposes. Just like a cup cannot do anything on its own, you do not have any ability to do the command of the Lord except to be where He wants you to be.

Answer the following questions about being a servant.

1. How much can a servant do by himself or herself? _____

2. When God works through a servant, how much can that servant do?

_____

3. What are two things a servant must do to be used by God?

_____

_____

A servant is a person who has to do two things: (1) be moldable and (2) remain in the

Master's (potter's) hands. Then the Master alone can use that instrument as He chooses. The servant can do nothing of Kingdom value by himself or herself. Just as Jesus said, "The Son can do nothing by himself" (John 5:19) and "Apart from me you can do nothing" (John 15:5). With God working through that servant, he or she can do anything God can do. Wow! Unlimited potential! Servanthood does require obedience. He must do what he is instructed, but the servant must remember who is accomplishing the work—God is.

If you have been working off the world's definition of *servant*, this concept should change your approach to serving God. You do not get orders and then go out and do them. You relate to God, respond to Him, and adjust your life to Him so that He can do whatever He wants to do through you.

Elijah

When Elijah challenged the prophets of Baal (a Canaanite fertility god) to prove once and for all whose God was the true God, he took a big risk in being a servant of God.

Read 1 Kings 18:16-39 and answer the following questions.

1. Elijah was God's servant. How many prophets of other gods did he face in this stand-off at Mount Carmel?

_____

2. What was the test Elijah proposed to prove whose was the One True God?

_____

3. What did Elijah do to the altar of the Lord?

_____

4. At whose initiative did Elijah offer this challenge? His own or God's?

_____

5. What did he plan to prove through this experience?

_____

6. How did all the people respond? _____

_____

7. What was God's work in this event? _____

_____

8. What was Elijah's work in this event? _____

_____

_____

Elijah was outnumbered 850 to 1. If God had not displayed His own work by coming in fire and consuming the sacrifice (and altar) as Elijah had proposed, Elijah would have utterly failed. That would probably have cost him his life. Elijah repaired the altar of the Lord. He had to stay with God and do everything God commanded him to do. He was acting in obedience to God's command and not based on his own initiative. He went where God told him, when God told him, and did what God told him. Then God accomplished His own purposes through him. Elijah wanted the people to identify the Lord as the True God. That is exactly how the people responded.

Did Elijah or God bring down the fire from Heaven? God did. What was Elijah doing? Being obedient. Elijah had no ability to do what God was about to do. When God did something only He could do, all the people knew that He was the True God. And, God did it through His obedient servant.

Reflection Time

As your study time permits, read the following thought provoking questions. Try to mentally answer each one before moving to the next one. You may want to jot a note to yourself on the response lines.

Elijah

1. Will there be a difference between the quality of service and the quantity of lasting results when God is working and when you are working?

_____

2. What are you doing in your life personally and in your church that you know cannot be accomplished unless God intervenes? Could much of what we are doing in our lives and in our churches be done without reference to God at all?

_____

3. When we finish a task and feel frustrated that lasting spiritual fruit is not visible, could the reason be that we are attempting very little that only God can do?

_____

"Don't Just Do Something"

We are a "doing" people. We always want to be doing something. Once in a while someone will say, "Don't just stand there, do something."

I think God is crying out and shouting to us, "Don't just do something. Stand there! Enter into a love relationship with Me. Get to know Me. Adjust your life to Me. Let Me love you and reveal Myself to you as I work through you." A time will come when the doing will be called for, but we cannot skip the relationship. The relationship with God must come first.

Jesus said, "I am the vine; you are the branches. If a man remains in me and I in him, he will bear much fruit; apart from me you can do nothing" (John 15:5). Do you believe Him? Without Him you can do nothing. He means that.

☀ **Turn to the diagram inside the back cover of this book. Read again all seven of the realities listed there. Personalize the *last* (seventh) reality and write it below using *I* and *me* instead of *you*.**

_____

_____

God wants you to come to a greater knowledge of Him by experience. He wants to establish a love relationship with you. He wants to involve you in His kingdom purposes. He wants to accomplish His work through you.

Find out where the Master is, then that is where you need to be.

Do you want to be a servant of God? Find out where the Master is, then that is where you need to be. Find out what the Master is doing, then that is what you need to be doing. Jesus said: "Whoever serves me must follow me; and where I am, my servant also will be. My Father will honor the one who serves me" (John 12:26).

☀ **Review today's lesson. Pray and ask God to identify one or more statements or Scriptures that He wants you to understand, learn, or practice. Then respond to the following:**

What was the most meaningful statement or Scripture you read today?

_____

_____

Reword the statement or Scripture into a prayer of response to God.

_____

_____

What does God want you to do in response to today's study?

_____

_____

Practice quoting your Scripture memory verse aloud and/or write it on separate paper.

- To be a servant of God I must be moldable and I must remain in the Master's hand.
- Apart from God, I can do nothing.
- With God working through me, I can do anything God can do.
- When I find out where the Master is, then I know that is where I need to be.
- I come to know God by experience as I obey Him and He accomplishes His work through me.

GOD WORKS THROUGH HIS SERVANTS, PART 1

You cannot stay the way you are and go with God.

We often act as though God tells us what He wants us to do and sends us off all by ourselves to try and do it. Then, any time we need Him we can call on Him, and He will help us. That is never the biblical picture. When He is about to do something, He reveals what He is about to do to His people. He wants to do it through His people, or through His servant.

When God is about to do something through you, He has to get you from where you are to where He is. So He comes and tells you what He is doing. (Later, I will try to help you understand how you can clearly know when God is speaking to you.) When you know what God is doing, then you know what you need to do—you need to join Him. The moment you know that God is doing something where you are, your life will be thrown in contrast to God. You cannot stay the way you are and go with God.

Seven Realities of Experiencing God

The illustration below (and inside the back cover of your book) will help you summarize the way you can respond to God's initiative in your life.

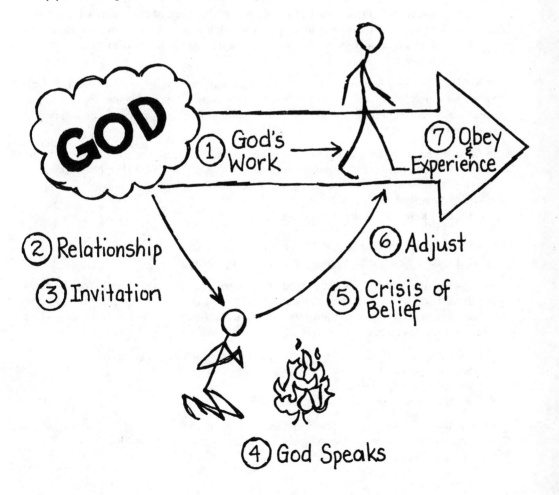

1. God is always at work around you.
2. God pursues a continuing love relationship with you that is real and personal.
3. God invites you to become involved with Him in His work.
4. God speaks by the Holy Spirit through the Bible, prayer, circumstances, and the church to reveal Himself, His purposes, and His ways.
5. God's invitation for you to work with Him always leads you to a crisis of belief that requires faith and action.
6. You must make major adjustments in your life to join God in what He is doing.
7. You come to know God by experience as you obey Him and He accomplishes His work through you.

A. Circle key words or phrases that help you recall the seven realities.

B. Write the key words or phrases on the following lines:

_____

_____

_____

_____

C. Read each reality slowly. Write below any questions you have about any of the realities you do not quite understand.

_____

_____

_____

D. Using only the words or phrases you wrote in item B, see if you can mentally summarize all seven of the realities. Check yourself before moving on to the next question.

E. Now, on a separate sheet of paper, try writing each of the realities from memory. They do not have to be word-for-word, but they should cover the important information of the realities. You may write your key words or phrases if that will help.

Most of this course will focus on one or more of these realities to help you understand them more completely. You will probably notice that I frequently repeat different aspects of this cycle. I use the repetition in different situations to help you learn how you can respond to God's activity in your life.

In the assignment above you could have selected many different words or phrases. Yours may be different, but I chose *God/work; love relationship; involved with Him; God speaks; crisis of belief; adjustments; obey.* You may have asked questions like:
• What is involved in a love relationship with God?
• How can I know when God is speaking?
• How do I know where God is at work?
• What kinds of adjustments does God require me to make?
• What is the difference between adjustment and obedience?

As I have worked with groups and individuals in many settings, I have been asked questions like these. I will try to answer as many questions during the remaining units of this course as I possibly can. I will answer many other questions in the optional videotape messages that go along with this course.

Three similarities in the lives of Bible characters through whom God worked are:
• When God spoke, they knew it was God.
• They knew what God was saying.
• They knew what they were to do in response.

Wouldn't you like for your relationship to God to be so that He would work through you that way? He wants to move you to that kind of relationship. I trust that this course will help you.

Moses' Example

Moses' call and ministry are good examples of how God worked with Bible characters. His early life and call to ministry are described in chapters 2, 3, and 4 of Exodus. Other passages of Scripture also help us see how Moses came to know and follow God's will. Using the seven points in the sequence on the back of this book, let's look at Moses' call and response. (You may want to read Ex. 2—4 as a background passage.)

> The Israelites groaned in their slavery and cried out, and their cry for help because of their slavery went up to God. God heard their groaning and he remembered his covenant with Abraham, with Isaac and with Jacob. So God looked on the Israelites and was concerned about them (Ex. 2:23-25).

1. God already was at work around Moses.

God took the initiative to come to Moses and initiate a love relationship with him at the burning bush. God told Moses that He would go with Moses into Egypt. Many texts throughout Exodus, Leviticus, Numbers, and Deuteronomy illustrate how God pursued a continuing love relationship with Moses. Here is one example:

2. God pursued a continuing love relationship with Moses that was real and personal.

> The Lord said to Moses, "Come up to me on the mountain and stay here, and I will give you the tablets of stone, with the law and commands I have written for their instruction". . . . When Moses went up on the mountain, the cloud covered it, and the glory of the Lord settled on Mount Sinai. . . . Moses entered the cloud as he went on up the mountain. And he stayed on the mountain forty days and forty nights" (Ex. 24:12, 15-16, 18).

> I have come down to rescue them [the Israelites] from the hand of the Egyptians and to bring them up out of that land into a good and spacious land. . . . So now, go. I am sending you to Pharaoh to bring my people the Israelites out of Egypt (Ex. 3:8, 10).

3. God invited Moses to become involved with Him in His work.

Answer the following questions about the three preceding statements.

1. Related to Israel, what was God already doing?

   _____

   _____

2. What evidence do you see that proves God wanted a personal and real relationship with Moses?

   _____

   _____

3. How did God want to involve Moses in the work He was already doing?

   _____

   _____

(1) God had a purpose that He was working out in Moses' world. Even though Moses was an exile in the desert, he was right on God's schedule, right in the fullness of God's timing, right in the middle of God's will. At the time God was about to deliver the children of Israel, the important factor was not what the will of God was for Moses. The important factor was the will of God for Israel. (2) God's purpose was to deliver the children of Israel. Moses was the one through whom God wanted to work to accomplish that. (3) Time and time again God invited Moses to talk with Him and to be with Him. God initiated and maintained a continuing relationship with Moses. This relationship was based on love, and daily God fulfilled His purposes through His 'friend' Moses. (For other examples of the love relationship, you may want to read Ex. 33:7—34:10 or Num. 12:6-8.)

Whenever God gets ready to do something, He always reveals to a person or His people what He is going to do. (See Amos 3:7.) God accomplishes His work through His people. This is the way God works with you. The Bible is designed to help you understand the ways of God. Then, when God starts to act in your life, you will recognize that it is God.

Since this is a two-part lesson, stop here and begin with statement 4 tomorrow.

"Surely the Sovereign Lord does nothing without revealing his plan to his servants the prophets." —Amos 3:7

Review today's lesson. Pray and ask God to identify one or more statements or Scriptures that He wants you to understand, learn, or practice. Then respond to the following:

What was the most meaningful statement or Scripture you read today?

_____

_____

Reword the statement or Scripture into a prayer of response to God.

_____

_____

What does God want you to do in response to today's study?

_____

_____

This two-part lesson will be summarized at the end of day 5.

DAY 5 GOD WORKS THROUGH HIS SERVANTS, PART 2

God reveals what He is about to do. That revelation becomes an invitation to join Him.

Yesterday, you studied the first three realities of God's working with Moses. Now look at the last four.

4. God spoke to reveal Himself, His purposes, and His ways.

There the angel of the Lord appeared to him in flames of fire from within a bush. . . . God called to him from within the bush, "Moses! Moses!" And Moses said, "Here I am."

"Do not come any closer," God said. "Take off your sandals, for the place where you are standing is holy ground." Then he said, "I am the God of your father, the God of Abraham, the God of Isaac and the God of Jacob."

The Lord said, "I have indeed seen the misery of my people in Egypt. I have heard them crying out because of their slave drivers, and I am concerned about their suffering. So I have come down to rescue them from the hand of the Egyptians and to bring them up out of that land into a good and spacious land" (Ex. 3:2-8).

"When a prophet of the Lord is among you, I reveal myself to him in visions, I speak to him in dreams. But this is not true of my servant Moses; he is faithful in all my house. With him I speak face to face" (Num. 12:6-8).

5. God's invitation for Moses to work with Him led to a crisis of belief that required faith and action.

Moses expressed this crisis of belief when he made the following statements to God:

Who am I, that I should go to Pharaoh and bring the Israelites out of Egypt?

Suppose I go to the Israelites and say to them, "The God of your fathers has sent me to you," and they ask me, "What is his name?" Then what shall I tell them?

What if they do not believe me or listen to me and say, "The Lord did not appear to you"?

O Lord, I have never been eloquent, neither in the past nor since you have spoken to your servant. I am slow of speech and tongue.

O Lord, please send someone else to do it (Ex. 3:11, 13; 4:1, 10, 13).

Moses' crisis called for faith and action.

By faith Moses, when he had grown up, refused to be known as the son of Pharaoh's daughter. He chose to be mistreated along with the people of God rather than to enjoy the pleasures of sin for a short time. . . . By faith he left Egypt, not fearing the king's anger; he persevered because he saw him who is invisible. By faith he kept the Passover and the sprinkling of blood, so that the destroyer of the firstborn would not touch the firstborn of Israel. By faith the people passed through the Red Sea as on dry land; but when the Egyptians tried to do so, they were drowned (Heb. 11:24-29).

The Lord had said to Moses in Midian, "Go back to Egypt, for all the men who wanted to kill you are dead." So Moses took his wife and sons, put them on a donkey and started back to Egypt (Ex. 4:19-20).

Many texts throughout Exodus, Leviticus, Numbers, and Deuteronomy illustrate how God revealed Himself to Moses. As Moses obeyed God, God accomplished through Moses what Moses could not do. Here is one example where Moses and the people came to know God as their Deliverer.

Then the Lord said to Moses, "Why are you crying out to me? Tell the Israelites to move on. Raise your staff and stretch out your hand over the sea to divide the water so that the Israelites can go through the sea on dry ground. I will harden the hearts of the Egyptians so that they will go in after them. And I will gain glory through Pharaoh and all his army....

Then Moses stretched out his hand over the sea, and all that night the Lord drove the sea back with a strong east wind and turned it into dry land. The waters were divided, and the Israelites went through the sea on dry ground, with a wall of water on their right and on their left. The Egyptians pursued them.

Then the Lord said to Moses, "Stretch out your hand over the sea so that the waters may flow back over the Egyptians and their chariots and horsemen." Moses stretched out his hand over the sea, and at daybreak the sea went back to its place.

But the Israelites went through the sea on dry ground, with a wall of water on their right and on their left. That day the Lord saved Israel from the hands of the Egyptians, and Israel saw the Egyptians lying dead on the shore. And when the Israelites saw the great power the Lord displayed against the Egyptians, the people feared the Lord and put their trust in him and in Moses his servant (Ex. 14:15-17, 21-23, 26-27, 29-31).

Answer the following questions about the preceding four statements.

4. What did God reveal about Himself, His purposes, and His ways?

_____

_____

_____

5a. What did Moses have trouble believing about God?

_____

_____

5b. How would you summarize Moses' faith as it is described in Hebrews 11?

_____

6. What adjustment(s) did Moses have to make?

_____

7. How do you think Moses must have felt when God delivered the Israelites

through him?

_____

_____

(4) God came and talked to Moses about His will. God wanted Moses to go to Egypt so He could deliver the Israelites through him. God revealed to Moses His holiness, His mercy, His power, His name, His purpose to keep His promise to Abraham and give Israel the promised land, and many other things not described in the Scriptures above. (5a) Moses offered many objections. He questioned whether God could do it through him (Ex. 3:11),

6. Moses had to make major adjustments in his life to join God in what He was doing.

7. Moses came to know God by experience as he obeyed God and God accomplished His work through Moses.

whether the Israelites would believe God had appeared to him (Ex. 4:1); and whether he was capable of speaking eloquently enough to get the job done (Ex. 4:10). In each case Moses was really doubting God more than himself. He faced the crisis of belief—Is God really able to do what He says? (5b) His faith is described in Hebrews, however, as a model of self-sacrifice and trust in an Almighty God. Once God let Moses know what He was about to do, that revelation became Moses' invitation to join Him.

God reveals what He is about to do. That revelation becomes an invitation to join Him.

---

(6) Moses made the necessary adjustments to orient his life to God. Moses had to come to the place where he believed God could do everything He said He would do. Then he had to leave his job and in-laws, and move to Egypt. After making these adjustments, he was in a position where he could obey God. That did not mean that he was going to do something all by himself for God. It meant that he was going to be where God was working, so that God could do what He had purposed to do in the first place. Moses was a servant who was *moldable,* and he *remained* at God's disposal to be used as God chose. God accomplished His purposes through him. When God does a God-sized work through your life, you will be humbled before Him. (7) Moses must have felt humility and unworthiness to be used in such a significant way. Moses obeyed and did everything God told him. Then God accomplished through Moses all He intended. Every step of obedience brought Moses (and Israel) to a greater knowledge of God (Ex. 6:1-8).

What Can One "Ordinary" Person Do?

"Elijah was a man just like us."

One of the wonderful Scriptures that has helped me at this point is: "Elijah was a man just like us. He prayed earnestly that it would not rain, and it did not rain on the land for three and a half years. Again he prayed, and the heavens gave rain, and the earth produced its crops" (Jas. 5:17-18). Elijah was an "ordinary" man just like we are ordinary. He prayed and God responded.

Peter and John

Uneducated but Mighty

When God healed the crippled beggar through Peter, he and John were called before the Sanhedrin to give an account of their actions. Filled with the Holy Spirit, Peter spoke boldly to the religious leaders. Notice the response of the leaders: "When they saw the courage of Peter and John and realized that they were unschooled, *ordinary men,* they were astonished and they took note that these men had been with Jesus" (Acts 4:13).

All of the persons that you see in the Scriptures were ordinary people. Their relationship with God and the activity of God made them extraordinary. Did you notice this statement— the leaders recognized that Peter and John "had been with Jesus"? Anyone who will take the time to enter into an intimate relationship with God can see God do extraordinary things through his or her life.

D. L. Moody

From shoe salesman to flaming evangelist

Dwight L. Moody was a poorly educated, unordained, shoe salesman who felt the call of God to preach the gospel. Early one morning he and some friends gathered in a hay field for a season of prayer, confession, and consecration. Henry Varley said, "The world has yet to see what God can do with and for and through and in a man who is fully and wholly consecrated to Him."

Moody was deeply moved by those words. Later, he listened to the great preacher Charles H. Spurgeon. Moody thought:

> "'The world had yet to see! with and for and through and in! A man!'
> Varley meant *any* man! Varley didn't say he had to be educated, or brilliant, or anything else! Just a *man!* Well, by the Holy Spirit in him, he'd
> [Moody] be *one* of those men. And then suddenly, in that high gallery,
> he saw something he'd never realized before,—it was not Mr. Spurgeon,
> after all, who was doing that work: it was God. And if God could use
> Mr. Spurgeon, why should He not use the rest of us, and why should
> we not all just lay ourselves at the Master's feet, and say to Him, 'Send
> me! use me!'"

Dwight L. Moody was an ordinary man who sought to be fully and wholly consecrated to Christ. Through this one ordinary life God began to do the extraordinary. Moody became one of the greatest evangelists of modern times. He preached in revival services across Britain and America where thousands and thousands came to Christ.

 Could God work in extraordinary ways through your life to accomplish significant things for His kingdom? Yes ❑ No ❑

You might say, "Well, I am not a D. L. Moody." You don't have to be a D. L. Moody. God doesn't want you to be a D. L. Moody. God wants you to be you and let Him do through you whatever He chooses. When you believe that nothing significant can happen through you, you have said more about your belief in God than you have said about yourself. You have said that God is not capable of doing anything significant through you. The truth is He is able to do anything He pleases with one ordinary person fully consecrated to Him.

When you believe that nothing significant can happen through you, you have said more about your belief in God than you have said about yourself.

God's Standards Are Different from Man's

Don't be surprised that God's standards of excellence are different from man's. How long was the public ministry of John the Baptist? Perhaps six months. What was Jesus' estimate of John's life? "I tell you, among those born of women there is no one greater than John" (Luke 7:28). None greater! He had six months wholly yielded to God, and the Son of God put that stamp of approval on his life.

John the Baptist

"None Greater"

Don't measure your life by the world's standards. Don't do it. Many denominations are doing it. Many pastors and staff leaders are doing it. Many churches are doing it. Think about it. By the world's standards, a person or church may look pretty good, yet in God's sight be utterly detestable. Similarly, a person or church may be wholly yielded to Him and very pleasing to Him and in the world's eyes be insignificant. Could a pastor who faithfully serves where God put him in a small rural community be pleasing to the Lord? Sure, if that is where God put him. God will look for and reward faithfulness whether the person has been given responsibility for little or much.

Don't measure your life by the world's standards.

An ordinary person is who God most likes to use. Paul said God deliberately seeks out the weak things and the despised things because it is from them that He can receive the greatest glory (1 Cor. 1:26-31). Then everyone will know that only God could have done it. If you feel weak, limited, ordinary, you are the best material through which God can work.

If you feel weak, limited, ordinary, you are the best material through which God can work.

 Review today's lesson. Pray and ask God to identify one or more statements or Scriptures that He wants you to understand, learn, or practice. Then respond to the following:

What was the most meaningful statement or Scripture you read today?

_____

_____

Reword the statement or Scripture into a prayer of response to God.

_____

_____

_____

What does God want you to do in response to today's study?

_____

_____

Review your Scripture memory verse and be prepared to recite it to a partner in your small-group session this week.

SUMMARY STATEMENTS

- God reveals what He is about to do.
- The revelation becomes an invitation to join Him.
- I can't stay the way I am and go with God.
- He is able to do anything He pleases with one ordinary person fully consecrated to Him.
- God's standards of excellence are different from man's.

LOOKING TO GOD

College Campus Bible Studies

Faith Baptist Church began to sense God leading us to an outreach ministry to the college campus. I had never done student work. Our church had never done student work. Our denominational student ministries department recommended we begin with a Bible study in the dorms. For over a year we tried to start a Bible study in the dorms and IT did not work.

One Sunday I pulled our students together and said, "This week I want you to go to the campus and watch to see where God is working and join Him." They asked me to explain. God had impressed on my heart these two Scriptures.
- Romans 3:10-11—"There is no one righteous, not even one; there is no one who understands, no one who seeks God" ;
- John 6:44—"No one can come to me [Jesus] unless the Father who sent me draws him."

I went on to explain, "According to these passages, no one is going to seek God on his own initiative. No one will ask after spiritual matters unless God is at work in his life. When you see someone seeking God or asking about spiritual matters, you are seeing God at work."

I told our students, "If someone starts asking you spiritual questions, whatever else you have planned, don't do it. Cancel what you are doing. Go with that individual and look to see what God is doing there." That week our students went out to see where God was at work and join Him.

On Wednesday one of the girls reported, "Oh, Pastor, a girl who has been in classes with me for two years came to me after class today. She said, 'I think you might be a Christian. I need to talk to you.' I remembered what you said. I had a class, but I missed it. We went to the cafeteria to talk. She said, 'Eleven of us girls have been studying the Bible, and none of us are Christians. Do you know somebody who can lead us in a Bible study?' "

As a result of that contact, we started three Bible study groups in the women's dorms and two in the men's dorm. For two years we tried to do something for God and failed. For three days we looked to see where God was working and joined Him. What a difference that made!

Verse to Memorize
This Week

Some trust in chariots and some in horses, but we trust in the name of the Lord our God.   —PSALM 20:7

GOD-CENTERED LIVING

Part of the Book of Genesis is the record of God accomplishing His purposes through Abraham. It is not the record of Abraham's walk with God. Can you see the difference of focus? The focus of the Bible is God. The essence of sin is a shift from a God-centeredness to a self-centeredness. The essence of salvation is a denial of self, not an affirming of self. We must come to a denial of self and a return to a God-centeredness with our lives. Then God has us where He can accomplish through us purposes He had before He created the world. Though more could be said, here are some descriptions of the life orientations available to you:

Self-centered:
- life focused on self
- proud of self and self's accomplishments
- self confidence
- depending on self and one's own abilities
- affirming self
- seeking to be acceptable to the world and its ways
- looking at circumstances from a human perspective
- selfish and ordinary living

God-centered:
- confidence in God
- dependence on God and His ability and provision
- life focused on God and His activity
- humble before God
- denying self
- seeking first the kingdom of God and His righteousness
- seeking God's perspective in every circumstance
- holy and godly living

In your own words write a definition of the following:

Self-centered _____

_____

_____

_____

God-centered _____

_____

_____

_____

In each of the following pairs of biblical examples, write a *G* before the one that illustrates God-centeredness. Write an *S* before the one that illustrates self-centeredness.

____ 1a. God placed Adam and Eve in a beautiful and bountiful garden. He told them not to eat from the tree of the knowledge of good and evil. Eve saw that the fruit was pleasing to the eye and desirable for gaining wisdom, so she ate it (Gen. 2:16-17; 3:1-7).

____ b. Potiphar's wife daily begged Joseph to come to bed with her. He told her he could not do such a wicked thing and sin against God. When she tried to force him, he fled the room and went to prison rather than yield to temptation (Gen. 39).

God had promised to give the land of Canaan to Israel. Moses sent 12 men into the Promised Land to explore it and bring back a report. The land was bountiful, but the people living there were seen as giants (Num. 13—14).

____ 2a. Ten of the spies said, "We can't attack those people; they are stronger than we are" (13:31).

____ b. Joshua and Caleb said, "If the Lord is pleased with us, he will lead us into that land . . . do not be afraid of the people of the land" (14:8, 9).

To know and do the will of God, you must deny self and return to a God-centered life.

Unit 2 · 27

Self-centeredness is a subtle trap. It makes so much sense (humanly speaking). Like King Asa you can avoid it at one time and fall right into the trap at another time. God-centeredness requires a daily death of self and submission to God (John 12:23-25). Illustrations of God-centeredness are 1-b, 2-b, 3-a. The others illustrate self-centeredness.

God's Purposes Not Our Plans

To live a God-centered life, you must focus your life on God's purposes not your own plans. You must seek to see from God's perspective rather than from your own distorted human perspective. When God starts to do something in the world, He takes the initiative to come and talk to somebody. For some divine reason, He has chosen to involve His people in accomplishing His purposes.

Answer the following questions. Look up and read the Scriptures listed if you do not already know the answer.

1. What was GOD about to do when He came to Noah and asked him to build an ark? (Gen. 6:5-14)

_____

2. What was GOD about to do to Sodom and Gomorrah when He came to Abraham? (Gen. 18:16-21; 19:13)

_____

3. What was GOD about to do when He came to Gideon? (Judg. 6:11-16)

_____

4. What was GOD about to do when He came to Saul (later called Paul) on the road to Damascus? (Acts 9:1-16)

_____

5. At each of these moments, what was the most important factor? Check one.
   ❏ What the individual wanted to do for God
   ❏ What GOD was about to do

God was about to destroy the world with a flood when He came to Noah. When God prepared to destroy Sodom and Gomorrah, He came to tell Abraham about it. God came to Gideon when He was about to deliver the Israelites from the oppression of Midian. God came to Saul when He was ready to carry the gospel message to the Gentiles around the known world. Without doubt, the most important factor in each situation was what God was about to do.

Let's use Noah for an example. What about all the plans he had to serve God? They would not make much sense in light of the coming destruction, would they? Noah was not calling God in to help him accomplish what he was dreaming he was going to do for God. You never find God asking persons to dream up what they want to do for Him.

We do not sit down and dream what we want to do for God and then call God in to help us accomplish it. The pattern in the Scripture is that we submit ourselves to God and:
• we wait until God shows us what He is about to do or
• we watch to see what God is doing around us and join Him.

Review today's lesson. Pray and ask God to identify one or more statements or Scriptures that He wants you to understand, learn, or practice. Underline them. Then respond to the following:

What was the most meaningful statement or Scripture you read today?

"Unless a kernel of wheat falls to the ground and dies, it remains only a single seed. But if it dies, it produces many seeds. The man who loves his life will lose it, while the man who hates his life in this world will keep it for eternal life."
—John 12:23-25

You never find God asking persons to dream up what they want to do for Him.

submit
wait
watch
join

_____

Reword the statement or Scripture into a prayer of response to God.

_____

What does God want you to do in response to today's study?

_____

_____

Write your Scripture memory verse for this week on the following lines.

_____

_____

Review your memory verse from last week.

SUMMARY STATEMENTS

- To know and do the will of God, I must deny self and return to a God-centered life.
- I must reorient my life to God.
- I must focus my life on God's purposes not my own plans.
- I must seek to see from God's perspective rather than from my own distorted human perspective.
- I must wait until God shows me what He is about to do through me.
- I will watch to see what God is doing around me and join Him.

GOD'S PLANS VERSUS OUR PLANS

DAY 2

Who delivered the children of Israel from Egypt? Moses or God? God did. God chose to bring Moses into a relationship with Himself so that He—God—could deliver Israel. Did Moses ever try to take matters about the children of Israel into his own hands? Yes.

In Exodus 2:11-15 (right) Moses began to assert himself in behalf of his own people. What might have happened if Moses had tried to deliver the children of Israel through a human approach? Thousands and thousands would have been slain. Moses tried to take Israelite matters into his own hands. That cost him 40 years of exile in Midian working as a shepherd (and reorienting his life to God-centered living).

When God delivered the children of Israel how many were lost? None. In the process God even led the Egyptians to give the Israelites their gold, silver, and clothes. Egypt was plundered, the Egyptian army was destroyed, and the Israelites did not lose a single person.

Why do we not realize that it is always best to do things God's way? We cause some of the wreck and ruin in our churches because we have a plan. We implement the plan and get out of it only what we can do. God (Jesus) is the head over the body—the church. Oh, that we would discover the difference when we let God be the Head of that body. He will accomplish more in six months through a people yielded to Him than we could do in 60 years without Him.

God's Ways

Read the following Scripture and look for God's response to those who will not follow His ways. Then answer the questions that follow.

" 'I am the Lord your God, who brought you up out of Egypt. Open wide your mouth and I will fill it. But my people would not listen to me; Israel would not submit to me. So I gave them over to their stubborn hearts to follow their own devices.' " (Ps. 81:10-12).

Understanding what God is about to do where I am is more important than telling God what I want to do for Him.

"One day, after Moses had grown up, he went out to where his own people were and watched them at their hard labor. He saw an Egyptian beating a Hebrew, one of his own people. Glancing this way and that and seeing no one, he killed the Egyptian and hid him in the sand. The next day he went out and saw two Hebrews fighting. He asked the one in the wrong, 'Why are you hitting your fellow Hebrew?'

"The man said, 'Who made you ruler and judge over us? Are you thinking of killing me as you killed the Egyptian?' Then Moses was afraid and thought, 'What I did must have become known.'

"When Pharaoh heard of this, he tried to kill Moses, but Moses fled from Pharaoh and went to live in Midian." —Exodus 2:11-15

1. What had God already done for Israel? _____

_____

2. What did God promise to His people? _____

_____

3. How did the people respond?_____

_____

4. What did God do? _____

_____

Now read the next two verses to see what could have been true for Israel. Then answer the question that follows.

> " 'If my people would but listen to me, if Israel would follow my ways, how quickly would I subdue their enemies and turn my hand against their foes!' " (Ps. 81:13-14).

5. What could have been true had Israel listened to and followed God?

_____

Locate in your Bible and read Hebrews 3:7-19. Then answer one more question.

6. Why were the children of Israel denied entrance to the promised land?

_____

We are His servants, and we adjust our lives to what He is about to do.

We adjust our lives to God so *He* can do through us what *He* wants to do. God is not our servant to make adjustment to our plans. We are His servants, and we adjust our lives to what He is about to do. If we will not submit, God will let us follow our own devices. In following them, however, we will never experience what God is waiting and wanting to do in our behalf or through us for others.

Israel was brought out of Egypt with many miraculous signs and wonders. Wouldn't you think they could trust God to do just about anything? When they got to the promised land they could not trust Him to deliver the promised land to them. For that reason, they spent the next 40 years wandering in the wilderness. In Psalm 81, God reminded Israel that He would have conquered the enemies *quickly* if they had only followed His plans rather than their own devices.

Think about and answer the following questions:

1. Has God changed in the way He works with people to carry out His plans and purposes?

_____

2. Would you rather follow your own plans and wander around in a spiritual wilderness or follow God's ways and quickly enter a spiritual promised land?

_____

You Need to Know What God Is About to Do

One year denominational leaders came to Vancouver to discuss long range plans for an emphasis which we had scheduled in the metropolitan area. Top people from several agencies were going to work with us to accomplish many wonderful things. Yet, in my mind I was asking, "But what if God has called our nation to judgment before that time?" I realized how much I needed to know what God had in mind for Vancouver. Planning what I wanted to do in the future could have been totally irrelevant.

When God called the prophets, He often had a two-fold message. The first desire of God was: "Call the people to return to Me." If the people failed to respond, they needed to hear the second message: "Let them know that they are closer to the moment of judgment than they have ever been." God's word to the prophet was, "Tell the people: This is what I have been doing. This is what I am doing right now. This is what I am about to do. Then call them to respond."

Do you suppose it was important that the prophets understand what God was about to do? When God was prepared to bring a terrible judgment to Jerusalem and destroy the entire city, was it important to know what God was about to do? Certainly!

How close do you think your country is to the judgment of God? Check one.
- ❑ 1. I do not believe God will bring judgment on my country.
- ❑ 2. I believe God's judgment is a long way off.
- ❑ 3. I cannot understand why God has waited this long. I believe we are on the verge of a major judgment from God.
- ❑ 4. I believe we are already experiencing a disciplinary judgment like that described in Isaiah 5:1-7.
- ❑ 5. I believe we have already come through an experience of God's judgment.

What evidence can you list to support your answer?

_____

_____

What affect does your belief have on the way you live your life?

_____

_____

In your group session you will have an opportunity to discuss your answers.

> Understanding what God is about to do where you are is more important than telling God what you want to do for Him.

What good would Abraham have done by telling God how he was planning to take a survey of Sodom and Gomorrah and go door-to-door witnessing the day before God was going to destroy the cities? What good would you do by making long-range plans in your church if, before you ever get to implement them, God brings judgment on your nation?

You need to know what God has on His agenda for your church, community, and nation at this time in history. Then you and your church can adjust your lives to God, so that He can move you into the mainstream of His activity before it is too late. Though God likely will not give you a detailed schedule, He will let you know one step at a time how you and your church need to respond to what He is doing.

Pray right now and ask for God's guidance on how you should respond to Him...
- in your personal life
- in your family
- in your church
- in your work
- in your community
- in our nation

You may want to jot some notes in the margin or on separate paper.

What was God about to do when He started to tell Martin Luther that "the just shall live by faith"? He was going to bring people all over Europe to an understanding that salvation was a free gift and that each person had direct access to Him. He was bringing about a great Reformation. As you study great movements of God in church history, you will notice in every case that God came to someone and the person released his life to God. Then God began to accomplish His purposes through that individual.

Martin Luther

When God began to speak to John and Charles Wesley, He was preparing for a sweeping revival in England that saved England from a bloody revolution like France had experienced. There stood a couple of men, along with George Whitfield and some others, through whom God was able to do a mighty work and turn England completely around.

John and Charles Wesley

George Whitfield

In your community there are some things that are about to happen in the lives of others. God wants to intercept those lives. Suppose He wants to do it through you. He comes to you and talks to you. But you are so self-centered, you respond, "I don't think I am trained. I don't think I am able to do it. And I . . ."

Do you see what happens? The focus is on self. The moment you sense that God is moving in your life, you give Him a whole list of reasons why He has got the wrong person or why the time is not right (Ex. 3:11; 4:1). I wish you would seek God's perspective. God knows that you can't do it! But He wants to do it Himself *through* you.

 Review today's lesson. Pray and ask God to identify one or more statements or Scriptures that He wants you to understand, learn, or practice. Underline them. Then respond to the following:

What was the most meaningful statement or Scripture you read today?

_____

_____

Reword the statement or Scripture into a prayer of response to God.

_____

_____

_____

What does God want you to do in response to today's study?

_____

_____

SUMMARY STATEMENTS

- Do things God's way.
- God will accomplish more in six months through a people yielded to Him than we could do in 60 years without Him.
- I am God's servant. I adjust my life to what He is about to do.
- Understanding what God is about to do where I am is more important than telling God what I want to do for Him.

DAY 3 — GOD TAKES THE INITIATIVE

God's revelation of His activity is an invitation for you to join Him.

God's Initiative Not Yours

All the way through the Scripture, God takes the initiative. When He comes to a person, He always reveals Himself and His activity. That revelation is always an invitation for the individual to adjust his life to God. None of the people God ever encountered could remain the same after the encounter. They had to make major adjustments in their lives in order to walk obediently with God.

God is the Sovereign Lord. I try to keep my life God-centered because He is the One who is the Pace Setter. He is always the One to take the initiative to accomplish what He wants to do. When you are God-centered, even the desires to do the things that please God come from God's initiative in your life (Phil. 2:13).

"It is God who works in you to will and to act according to his good purpose."
—Philippians 2:13

What often happens when we see God at work? We immediately get self-centered rather than God-centered. Somehow we must reorient our lives to God. We must learn to see things from His perspective. We must allow Him to develop His character in us. We must let Him reveal His thoughts to us. Only then can we get a proper perspective on life.

If you keep your life God-centered, you will immediately put your life alongside His activity. When you see God at work around you, your heart will leap within you and say, "Thank You, Father, thank You for letting me be involved where You are." When I am in the middle of the activity of God and God opens my eyes to let me see where He is working, I always assume that God wants me to join Him.

 Answer the following questions by checking your responses.

1. Who takes the initiative in your knowing and doing the will of God?
❏ a. I do. God waits on me until I decide what I want to do for Him.
❏ b. God does. He invites me to join Him in what He is about to do.

2. Which of the following are ways God may reveal His plan or purpose to you? Check all that apply.
❏ a. He lets me see where He is already working around me.
❏ b. He speaks to me through Scripture and impresses me with a practical application of the truth to my life.
❏ c. He gives me an earnest desire that only grows stronger as I pray.
❏ d. He creates circumstances around me that open a door of opportunity.

God always takes the initiative (1b). He does not wait to see what we want to do for Him. After He has taken the initiative to come to us, He does wait until we respond to Him by adjusting ourselves to Him and making ourselves available to Him. In question 2 all four are ways God may reveal His plan or purpose to you. There are others as well. The last two (c and d), however, must be carefully watched. A self-centered life will have a tendency to confuse its selfish desire with God's will. Circumstances cannot always be a clear direction for God's leadership either. "Open" and "closed doors" are not always indications of God's directions. In seeking God's direction, check to see that prayer, the Scripture, and circumstances agree in the direction you sense God leading you.

Now, you may still be saying, "That all sounds good, but I need some practical help in learning how to apply these concepts." In every situation God demands that you depend on Him, not a method. The key is not a method but a relationship to God. Let me see if I can help you by telling you about a man who learned to walk with God by prayer and faith.

George Mueller's Walk of Faith

George Mueller was a pastor in England during the nineteenth century. He was concerned that God's people had become very discouraged. They no longer looked for God to do anything unusual. They no longer trusted God to answer prayers. They had so little faith.

George Mueller

God began to lead George to pray. George's prayers were for God to lead him to a work that could only be explained by the people as an act of God. George wanted the people to learn that their God was a faithful, prayer-answering God. He came upon the verse in Psalm 81:10 that you read in yesterday's lesson—"Open wide your mouth and I will fill it." God began to lead him in a walk of faith that became an outstanding testimony to all who hear of his story.

When George felt led of God to do some work, he prayed for resources needed and told no one of the need. He wanted all to know that God had provided for the need only in answer to prayer and faith. During his ministry in Bristol, George started the Scriptural Knowledge Institute for distribution of Scripture and for religious education. He also began an orphanage. By the time of his death, George Mueller had been used by God to build four orphan houses that cared for 2,000 children at a time. Over 10,000 children had been provided for through the orphanages. He distributed over eight million dollars that had been given to him in answer to prayer. When he died at 93, his worldly possessions were valued at $800.[1]

How did he know and do the will of God?

☀ **Read the following statement and list the things he did that helped him know what to do. Then list the things that led him to make mistakes in knowing God's will.**

> "I never remember. . . a period. . . that I ever sincerely and patiently sought to know the will of God by the teaching of the Holy Ghost, through the instrumentality of the Word of God, but I have been always directed rightly. But if honesty of heart and uprightness before God were lacking, or if I did not patiently wait upon God for instruction, or if I preferred the counsel of my fellow men to the declarations of the Word of the living God, I made great mistakes."

What helped George Mueller know God's will?

_____

_____

What led to mistakes in knowing God's will:_____

_____

_____

George Mueller mentioned these things that helped him:
• He sincerely sought God's direction.
• He waited patiently on God until he had a word from God.
• He looked to the Holy Spirit (Ghost) to teach him through the word.

He knew the following things led to his making mistakes:
• Lacking honesty of heart
• Lacking uprightness before God
• Impatience to wait for God
• Preferred the counsel of men over the declarations of Scripture

Here is how he summed up the way he entered into a "heart" relationship with God and learned to discern God's voice:

1. I seek at the beginning to get my heart into such a state that it has no will of its own in regard to a given matter. Nine-tenths of the trouble with people generally is just here. Nine-tenths of the difficulties are overcome when our hearts are ready to do the knowledge of what His will is.

2. Having done this, I do not leave the result to feeling or simple impression. If so, I make myself liable to great delusions.

3. I seek the Will of the Spirit of God through, or in connection with, the Word of God. The Spirit and the Word must be combined. If I look to the Spirit alone without the Word, I lay myself open to great delusions also. If the Holy Ghost guides us at all, He will do it according to the Scriptures and never contrary to them.

4. Next I take into account providential circumstances. These often plainly indicate God's Will in connection with His Word and Spirit.

5. I ask God in prayer to reveal His Will to me aright.

6. Thus, (1) through prayer to God, (2) the study of the Word, and (3) reflection, I come to a deliberate judgment according to the best of my ability and knowledge, and if my mind is thus at peace, and continues so after two or three more petitions, I proceed accordingly.

Check the correct answer for each of the following questions.

1. How did Mueller begin in his search for God's will?
   ❏ a. He tried to decide what he wanted to do for God.
   ❏ b. He tried to make sure he had no will of his own.
   ❏ c. He tried to get to the place he wanted only God's will.
   ❏ d. Both b and c.

2. What did Mueller say leads to possible delusions or false directions?
   ❏ a. Basing the decision on feelings alone.
   ❏ b. Following the slightest impressions.
   ❏ c. Looking to the Spirit alone for direction.
   ❏ d. All of the above.

3. In which of the following pairs of things did Mueller look for agreement?
   ❏ a. His desires and circumstances.
   ❏ b. The Spirit and the Word.
   ❏ c. The counsel of others and his desires.
   ❏ d. Circumstances and a sense of peace.

4. What was the final test whereby Mueller came to a judgment about God's will?
   - ❏ a. He identified whether the "door" was open or closed.
   - ❏ b. He asked a pastor friend what he thought.
   - ❏ c. He proceeded with a hunch and watched to see if it worked.
   - ❏ d. He used prayer, Bible study, and reflection to find lasting peace about a proposed direction.

Answers are 1-d, 2-d, 3-b, 4-d. I hope this has helped. Don't get discouraged if it still seems vague. We have much more time to work together. Tomorrow I will start by giving you a real-life example of how God works.

✺ **Review today's lesson. Pray and ask God to identify one or more statements or Scriptures that He wants you to understand, learn, or practice. Underline them. Then respond to the following:**

What was the most meaningful statement or Scripture you read today?

_____

_____

Reword the statement or Scripture into a prayer of response to God.

_____

_____

_____

What does God want you to do in response to today's study?

_____

_____

Practice quoting your Scripture memory verses aloud or write them on separate paper.

SUMMARY STATEMENTS

- God's revelation of His activity is an invitation for me to adjust my life to Him and join in His work.
- "I seek at the beginning to get my heart into such a state that it has no will of its own in regard to a given matter."
- "I do not leave the result to feeling or simple impression."
- "I seek the Will of the Spirit of God through, or in connection with, the Word of God."

GOD SPEAKS TO HIS PEOPLE

DAY 4

God has not changed. He still speaks to His people.

Years ago I spoke to a group of young pastors. When I finished the first session, a pastor took me aside and said, "I vowed to God I would never, ever again listen to a man like you. You talk as though God is personal and real and talks to you. I just despise that."

I asked him, "Are you having difficulty having God speak to you?" He and I took time to talk. Before long, we were on our knees. He was weeping and thanking God that God had spoken to him. Oh, don't let anyone intimidate you about hearing from God.

✺ **Read the following Scriptures, answer the questions that follow.**

Hebrews 1:1—"In the past God spoke to our forefathers through the prophets at many times and in various ways, but in these last days he has spoken to us by his Son."

John 14:26—"The Counselor, the Holy Spirit, whom the Father will send in my name, will teach you all things and will remind you of everything I have said to you."

John 16:13-14—"When he, the Spirit of truth, comes, he will guide you into all truth. He will not speak on his own; he will speak only what he hears, and he will tell you what is yet to come. He will bring glory to me by taking from what is mine and making it known to you."

John 8:47—"He who belongs to God hears what God says. The reason you do not hear is that you do not belong to God."

1. In the Old Testament ("times past") how did God speak and through whom?

_____

2. In New Testament times ("these last days") how did God speak?

_____

3. In John 14:26 whom did Jesus promise the Father would send in His name?

_____

4. What is the work of the Holy Spirit described in John 14:26 and 16:13-14?

_____

5. Who is the one who hears what God says?

_____

6. What does John 8:47 have to say about a person who does not hear what God says?

_____

Write a summary of what these Scriptures say about God's speaking.

_____

_____

_____

In the Old Testament God spoke at many times and in a variety of ways. Through Jesus, God Himself spoke to His people during His lifetime. Now God speaks through the Holy Spirit. The Holy Spirit will teach you all things, will call to your memory the things Jesus said, will guide you into all truth, will speak what He hears from the Father, will tell you what is yet to come, and glorify Christ as He reveals Christ to you.

Does God really speak to His people in our day? Will He reveal to you where He is working when He wants to use you? Yes! God has not changed. He still speaks to His people. If you have trouble hearing God speak, you are in trouble at the very heart of your Christian experience.

How Do I Know When God Speaks?

Sin has so affected us (Rom. 3:10-11), you and I cannot understand the truth of God unless the Holy Spirit of God reveals it. He is the Teacher. When He teaches you the Word of God, sit before Him and respond to Him. As you pray, watch to see how He uses the Word of God to confirm in your heart a word from God. Watch what He is doing around you in circumstances. The God who is speaking to you as you pray and the God who is speaking to you in the Scriptures is the God who is working around you.

If you have trouble hearing God speak, you are in trouble at the very heart of your Christian experience.

Look on the inside back cover at the fourth statement. Then answer the following questions.

1. When Jesus returned to heaven, which Person of the trinity was sent to speak to God's people? Check one.
   ❏ a. God the Father
   ❏ b. Jesus
   ❏ c. The Holy Spirit

2. What are four ways through which He speaks?

_____

3. When He speaks, what does He reveal?

_____

God speaks by the Holy Spirit through the Bible, prayer, circumstances, and the church to reveal Himself, His purposes, and His ways. Later in the course, we will spend several units studying these ways God speaks. I cannot give you a formula, however, and say this is how you can know when God is speaking to you. I will share with you from the Scripture what the Scriptures say. The evidence of the Scriptures can encourage you at this point. When God chose to speak to an individual in the Bible, the person knew it was God, and he knew what God was saying.

In John 10:2-4 and 14 Jesus said:
- " 'The man who enters by the gate is the shepherd of his sheep.
- The sheep listen to his voice.
- His sheep follow him because they know his voice.
- I am the good shepherd; I know my sheep and my sheep know me.' "

The key to knowing God's voice is not a formula. It is not a method you can follow. Knowing God's voice comes from an intimate love relationship with God. That is why those who do not have the relationship ("do not belong to God") do not hear what God is saying (John 8:47). You are going to have to watch to see how God uniquely communicates with you. You will not have any other crutch. You will have to depend on God alone. Your relationship to Him is of upmost importance.

Which of the following best describes the way you will know the voice of God when He speaks? Check your response.

    ❏ a. God will give me a miraculous sign. Then I will know God has spoken to me.
    ❏ b. Out of an intimate relationship with God, I will come to recognize God's voice.
    ❏ c. When I learn and follow the correct formula, I will hear God speaking.
    ❏ d. I can open the Bible, pick out a verse that I want to use, and claim that I have a word from God for my circumstance.

What is the key to knowing God's voice? _____

The _relationship_ is the key to knowing God's voice, to hearing when God speaks. _B_ is the correct answer to the preceding question. Now what about _a, c,_ and _d_? Sometimes in Scripture God did give a miraculous sign to assure the person that the word was from Him. Gideon is one example (Judg. 6). Asking God for a sign is often an indication of unbelief. When the scribes and Pharisees asked Jesus for a miraculous sign, Jesus condemned them as a "wicked and adulterous generation" (Matt. 12:38-39). They were so self-centered and sinful, they could not even recognize that God was there in their midst. (See Luke 19:41-44.)

A "correct formula" is not the way either. How many other burning bushes like Moses experienced were there? None. God does not want you to become an expert at using a formula. He wants an intimate love relationship with you. He wants you to depend on Him alone. Hearing God does not depend on a method or formula but a relationship.

Some may wonder why answer _d_ is not acceptable. They may ask, "Can't I get a word from God from the Bible?" Yes you can! But only the Holy Spirit of God can reveal to you which truth of Scripture is a word from God in a particular circumstance. Notice how self-centered answer _d_ is? "_I_ open . . . _I_ pick . . . _I_ claim . . . " Even if the circumstance is similar to yours, only God can reveal His word for your circumstance.

You also need to be very careful about claiming you have a word from God. Claiming to have a word from God is serious business. If you have been given a word from God, you must continue in that direction until it comes to pass (even 25 years like Abram). If you have not been given a word from God yet you say you have, you stand in judgment as a false prophet:

> "You may say to yourselves, 'How can we know when a message has not been spoken by the Lord?' If what a prophet proclaims in the name of the Lord does not take place or come true, that is a message the Lord has not spoken. That prophet has spoken presumptuously" (Deut. 18:21-22).

In the Old Testament law the penalty for a false prophet was death (Deut. 18:20). That certainly is a very serious charge. Do not take a word from God lightly.

God loves you. He wants to have an intimate relationship with you. He wants you to depend only on Him when you are seeking a word from Him. He wants you to learn to hear His voice and know His will. Your relationship to Him is the key to hearing when God speaks to you.

Consider praying the following prayer: "God, I pray that I will come to such a relationship with You that when you speak, I will hear and respond."

Review today's lesson. Pray and ask God to identify one or more statements or Scriptures that He wants you to understand, learn, or practice. Underline them. Then respond to the following:

What was the most meaningful statement or Scripture you read today?

_____

_____

Reword the statement or Scripture into a prayer of response to God.

_____

_____

What does God want you to do in response to today's study?

_____

_____

SUMMARY STATEMENTS

- God has not changed. He still speaks to His people.
- If I have trouble hearing God speak, I am in trouble at the very heart of my Christian experience.
- God speaks by the Holy Spirit through the Bible, prayer, circumstances, and the church to reveal Himself, His purposes, and His ways.
- Knowing God's voice comes from an intimate love relationship with God.

DAY 5   GOD SPEAKS WITH A PURPOSE

God develops character to match the assignment.

We usually want God to speak to us so He can give us a devotional thought to make us feel good all day. If you want the God of the universe to speak to you, you need to be ready for Him to reveal to you what He is doing where you are. In the Scripture, God is not often seen coming and speaking to people just for conversation's sake. He was always up to something. When God speaks to you through the Bible, prayer, circumstances, the church, or in some other way, He has a purpose in mind for your life.

Abram

When God spoke to Abram (Gen. 12), what was God about to do? He was about to begin to build a nation. Notice the timing of God. Why did God speak to Abram when He did? Because it was then that God wanted to start to build a nation. The moment Abram knew what God was about to do, he had to make an adjustment in his life to God. He had to immediately follow what God said.

The moment God speaks to you is the very moment God wants you to respond to Him.

The moment God speaks to you is the very moment God wants you to respond to Him. Some of us assume that we have the next three to four months to think about it and to try to decide whether this is really God's timing. The moment God speaks to you *is* God's timing. That is why He chooses to speak when He does. He speaks to His servant when He is ready to move. Otherwise He wouldn't speak to you. As God comes into the mainstream of your life, the timing of your response is crucial. When God speaks to you, you need to believe and trust God.

The moment God speaks to you is God's timing.

How long was it from the time that He spoke to Abram (later named Abraham) that Isaac, the child of promise, was born? Twenty-five years! (See Gen. 12:4 and 21:5.) Why did God wait twenty-five years? Because it took God twenty-five years to make a father suitable for Isaac. God was concerned, not so much about Abram, but about a nation. The quality of the father will affect the quality of all the generations that follow. As goes the father, so goes the next several generations. God took time to build Abram into a man of character. Abram had to begin to adjust his life to God's ways immediately. He could not wait until Isaac was born and then try to become the father God wanted him to be.

 Mark the following statements as T (true) or F (false).

_____1. God speaks to me just so I can have a devotional thought to make me feel good all day.

_____2. God speaks to me when He has a purpose in mind for my life.

_____3. When God speaks to me, I can take plenty of time deciding when and how I should respond.

_____4. When God speaks to me, I must respond immediately by adjusting my life to Him, His purposes, and His ways.

_____5. The moment God speaks is God's timing.

We are so oriented to quick response that we abandon the word from God long before He has a chance to develop our character. When God speaks, He has a purpose in mind for your life. The time He speaks is the time you need to begin responding to Him. False: 1 and 3; True: 2, 4, and 5.

God Develops Character to Match the Assignment

When God called Abram, He said, "I will make your name great" (Gen. 12:2). That means: "I will develop your character to match your assignment." Nothing is more pathetic than having a small character in a big assignment. Many of us don't want to give attention to our character, we just want the big assignment from God.

Suppose a pastor is waiting for a big church to call him to be pastor. Then a small church calls and says, "Will you come and be bivocational and help us out here on the west side of Wyoming?"

"Well, no," the prospective pastor responds. He thinks, "I am here waiting for God to give me an assignment. I have done so much training, I can't waste my life by working a secular job when I can serve a church full-time. I think that I deserve something much more significant than that."

 How would you classify that response? Check one.
❏ That is a God-centered response.
❏ That is a self-centered response.

Do you see how self-centered that viewpoint is? Human reasoning will not give you God's perspective. If you can't be faithful in a little, God will not give you the larger assignment. He may want to adjust your life and character in smaller assignments in order to prepare you for the larger ones. That is where God starts to work. When you make the adjustments and start to obey Him, you come to know Him by experience. This is the goal of God's activity in your life—that you come to KNOW Him. Do you want to experience God mightily working in your life and through your life? Then adjust your life to God in the kind of relationship where you follow Him wherever He leads you—even if the assignment seems to be small or insignificant. Wouldn't you rather hear: "Well done, good and faithful servant!" (Matt. 25:21).

Now, you may ask, "Do I automatically assume that a request like the pastor received to the west side of Wyoming is from God because it is a small assignment?" No. Whether the assignment is large or small in your eyes, you will still have to find out whether it is from God or not. However, you always need to let God tell you that. Do not rule out an assignment, large or small, on the basis of your own preconceived ideas. Remember—you will know through the relationship with God. Don't try to bypass the relationship.

 Before we move to our next topic, respond to this: Suppose you had planned to go fishing or watch Monday night football or go to the shopping mall. Then God confronts you with an opportunity to join Him in something He wants to do. What would you do? Check your response:

"Well done, good and faithful servant! You have been faithful with a few things; I will put you in charge of many things. Come and share your master's happiness!"
—Matthew 25:21

You will know through the relationship.

❏ 1. I would finish my plans and then fit God's plans into the next available time in my schedule.

❏ 2. I would assume that, since God already knew my plans, this new assignment must not be from Him.

❏ 3. I would try to work out a way to do both what I want and what God wants.

❏ 4. I would adjust my plans to join God in what He was about to do.

Lordship

I have known some people who wouldn't interrupt a fishing trip or a football game for anything in the world. In their mind they say they want to serve God, but they keep eliminating from their life anything that is going to interfere with their own plans. They are so self-centered that they do not recognize the times when God comes to them. If you are God-centered, you will adjust your circumstances to what God wants to do.

> He has a right to interrupt your life. He is Lord. When you accepted Him as Lord, you gave Him the right to help Himself to your life anytime He wants.

Suppose that five times out of ten when the Master had something for the servant to do the servant said, "I am sorry. That is not on my schedule." What do you suppose the Master would do? The Master would discipline the servant. If the servant did not respond to the discipline, sooner or later that servant would find that the Master is no longer coming to him with assignments.

You may be saying, "Oh, I wish I could experience God working through me the way He has worked through John (or Sue)." But every time God comes to John, John adjusts his life to God and is obedient. When John has been faithful in little assignments, God has given him more important assignments.

If you are not willing to be faithful in a little, God cannot give you a larger assignment.

If you are not willing to be faithful in a little, God cannot give you a larger assignment. The smaller assignments of God are always used of God to develop character. God always develops character to match His assignment. If God has a great assignment for you, He has to develop a great character to match that assignment before He can give you the assignment.

☀ **Reflect over these matters of Lordship and God's developing character for the assignment. Answer the following questions:**

1. What kind of assignments have you wanted the Lord to give you? Have you been frustrated or disappointed in this area of your life?

_____

_____

2. Can you think of a time when God probably wanted to use you in an assignment and you chose not to follow His leading? If so, briefly describe the situation.

_____

_____

3. Is the Holy Spirit saying anything to you right now about your character? If so, what is He saying?

_____

_____

4. Do your actions acknowledge Christ as Lord of your life? If not, what response do you want to make to His claims on your life right now?

_____

_____

God needs time to prepare you for an assignment.

When God tells you a direction, you accept it, and understand it clearly, then give God all the time He needs to make you the kind of person that He could trust with that assignment.

Do not assume that the moment He calls you you are ready for the assignment.

How long was it after God (through Samuel) anointed David king, that David mounted the throne? Maybe ten or twelve years. What was God doing in the meantime? He was building David's relationship with Himself. As goes the king, so goes the nation. You cannot bypass character.

David

How long was it after the living Lord called the Apostle Paul that Paul went on his first missionary journey? Maybe ten or eleven years. The focus is not on Paul; the focus is on God. God wanted to redeem a lost world, and He wanted to begin to redeem the Gentiles through Paul. God needed that much time to prepare Paul for the assignment.

Paul

Is it for your sake that God takes time to prepare you? No, not for you alone, but also for the sake of those He wants to reach through you. For their sake, give yourself to the kind of relationship to God we are discussing. Then, when He puts you in an assignment, He will achieve everything He wants in the lives of those you touch.

Review today's lesson. Pray and ask God to identify one or more statements or Scriptures that He wants you to understand, learn, or practice. Then respond to the following:

What was the most meaningful statement or Scripture you read today?

_____

_____

_____

Reword the statement or Scripture into a prayer of response to God.

_____

_____

_____

_____

What does God want you to do in response to today's study?

_____

_____

_____

Write your Scripture memory verse (Ps. 20:7) on the following lines.

_____

_____

Review your other Scripture memory verses and be prepared to recite them to a partner in your small-group session this week.

SUMMARY STATEMENTS

- The moment God speaks to me is the very moment God wants me to respond to Him.
- The moment God speaks to me is God's timing.
- God develops my character to match the assignment He has for me.
- He has a right to interrupt my life. He is Lord. When I accepted Him as Lord, I gave Him the right to help Himself to my life anytime He wants.

---

[1]For further reading on George Mueller see, *Answers to Prayer from George Mueller's Narratives,* Compiled by A. E. C. Brooks, Moody Press; *George Mueller* by Faith Coxe Bailey, Moody Press.

GOD PURSUES A LOVE RELATIONSHIP

Carrie's Cancer*

When one of my children could not get his own way, he used to say, "You don't love me." Was that true? No, it wasn't true. My love had not changed. At that moment, however, my love was expressing itself differently than he wanted it.

When our only daughter Carrie was sixteen, the doctors told us she had cancer. We had to take her through chemotherapy and radiation. We suffered along with Carrie as we watched her experience the sickness that goes along with the treatments. Some people face such an experience by blaming God and questioning why He doesn't love them any more. Carrie's cancer treatments could have been a very devastating experience for us. Was God loving us still? Yes. Had His love changed? No, His love had not changed.

When you face circumstances like this, you can question and ask Him to show you what is going on. We did that. We had to ask Him what we should do. We asked all those questions; but I never said, "Lord, I guess you don't love me."

At times I went before the Heavenly Father, and I saw behind my daughter the cross of Jesus Christ. I said, "Father, don't ever let me look at circumstances and question your love for me. Your love for me was settled on the cross. That has never changed and will never change for me." Our love relationship with the Heavenly Father sustained us through a very difficult time.

No matter what the circumstances are, His love never changes. Long before this experience with Carrie, I had made a determination: no matter what the circumstances, I would never look at those circumstances except against the backdrop of the cross. In the death and resurrection of Jesus Christ, God forever convinced me that He loved me. The cross, the death of Jesus Christ, and His resurrection are God's final, total, and complete expression that He loves us. Never allow your heart to question the love of God. Settle it on the front end of your desiring to know Him and experience Him, that He loves you. He created you for that love relationship. He has been pursuing you in that love relationship. Every dealing He has with you is an expression of His love for you. God would cease to be God if He expressed Himself in any way other than *perfect love*!

* Carrie is now doing very well and has finished her university degree. God is so good to us. April 1992

Verse to Memorize
This Week

Jesus replied: "Love the Lord your God with all your heart and with all your soul and with all your mind. This is the first and greatest commandment." —MATTHEW 22:37-38

CREATED FOR A LOVE RELATIONSHIP

In the first two units I introduced you to some basic principles for knowing and doing the will of God. The seven realities you have examined summarize the kind of relationship through which God works to accomplish His purposes. As I said earlier, this course is not written to teach you a program, a method, or a formula for knowing and doing the will of God. It is written to point you to a *relationship* with God. God will then work through that relationship to accomplish through you what He pleases.

By way of review, see if you can fill in the blanks in the seven realities below with the correct words. If you need help, you may look on the inside back cover of your book.

1. _____ is always at work around you.

2. God pursues a continuing love _____ with you that is real and _____.

3. God invites you to become _____ with Him in His _____.

4. God speaks by the _____ _____ through the Bible, _____, circumstances, and the _____ to reveal Himself, His _____, and His ways.

5. God's invitation for you to work with Him always leads you to a crisis of _____ that requires _____ and action.

6. You must make major _____ in your life to join God in what He is doing.

7. You come to know God by _____ as you _____ Him and He accomplishes His work through you.

This unit will focus on the second reality. Write the second reality below but replace the word *you* with *me*.

_____

_____

_____

Check your work using the inside back cover.

A Love Relationship

During this unit, I want to help you see that God Himself pursues a love relationship with you. He is the One who takes the initiative to bring you into this kind of relationship. He created you for a love relationship with Himself. That is the very purpose of your life. This love relationship can and should be real and personal to you.

If you were standing before God, could you describe your relationship to Him by saying, "I love You with all my heart and all my soul and all my mind and all my strength"? Yes ❑ No ❑ Why?

_____

_____

One of our church members always was having difficulty in his personal life, his family, at work, and in the church. One day I went to him and asked, "Can you describe your relationship with God by sincerely saying, 'I love You with all of my heart'?"

The strangest look came over his face. He said, "Nobody has ever asked me that. No, I could not describe my relationship with God that way. I could say I obey Him, I serve Him, I worship Him, and I fear Him. But I cannot say that I love Him."

Can you describe your relationship with God by sincerely saying, "I love You with all of my heart"?

I realized that everything in his life was out of order, because God's basic purpose for his life was out of order. God created us for a love relationship with Him. If you cannot describe your relationship with God by saying that you love Him with all your being, then you need to ask the Holy Spirit to bring you into that kind of a relationship.

※ **If you need to and are willing, pause right now and ask the Holy Spirit to bring you into a whole-hearted love relationship with God.**

Spend time in prayer expressing your love to God. Thank Him for the ways He has shown His love to you. Be specific in listing the ways. You may even want to list some in the left margin. Praise Him for His loving-kindness.

If I were to try to summarize the entire Old Testament, it would be expressed in this verse: "Hear, O Israel: The Lord our God, the Lord is one. Love the Lord your God with all your heart and with all your soul and with all your strength" (Deut. 6:4-5).

This heart-cry of God is expressed throughout the Old Testament. The essence of the New Testament is the same. Quoting from Deuteronomy, Jesus said the greatest commandment in the law is: "Love the Lord your God with all your heart and with all your soul and with all your mind and with all your strength" (Mark 12:30). Everything depends on this! Everything in your Christian life, everything about knowing Him and experiencing Him, everything about knowing His will, depends on the quality of your love relationship to God. If that is not right, nothing in your life will be right.

The Greatest Commandment

Everything in your Christian life, everything about knowing Him and experiencing Him, everything about knowing His will, depends on the quality of your love relationship to God.

※ **Read the following Scriptures that speak of a love relationship. As you read, emphasize the word *love* (or any form of it, such as "loves") by circling it each time it appears.**

Deuteronomy 30:19-20—"This day I call heaven and earth as witnesses against you that I have set before you life and death, blessings and curses. Now choose life, so that you and your children may live and that you may love the Lord your God, listen to his voice, and hold fast to him. For the Lord is your life."

John 3:16—"God so loved the world that he gave his one and only Son, that whoever believes in him shall not perish but have eternal life."

John 14:21—"Whoever has my commands and obeys them, he is the one who loves me. He who loves me will be loved by my Father, and I too will love him and show myself to him."

Romans 8:35, 37, 39—"Who shall separate us from the love of Christ? Shall trouble or hardship or persecution or famine or nakedness or danger or sword? . . . No, in all these things we are more than conquerors through him who loved us. . . . [Nothing] will be able to separate us from the love of God that is in Christ Jesus our Lord."

1 John 3:16—"This is how we know what love is: Jesus Christ laid down his life for us. And we ought to lay down our lives for our brothers."

1 John 4:9-10, 19—"This is how God showed his love among us: He sent his one and only Son into the world that we might live through him. This is love: not that we loved God, but that he loved us and sent his Son as an atoning sacrifice for our sins. . . . We love because he first loved us."

※ **Using the preceding Scriptures, answer the following questions:**

1. Who is your "life"? _____

2. In what ways has God demonstrated His love for us? _____

_____

3. How can we show our love for Him? _____

_____

_____

4. What does God promise to do in response to our loving Him?

_____

_____

_____

_____

5. Who loved first—we or God? _____

Answers: (1) The Lord is your life. (2) He has drawn us to Himself. He sent His only Son to provide eternal life for us. Jesus laid down His life for us. (3) Choose life; listen to His voice; hold fast to Him; believe in His only Son; obey His commands and teachings; be willing to lay down our lives for our brothers. (4) We and our children will live under His blessings. By believing in Jesus, we have eternal life. The Father will love us. God will come to make His home with us. He will make us more than conquerors over all difficulties. We never will be separated from His love. (5) God loved us first. "God is love" (1 John 4:16). His very nature is love.

What is the one thing God wants from you? He wants you to love Him with all your being. Your experiencing God depends on your having this relationship of love. A love relationship with God is more important than any other single factor in your life.

A love relationship with God is more important than any other single factor in your life.

Review today's lesson. Pray and ask God to identify one or more statements or Scriptures that He wants you to understand, learn, or practice. Underline it (them). Then respond to the following:

What was the most meaningful statement or Scripture you read today?

_____

_____

Reword the statement or Scripture into a prayer of response to God.

_____

_____

_____

What does God want you to do in response to today's study?

_____

Write your Scripture memory verse for this unit on the following lines and review your verses from other units. Remember, you may select a different verse.

_____

_____

_____

On day 3 you will be given an assignment that may require some advanced planning. Turn to page 50 and read "Day 3's Assignment" so you can prepare.

SUMMARY STATEMENTS

- My Christian life depends on the quality of my love relationship to God.
- God created me for a love relationship with Him.
- Everything God says and does is an expression of love.
- A love relationship with God is more important than any other single factor in my life.

A LOVE RELATIONSHIP WITH GOD

To be loved by God is the highest relationship, the highest achievement, and the highest position in life.

Picture in your mind a tall ladder leaning against a wall. Now think about your life as a process of climbing that ladder. Wouldn't it be a tragedy to get to the top of the ladder and find you placed it against the wrong wall? One life to live and you missed it!

Earlier in the course we talked about your life being God-centered. That means your life must be properly related to God. This is the love relationship for which you were created—a God-centered love relationship. Your relationship to God (Father, Son, and Spirit) is the single most important aspect of your life. If it is not right, nothing else is important.

If you knew that all you had was a relationship with Him, would you be totally and completely satisfied? Many people would say, "Well, I would like to have that relationship, but I sure would like to do something" or "I sure would like for Him to give me a ministry or give me something to do." We are a "doing" people. We feel worthless or useless if we are not busy doing something. The Scripture leads us to understand that God is saying, "I want you to love me above everything else. When you are in a relationship of love with Me, you have everything there is." To be loved by God is the highest relationship, the highest achievement, and the highest position in life.

That does not mean you will never do anything as an expression of your love for Him. God will call you to obey Him and do whatever He asks of you. However, you do not need to be doing something to feel fulfilled. You are fulfilled completely in a relationship with God. When you are filled with Him, what else do you need?

Read the following hymn by Rhea F. Miller. Circle all things that may compete with Jesus for a person's love and attention.

> I'd rather have Jesus than silver or gold,
> I'd rather be His than have riches untold;
> I'd rather have Jesus than houses or lands,
> I'd rather be led by His nail-pierced hand.
>
> I'd rather have Jesus than men's applause,
> I'd rather be faithful to His dear cause;
> I'd rather have Jesus than world-wide fame,
> I'd rather be true to His holy name.
>
> He's fairer than lilies of rarest bloom,
> He's sweeter than honey from out the comb;
> He's all that my hungering spirit needs,
> I'd rather have Jesus and let Him lead.
>
> REFRAIN
> Than to be the king of a vast domain
> Or be held in sin's dread sway;
> I'd rather have Jesus than anything
> This world affords today.[1]

Reflect on the meaning of the words. If you could only have one or the other in each of the following pairs, which would you honestly choose? Check your response.

1. I would rather have ❏ Jesus
   ❏ Silver, gold, riches untold, houses and lands

2. I would rather have ❏ Jesus
   ❏ Men's applause and world-wide fame

3. I would rather have ❏ Jesus
   ❏ Be the king of a vast domain

Do you really want to love the Lord your God with all of your heart? He will allow no competitors. He says:

"You cannot serve both God and Money."

> No one can serve two masters. Either he will hate the one and love the other, or he will be devoted to the one and despise the other. You cannot serve both God and Money (Matt. 6:24).

When the Lord your God brings you into the land he swore to your fathers, to Abraham, Isaac and Jacob, to give you—a land with large, flourishing cities you did not build, houses filled with all kinds of good things you did not provide, wells you did not dig, and vineyards and olive groves you did not plant—then when you eat and are satisfied, be careful that you do not forget the Lord, who brought you out of Egypt, out of the land of slavery. Fear the Lord your God, serve him only and take your oaths in his name. Do not follow other gods, the gods of the peoples around you; for the Lord your God, who is among you, is a jealous God (Deut. 6:10-15).

Out of His love for you, He will provide all else that you need—when you love Him and Him alone. (See Matt. 6:31-33.)

Created Not for Time, but Eternity

God did not create you for time; He created you for eternity. Time (your lifetime on earth) provides the opportunity to get acquainted with Him. It is an opportunity for Him to develop your character in His likeness. Then eternity will have its fullest dimensions for you.

If you just live for time (the here and now), you will miss the ultimate purpose of creation. If you live for time, you will allow your past to mold and shape your life today. Your life as a child of God ought to be shaped by the future (what you will be one day). God uses your present time to mold and shape your future usefulness here on earth and in eternity.

What are some of the things in your past that are having a strong limiting influence on your life today? These may include handicaps, a troubled family background, failures, shame over some personal or family "secret," or such things as pride, success, fame, recognition, excessive wealth, and so forth.

_____

_____

Do you think you are primarily being shaped by your past or by your future? Why?

_____

_____

Paul struggled with this problem. Here was his approach to dealing with his past and present:

Philippians 3:4-14

4If anyone else thinks he has reasons to put confidence in the flesh, I have more: 5circumcised on the eighth day, of the people of Israel, of the tribe of Benjamin, a Hebrew of Hebrews; in regard to the law, a Pharisee; 6as for zeal, persecuting the church; as for legalistic righteousness, faultless.

7But whatever was to my profit I now consider loss for the sake of Christ. 8What is more, I consider everything a loss compared to the surpassing greatness of knowing Christ Jesus my Lord, for whose sake I have lost all things. I consider them rubbish, that I may gain Christ 9and be found in him, not having a righteousness of my own that comes from the law, but that which is through faith in Christ—the righteousness that comes from God and is by faith. 10I want to know Christ and the power of his resurrection and the fellowship of sharing in his sufferings, becoming like him in his death, 11and so, somehow, to attain to the resurrection from the dead.

12Not that I have already obtained all this, or have already been made perfect, but I press on to take hold of that for which Christ Jesus took hold of me. 13Brothers, I do not consider myself yet to have taken hold of it. But one thing I do: Forgetting what is behind and straining toward what is ahead, 14I press on toward the goal to win the prize for which God has called me heavenward in Christ Jesus.

Answer the following questions based on Paul's statement in Philippians 3:4-14.

"When you eat and are satisfied, be careful that you do not forget the Lord. . . . the Lord your God, who is among you, is a jealous God."

"Do not worry, saying, 'What shall we eat?' or 'What shall we drink?' or 'What shall we wear?' For the pagans run after all these things, and your heavenly Father knows that you need them. But seek first his kingdom and his righteousness, and all these things will be given to you as well."
—Matthew 6:31-33

Paul

1. What are some of the things in Paul's past that could have influenced his present?

_____

_____

2. How did Paul value these things? (v. 8)

_____

3. Why did Paul discredit his past this way? (vv. 8-11)

_____

4. What did Paul do to prepare for a *future* prize? (vv. 13-14)

Forget _____

Strain toward _____

Press on toward _____

Answers: (1) He was a true and faithful Jew from the royal tribe of Benjamin. He was faultless in keeping the laws of the Pharisees. He was zealous for God. (2) He considered them as rubbish and loss. (3) Paul wanted to know Christ, be found in Him, and become like Him to attain a *future* blessing (resurrection from the dead). (4) He forgets the past. He strains toward the future. He presses toward the future goal of a heavenly prize.

Paul's real desire was to know Christ and become like Him. You, too, can so order your life under God's direction that you come to know Him, love Him only, and become like Christ. Let your present be molded and shaped by what you are to become in Christ. You were created for eternity!

Investing in the Future

You need to begin orienting your life to the purposes of God. His purposes go far beyond time and into eternity. Make sure you are investing your life, time, and resources in things that are lasting and not things that will pass away. If you don't recognize that God created you for eternity, you will invest in the wrong direction. You need to store up treasures in heaven. (See Matt. 6:19-21, 33.)

This is why a love relationship with God is so important. He loves you. He knows what is best for you. Only He can guide you to invest your life in worthwhile ways. This guidance will come as you "walk" with Him and listen to Him.

In what are you investing your life, your time, and your resources? Make two lists below. On the left list things that will pass away. On the right list things that have eternal value.

<table>
<tr><td></td><td></td></tr>
</table>

Think and pray about any adjustments you may need to make in the way you invest your life. Ask God for His perspective on your life. Below write any adjustments you sense God wants you to make.

_____

_____

_____

> "Do not store up for yourselves treasures on earth, where moth and rust destroy, and where thieves break in and steal. But store up for yourselves treasures in heaven, where moth and rust do not destroy, and where thieves do not break in and steal. For where your treasure is, there your heart will be also.... But seek first his kingdom and his righteousness, and all these things will be given to you as well."
>
> —Matthew 6:19-21, 33

Review today's lesson. Pray and ask God to identify one or more statements or Scriptures that He wants you to understand, learn, or practice. Underline it (them). Then respond to the following:

What was the most meaningful statement or Scripture you read today? _____

_____

_____

_____

Reword the statement or Scripture into a prayer of response to God. _____

_____

_____

_____

What does God want you to do in response to today's study? _____

_____

_____

SUMMARY STATEMENTS

- To be loved by God is the highest relationship, the highest achievement, and the highest position in life.
- God did not create me for time; He created me for eternity.
- I will let my present be molded and shaped by what I am to become in Christ.
- "Seek first his kingdom and his righteousness."
- I will make sure I am investing in things that are lasting.
- Only He can guide me to invest my life in worthwhile ways.

WALKING WITH GOD

DAY 3

When your relationship is as it ought to be, you will always be in fellowship with the Father.

Adam and Eve

God created the first man and woman, Adam and Eve, for a love relationship with Himself. After Adam and Eve had sinned, they heard God walking in the garden in the cool of the day. They hid from Him because of their fear and shame. Try to sense the heart of a loving Father when He asked that wonderful love question, "Where are you?" (Gen. 3:9). God knew that something had happened to the love relationship.

When your relationship is as it ought to be, you will always be in fellowship with the Father. You will be there in His presence expecting and anticipating the relationship of love. When Adam and Eve were not there, something had gone wrong.

Quiet Time with God

Early each day, I have an appointment with God. I often wonder what happens when the God who loves me comes to meet me there. How does He feel when He asks, "Henry, where are you?" and I am just not there. I have found this to be true in my own walk with the Lord: I keep that time alone with God, not in order to have a relationship, but because I have a relationship. Because I have that love relationship with the Lord, I want to meet with Him in my quiet time. I want to spend the time there. Time with Him enriches and deepens the relationship I have with Him.

I hear many persons say, "I really struggle trying to have that time alone with God." If that is a problem you face, let me suggest something to you. Make the priority in your life to come to love Him with all your heart. That will solve most of your problem with your quiet time. Your quiet time is because you know Him and, therefore, love Him, not only in order to learn about Him. The Apostle Paul said it was "Christ's love" that compelled or constrained him (2 Cor. 5:14).

☀ **Suppose you were dating a person you loved and intended to marry. What is the *primary* reason you date (spend time with) that person? Check only ONE response:**
❑ 1. Because I would want to find out about his likes and dislikes.
❑ 2. Because I would want to find out about her family background.
❑ 3. Because I would want to find out about his knowledge and education.
❑ 4. Because I love her and enjoy being with her.

When two people love each other and plan to marry, they are concerned about finding out information about each other. That is not, however, the primary reason why they date. They spend time together because they love each other and enjoy being together.

Similarly, you will learn much about God, His Word, His purposes, and His ways as you spend time with Him. You will come to know Him during the day as you experience Him working in and through your life. Learning about Him is not, however, why you should want to have a quiet time with Him. The more you know Him and experience His love, the more you will love Him. Then you will want that time alone with Him, because you do love Him and enjoy His fellowship.

Day 3's assignment

Today's lesson is shorter than normal in order to allow time for the following assignment. You may be able to do it today, but you may choose to set aside time later in the week. Plan to complete the assignment sometime prior to your next small-group session. This assignment may require some planning or adapting. Feel free to adjust the assignment to your personal needs and circumstances.

☀ **Adam and Eve walked with God in the cool of the day. I want you to set aside at least 30 minutes for a time to "walk with God." If your location, physical condition, and weather permit, find a place outside to walk. Use this time to get out of your routine. You may even want to plan a special trip for part of a day just to be alone with God. The place could be:**

—your neighborhood
—a city park
—a garden
—a lakeshore

—a wooded area in the country
—a sandy beach
—a mountain road
—anywhere

Spend the time walking and talking with God. If the location permits, you may even want to talk out loud. Focus your thoughts on the love of your heavenly Father. Praise Him for His love and mercy. Thank Him for expressions of His love to you. Be specific. Express to God your love for Him. Take time to worship Him and adore Him.

After your walk, use the space below to write about your feelings. If they apply, answer some of the following:
• How did you feel as you walked and talked with God?
• What aspect of your love relationship with God did you become aware of?
• If this was a difficult or an emotionally uneasy time, why do you think it was?
• What happened that was especially meaningful or joyful?

_____

_____

_____

_____

_____

Practice quoting your Scripture memory verses aloud or write them on separate paper.

SUMMARY STATEMENTS

• When my relationship is as it ought to be, I will always be in fellowship with the Father.
• I will make the priority in my life to come to love Him with all my heart.
• I will have my quiet time because I know Him and love Him, not in order to learn about Him.

God always takes the initiative in this love relationship. God must take the initiative and come to us if we are to experience Him. This is the witness of the entire Bible. He came to Adam and Eve in the garden. In love He fellowshipped with them, and they with Him. He came to Noah, Abraham, Moses, and the prophets. God took the initiative for each person in the Old Testament to experience Him in a personal fellowship of love. This is true of the New Testament as well. Jesus came to the disciples, and chose them to be with Him and experience His Love. He came to Paul on the Damascus Road. In our natural human state, we do not seek God on our own initiative.

God takes the initiative. He chooses us, loves us, and reveals His eternal purposes for our lives.

No One Seeks God on His Own Initiative

Read Romans 3:10-12 (right) and answer the following questions.

1. How many people are righteous on their own? _____

2. How many people understand spiritual things on their own? _____

3. How many people seek after God on their own? _____

4. How many people do good on their own? _____

No one; not even one! Sin has affected us so deeply that no one seeks after God on his own initiative. Therefore, if we are to have any relationship with Him or His Son, God will have to take the initiative. This is exactly what He does.

"There is no one righteous, not even one; there is no one who understands, no one who seeks God. All have turned away, they have together become worthless; there is no one who does good, not even one."
—Romans 3:10-12

God Draws Us to Himself

Read the Scripture on the right and answer the following questions:

1. Who can come to Jesus without being drawn by the Father? _____

2. What does a person do who listens to the Father and learns from Him?

_____

3. What is the only way a person can come to Jesus? _____

_____

Jeremiah 31:3—"The Lord appeared to us in the past saying: 'I have loved you with an everlasting love; I have drawn you with loving-kindness.'"

Hosea 11:4—"I led them with cords of human kindness, with ties of love; I lifted the yoke from their neck and bent down to feed them."

"No one can come to me [Jesus] unless the Father who sent me draws him. . . . Everyone who listens to the Father and learns from him comes to me. . . . This is why I told you that no one can come to me unless the Father has enabled him."
—John 6:44, 45, 65

The love that God focuses on your life is an everlasting love. Because of that love, He has drawn you to Himself. He has drawn you with cords of love when you were not His friend, when you were His enemy. He gave His own Son to die for you. To firmly anchor the experiencing of God and knowing His will, you must be absolutely convinced of God's love for you.

How do you know God loves you? What are some reasons you can give that convince *you* that God loves you?

_____

_____

_____

God came to Saul, known later as Paul (Acts 9:1-19). Saul was actually opposing God and His activities, and fighting against God's Son Jesus. Jesus came to Paul and revealed the Father's purposes of love for him. This also is true in our lives. We do not choose Him. He chooses us, loves us, and reveals His eternal purposes for our lives.

Paul

Jesus said to those who were His disciples: "You did not choose me, but I chose you and appointed you. . . . As it is, you do not belong to the world, but I have chosen you out of the world" (John 15:16, 19). Didn't Peter choose to follow Jesus? No. Jesus chose Peter. Peter responded to the invitation of God. God took the initiative.

Disciples

Jesus and Peter

"When Jesus came to the region of Caesarea Philippi, he asked his disciples, 'Who do people say the Son of Man is?'

"They replied, 'Some say John the Baptist; others say Elijah; and still others, Jeremiah or one of the prophets.'

'But what about you?' he asked. 'Who do you say I am?'

"Simon Peter answered, 'You are the Christ, the Son of the living God.'

"Jesus replied, 'Blessed are you, Simon son of Jonah, for this was not revealed to you by man, but by my Father in heaven.'"

—Matthew 16:13-17

Jesus said that Peter was responding to God's initiative in his life (Matt. 16:13-17). Jesus asked the disciples who men said He was. Then He asked them who they said He was. Peter answered correctly, "You are the Christ." Then Jesus made a very significant statement to Peter, "This was not revealed to you by man, but by my Father in heaven."

Who had revealed to Peter that Jesus was the Christ, the promised Messiah?

_____

In essence Jesus was saying, "Peter, you could never have known and confessed that I am the Christ unless My Father had been at work in you. He caused you to know who I am. You are responding to the Father's activity in your life. Good!"

Do you realize that God determined to love you? Apart from that you never would have become a Christian. He had something in mind when He called you. He began to work in your life. You began to experience a love relationship with God where He took the initiative. He began to open your understanding. He drew you to Himself.

What did you do? Check your response.
❏ 1. I responded to His invitation to a love relationship.
❏ 2. I rejected His offer of a love relationship.

When you responded to His invitation, He brought you into a love relationship with Himself. But you would never know that love, be in the presence of that love, or be aware of that love if God had not taken the initiative.

> You cannot know the activity of God unless
> He takes the initiative to reveal it to you.

Number the following items from 1 to 4 in the order they occur in the development of a love relationship with God.

_____a. God comes into my life and fellowships with me.

_____b. I respond to God's activity in my life and invite Him to do in my life what He pleases.

_____c. God shows me His love and reveals Himself to me.

_____d. God chooses me because of His love.

Some of these actions almost seem to happen at the same time. Yet, we can be sure of this—God takes the initiative; then we respond. I numbered the items a-4, b-3, c-2, and d-1. God *always* takes the initiative in loving us.

The following Scriptures speak of God's initiative in the love relationship. Read each passage. Then write a brief summary statement about how God acts (acted) or what He does (did) to take the initiative.

Deuteronomy 30:6—"The Lord your God will circumcise your hearts and the hearts of your descendants, so that you may love him with all your heart and with all your soul, and live."

_____

Luke 10:22—"All things have been committed to me by my Father. No one knows who the Son is except the Father, and no one knows who the Father is except the Son and those to whom the Son chooses to reveal him."

_____

John 15:16—"You did not choose me, but I chose you and appointed you to go and bear fruit—fruit that will last."

_____

Philippians 2:13—"It is God who works in you to will and to act according to his good purpose."

_____

1 John 3:16—"This is how we know what love is: Jesus Christ laid down his life for us."

_____

Revelation 3:20—"Here I am! I stand at the door and knock. If anyone hears my voice and opens the door, I will come in and eat with him, and he with me."

_____

Write one of these words in the blank to make the following statement true.

never   sometimes   frequently   always

God _____ takes the initiative to establish a love relationship with me.

Review today's lesson. Pray and ask God to identify one or more statements or Scriptures that He wants you to understand, learn, or practice. Underline it (them). Then respond to the following:

What was the most meaningful statement or Scripture you read today?

_____

_____

Reword the statement or Scripture into a prayer of response to God.

_____

_____

What does God want you to do in response to today's study?

_____

_____

SUMMARY STATEMENTS

- In this love relationship, God always takes the initiative.
- I do not choose Him. He chooses me, loves me, and reveals His eternal purposes for my life.
- I cannot know the activity of God unless He takes the initiative to let me know.

A REAL, PERSONAL, PRACTICAL RELATIONSHIP

DAY 5

The relationship God wants to have with you will be real and personal. Some ask the question; "Can a person actually have a real, personal, and practical relationship with God?" They seem to think that God is far off and unconcerned about their day-to-day living. That is not the God we see in the Scriptures.

God's plan for the advancement of His kingdom depends on His relationship to His people.

☀ **Read one Scripture passage. Then _describe_ at least _one fact_ that indicates the relationship the person(s) had with God was real, personal, and/or practical. If you are already familiar with the story, you may answer from your present knowledge of the passage. Then do the same for the next passage. I have completed the first as an example.**

Adam and Eve after they sinned—Genesis 3:20-21 _They were naked._

God made garments of skin for them.

Hagar when she fled from Sarai—Genesis 16:1-13 _____

_____

Solomon and his request for discernment—1 Kings 3:5-13; 4:29-30 _____

_____

The Twelve that Jesus sent out to preach—Mark 6:7-13 _____

_____

Peter in prison awaiting trial—Acts 12:1-17 _____

_____

John on the island of Patmos—Revelation 1:9-20 _____

_____

Adam and Eve

From Genesis to Revelation, we see God relating to people in real, personal, intimate, and practical ways. God had intimate fellowship with Adam and Eve, walking in the garden with them in the cool of the day. When they sinned, God came after them to restore the love relationship. He met a very practical need by providing clothing to cover their nakedness.

Hagar

Hagar had been used, mistreated, and abused by Sarai. She fled for her life. When she reached the end of her own resources, when she had no where else to turn, when all hope was gone, God came to her. In her relationship to God, she learned that God saw her, knew her needs, and would lovingly provide for her. God is very personal.

Solomon

Solomon's father David had been a man who sought the Lord with his whole heart. Solomon had a heritage of faith and obedience to follow. He had the opportunity to ask and receive anything he wanted from God. Solomon demonstrated his love for God's people by asking for a discerning heart. God granted his request and gave him wealth and fame as well. Solomon found his relationship with God to be very practical.

The Twelve

The disciples also had a real, personal, and practical relationship with Jesus—the Son of God. Jesus had chosen them to be with Him. What a pleasure it must have been to have such an intimate relationship with Jesus! When they were given a very difficult assignment, Jesus did not send them out helpless. He gave them authority they had never known before over evil spirits.

Peter

In some places of the world obedience to the Lord results in imprisonment. This was Peter's experience. In answer to prayer, the Lord miraculously delivered him. This was so dramatic and practical, Peter first thought it was a dream. The praying Christians thought he was an angel. Soon, they all discovered that the Lord's deliverance was real. That deliverance probably saved Peter's life.

John

In exile on the island of Patmos, John was spending the Lord's Day in fellowship with God. During this time of fellowship in the Spirit, the revelation of Jesus Christ came to John to "show his servants what must soon take place" (Rev. 1:1). This message has been a genuine challenge and encouragement to the churches from John's day to this.

Do you sense, as you read the Scripture, that God became real and personal to people? Do you sense that their relationship with God was practical? Was He also real and personal to Noah? to Abraham? to Moses? to Isaiah? Yes! Yes! Yes! Has God changed? No! This was true in the Old Testament. It was true during the time of Jesus' life and ministry. It was true after the coming of the Holy Spirit at Pentecost. Your life also can reflect that kind of real, personal, and practical relationship as you respond to God's working in your life.

☀ **Briefly describe an experience in your own life when God was real, personal, and/or practical in His relationship to you.**

_____

_____

_____

_____

Love must be real and personal. A person cannot love without another "someone" to love. A love relationship with God takes place between two real beings. A relationship with God is real and personal. This has always been His desire. All His efforts are expended to bring this desire to reality. God is a Person pouring His life into yours.

If, for some reason, you cannot think of a time when your relationship to God has been real, personal, and practical, you need to spend some time evaluating your relationship to Him. Go before the Lord in prayer and ask Him to reveal the true nature of your relationship to Him. Ask Him to bring you into that kind of relationship. If you come to the realization that you have never entered a saving relationship with God, turn to the activity on page 8 for help in settling that most important issue now.

God's Presence and Work in Your Life Is Practical

Some people say to me, "Henry, what you are suggesting about doing God's will is not practical in our day." I always have to differ with them. God is a very practical God. He was in Scripture. He is the same today. When He provided manna, quail, and water for the children of Israel, He was being practical. When Jesus fed five thousand He was being practical. The God I see revealed in Scripture is real, personal, and practical. I just trust God to be practical and real to me, too.

God is practical.

The constant presence of God is the most practical part of your life and ministry. Unfortunately we often assign God to a limited place in our lives. Then we call on Him whenever we need help. That is the exact opposite of what we find in the Word of God. He is the One who is working in our world. He invites you to relate to Him, so He can accomplish His work through you. His whole plan for the advance of the Kingdom depends on His working in real and practical ways through His relationship to His people.

The constant presence of God is the most practical part of your life and ministry.

Knowing and experiencing God through a real and personal relationship was practical in the Scriptures. Be patient as we work together. I believe you will find that this kind of walk with God will be exceedingly practical. God can make a practical difference in your relationships in your family, your church, and other people. You can encounter God in such a way that you know you are experiencing Him.

Can you describe your relationship with God as real, personal, and practical? Why?

_____

_____

Fill in the blank to complete the second reality of experiencing God. Make it personal.

1. God is always at work around me.

2. God _____ a continuing _____

_____

Review today's lesson. Pray and ask God to identify one or more statements or Scriptures that He wants you to understand, learn, or practice. Underline it (them). Then respond to the following:

What was the most meaningful statement or Scripture you read today? _____

_____

_____

Reword the statement or Scripture into a prayer of response to God. _____

_____

_____

What does God want you to do in response to today's study? _____

_____

_____

Review your Scripture memory verses and be prepared to recite them to a partner in your small-group session this week.

If you have not taken time to "walk with God" and write about the experience on Day 3, try to do so before your small-group session this week.

SUMMARY STATEMENTS

- The relationship God wants to have with me will be real and personal.
- God's whole plan for the advance of the Kingdom depends on His working in real and practical ways through His personal relationship with His people.

LOVE AND GOD'S INVITATION

Jack Conner: Mission Pastor

UNIT

4

When Faith Baptist Church started its first mission, we called Jack Conner as our mission pastor; but we had no money for moving expenses and no money for a salary. Jack had three children in school, so we felt that we ought to pay him at least $850 a month. We began to pray that God would provide for his move and his needs. I had never guided a church to do that before. We had now stepped out in faith, believing that God wanted him to pastor our mission in Prince Albert. Except for a few people in California, I didn't know anybody who could help us financially. I began to ask myself, "How in the world will God make this provision?" Then it dawned on me that as long as God knew where I was, He could cause anybody in the world to know where I was. As long as He knew my need, He could place that need on the heart of anybody He chose.

Jack passed immigration and started his move of faith, convinced that God had called him. I then received a letter from First Baptist Church, Fayetteville, Arkansas. They said, "God has laid it on our heart to send one percent of our mission giving to Saskatchewan missions. We are sending a check to use however you choose." I did not know how in the world they got involved with us at that time, but a check came for $1,100.

One day I received a phone call at home. The person's pledge completed the $850 a month we needed to provide Jack's salary for one year. Just as I got off the phone, Jack drove into our driveway.

I asked, "Jack, what did it cost to move you?"

He said, "Well, Henry, as best I can tell it cost me $1,100."

We began that first step of faith by believing that the God who knows where we are is the God who can touch anybody, anywhere and cause him/her to know where we are. We made the adjustments and were obedient. We believed that the God who called Jack also said, "I AM Provider." When we were obedient, God demonstrated Himself to be our Provider. That experience led us to a deeper love relationship with an all-sufficient God.

Verse to Memorize
this Week

Whoever has my commands and obeys them, he is the one who loves me. He who loves me will be loved by my Father, and I too will love him and show myself to him —JOHN 14:21

This unit continues our focus on the love relationship with God. You will find that the call to relationship is also a call to be on mission with Him. If you want to know God's will, you must respond to His invitation to love Him wholeheartedly. God works through those He loves to carry out His kingdom purposes in the world. During this unit, we will begin to look at how God invites you to become involved with Him in His work.

Knowing God by Experience

You will never be satisfied to just know *about* God. Knowing God only comes through experience as He reveals Himself to you. When Moses was at the burning bush, he asked God, "Suppose I go to the Israelites and say to them, 'The God of your fathers has sent me to you,' and they ask me, 'What is his name?' Then what shall I tell them?" (Ex. 3:13).

God responded, "I AM WHO I AM. This is what you are to say to the Israelites: 'I AM has sent me to you' " (Ex. 3:14). When God said, "I AM WHO I AM," He was saying, "I AM the Eternal One. I will be what I will be." He was saying "I am everything you will need." During the next 40 years, Moses came to know God experientially as Jehovah or Yahweh, the Great I AM.

I AM WHO I AM

Names of God

In the Bible God took the initiative to reveal Himself to people by experience. Frequently when God revealed Himself to a person, the person gave God a new name or described Him in a new way. For the Hebrew, a person's name represented his character or described his nature. This is why we frequently see new names or titles for God following an event where a Bible character experienced God. To know God by name required a personal experience of His presence.

Biblical names, titles, and descriptions of God identify how Bible characters personally came to know God. The Scripture is a record of God's revelation of Himself to man. Each name for God is a part of that revelation.

For example: Joshua and the Israelites were fighting the Amalekites. Moses was overseeing the battle from a nearby mountain. While he held his hands up to God, the Israelites were victorious. When he let his hands down they began to lose. God defeated the Amalekites through Israel that day. Moses built an altar and gave it the name "The Lord is my Banner." A banner is the standard that goes out in front of an army to indicate who it represents. "The Lord is my Banner" says we are God's people; He is our God. Moses' uplifted hands gave constant glory to God indicating that the battle was His and Israel was His. Israel came to know God in a better way as they realized anew—We are God's people; the Lord is our Banner. (See Ex. 17:8-15.)

The Lord is my Banner

For another example read Genesis 22:1-18 and answer the following:

1. What did God ask Abraham to do? (v. 2)

_____

2. What do you think verse 8 indicates about Abraham?

_____

3. What did God do for Abraham? (v. 13)

_____

4. What name did Abraham give the place? (v. 14)

_____

5. Why did God promise to bless Abraham? (vv. 15-18)

God was in the process of developing Abraham's character to be the father of a nation. He put Abraham's faith and obedience to the test. This brought Abraham to a crisis of belief. Abraham had faith that the Lord would provide (v. 8). He made the adjustment of his life to act on his belief that God was Provider. He obeyed God. When God provided a ram,

The Lord Will Provide

Abraham came to an intimate knowledge of God through the experience of God as his Provider.

Look at the seven realities on the inside back cover of this book. How does Abraham's experience of God follow that sequence?

_____

_____

_____

_____

_____

At the beginning of this unit you read how Faith Baptist Church and Jack Conner came to know God as Provider. God reveals Himself to us through our experience of Him at work in our lives.

Provider of Partners

As a pastor of college students, I called the students in and talked with them regularly. I knew they were in a period of rapid change. I wanted to help them as they made major decisions in their lives. A wonderful girl who was studying nursing came to my office. I had been praying for Sherri and what God might be doing in her life. We talked about her alcoholic father. We talked about her decision of whether or not to continue in nursing. Then I looked at Sherri and said, "Sherri, I want you to know that God has laid on my heart that I need to pray for a husband for you."

She asked, "Are you serious?"

I said, "Sherri, I want you to know I *am* serious. Because you have had an alcoholic father and have experienced all the turmoil and heartache that you have, I believe God wants to give you a wonderful man to love you for who you are. I want you to know that, beginning today, I am praying that God will give you a wonderful, loving husband."

She wept. She and I began to pray that God would provide her a partner. About three months later, God brought into our church a wonderful young man who was an engineering student. They fell in love, and I performed their wedding ceremony. They now have at least two children and are serving the Lord very faithfully. The last I heard, Sherri was as happy as could be.

How did Sherri know that God was the God who could provide a husband? She claimed who God was and then proceeded to watch and pray. She was open to receive the one God would give her. She had to obey and receive when God revealed His choice to her. Then she came to know God as the Provider of Partners.

Describe an event through which you know you experienced God at work in your life.

_____

_____

_____

What name could you use to describe the God you experienced?

_____

Read the following list of names, titles, and descriptions of God. Circle those that describe God in ways you have personally experienced Him.

my advocate (Job 16:19)	bread of life (John 6:35)
Comforter in sorrow (Jer. 8:18)	my confidence (Ps. 71:5)
Wonderful Counselor (Isa. 9:6)	defender of widows (Ps. 68:5)
my strong deliverer (Ps. 140:7)	Faithful and True (Rev. 19:11)
our Father (Isa. 64:8)	a consuming fire (Deut. 4:24)
a sure foundation (Isa. 28:16)	my friend (Job 16:20)
God Almighty (Gen. 17:1)	God of all comfort (2 Cor. 1:3)
God who avenges me (Ps. 18:47)	God who saves me (Ps. 51:14)
our guide (Ps. 48:14)	head of the church (Eph. 5:23)
our Help (Ps. 33:20)	my hiding place (Ps. 32:7)
a great high priest (Heb. 4:14)	Holy One among you (Hos. 11:9)

my hope (Ps. 71:5)	Jealous (Ex. 34:14)
righteous Judge (2 Tim. 4:8)	King of kings (1 Tim. 6:15)
our leader (2 Chron. 13:12)	your life (Col. 3:4)
light of life (John 8:12)	Lord of lords (1 Tim. 6:15)
Lord of the harvest (Matt. 9:38)	mediator (1 Tim. 2:5)
the most holy (Dan. 9:24)	our peace (Eph. 2:14)
Prince of Peace (Isa. 9:6)	my Redeemer (Ps. 19:14)
refuge and strength (Ps. 46:1)	my salvation (Ex. 15:2)
my Savior (Ps. 42:5)	the good shepherd (John 10:11)
Sovereign Lord (Luke 2:29)	my stronghold (Ps. 18:2)
my support (2 Sam. 22:19)	good teacher (Mark 10:17)

As time permits, make brief notes (in the margin) of a few experiences through which you have come to know God in these ways.

Did you see that you have come to know God through experience? Could you circle any of the names and not think of an experience where God acted in that way? For instance, you could not have known God as the "Comforter in sorrow" unless you had *experienced* His comfort during a time of sorrow. You come to know God when He reveals Himself to you. You come to know Him as you experience Him. That is why we have titled this course *Experiencing God.*

How do you come to know God personally and intimately?

_____

You come to know God more intimately as He reveals Himself to you through your experiences with Him.

Review today's lesson. Pray and ask God to identify one or more statements or Scriptures that He wants you to understand, learn, or practice. Underline it (them). Then respond to the following:

What was the most meaningful statement or Scripture you read today?

_____
_____
_____

Reword the statement or Scripture into a prayer of response to God.

_____
_____
_____

What does God want you to do in response to today's study?

_____
_____

Write your Scripture memory verse for this unit on the following lines and review your verses from other units.

_____
_____
_____
_____

SUMMARY STATEMENTS

- Knowing God only comes through experience as He reveals Himself to me.
- I know God more intimately as He reveals Himself to me through my experiences with Him.

"O Lord, our Lord, how majestic is your name in all the earth!" (Ps. 8:1).

Yesterday you learned that you come to know God by experience at His initiative. You learned that a Hebrew name described a person's character or nature. The name was closely associated with the person and his presence. Thus, to call on one's name was to seek his presence. God's name is majestic and worthy of our praise. Acknowledging God's name amounts to recognizing God for who He is. Calling on His name indicates you are seeking His presence. Praising His name is praising *Him*. God's names in Scripture can become a call to worship for you.

Spend this day in worship of God through His names. To focus your attention on His name is to focus attention on the God of the name. His name represents His presence. To worship is to reverence and honor God, to acknowledge Him as worthy of your praise. The Psalms are rich in their instructions to direct your worship toward God through His name.

Read the following Scriptures and circle or underline the word or phrase that describes ways you can direct your worship toward God through His names.

"Sing unto the Lord, bless his name" (Ps. 96:2, KJV).

"Revive us, and we will call on your name" (Ps. 80:18).

"I will declare your name to my brothers" (Ps. 22:22).

"Give me an undivided heart, that I may fear your name" (Ps. 86:11).

"Save us, O Lord our God, and gather us from the nations, that we may give thanks to your holy name and glory in your praise" (Ps. 106:47).

"All the nations you have made will come and worship before you, O Lord; they will bring glory to your name" (Ps. 86:9).

"Glory in his holy name; let the hearts of those who seek the Lord rejoice (Ps. 105:3).

"I will praise you forever for what you have done; in your name I will hope, for your name is good" (Ps. 52:9).

"Those who know your name will trust in you, for you, Lord, have never forsaken those who seek you" (Ps. 9:10).

"Thus will I bless thee while I live: I will lift up my hands in thy name" (Ps. 63:4, KJV).

"But let all who take refuge in you be glad; let them ever sing for joy. Spread your protection over them, that those who love your name may rejoice in you" (Ps. 5:11).

"In God we make our boast all day long, and we will praise your name forever" (Ps. 44:8).

"Blessed are those who have learned to acclaim you, who walk in the light of your presence, O Lord. They rejoice in your name all day long; they exult in your righteousness" (Ps. 89:15-16).

"In the night I remember your name, O Lord, and I will keep your law" (Ps. 119:55).

"Cover their faces with shame so that men will seek your name, O Lord" (Ps. 83:16).

"I will give thanks to the Lord because of his righteousness and will sing praise to the name of the Lord Most High" (Ps. 7:17).

"All the earth bows down to you; they sing praise to you, they sing praise to your name" (Ps. 66:4).

"In him our hearts rejoice, for we trust in his holy name" (Ps. 33:21).

WAYS TO WORSHIP GOD

bless *His name*	glory in *His name*	rejoice in *His name*
call upon *His name*	hope in *His name*	remember the name
declare *His name*	know *His name*	seek *His name*
fear *His name*	lift up hands in *His name*	sing praise to *His name*
give thanks to *His name*	love *His name*	sing to *His name*
glorify *His name*	praise *His name*	trust in *His name*

Use these ways to worship God right now. Turn to Appendix A, "Names, Titles, and Descriptions of God," (p. 220). Spend the remainder of your study time today in worship. The names direct your attention to Him, who He is, and what He does. Praise Him for who He is. Thank Him for what He has done. Glorify Him. Love and adore Him.

Seek Him. Trust Him. Sing to Him. Take as much time as you like for this period of worship. Make this a meaningful time to experience your love relationship with the Lord.

Briefly summarize what you thought, felt, or experienced during this time of worship. What was the most meaningful part of this time of worship?

_____

_____

_____

_____

LOVE GOD

God takes the initiative to pursue a love relationship with you. This love relationship, however, is not a one-sided affair. He wants you to know Him and worship Him. Most of all, He wants you to love Him.

Read this unit's suggested memory verse in the right margin and answer these questions.

1. Who is the one who loves Jesus? What does he have and do?

_____

2. How does the Father respond to the one who loves Jesus?

_____

3. What two things will Jesus do for the one who loves Him?

_____

_____

Jesus said, "If you love me, you will obey what I command" (John 14:15). When you obey Jesus, you show that you love Him and trust Him. The Father loves those who love His Son. For those who love Him, Jesus said He would love them and show Himself to them. Obedience is the outward expression of your love of God.

The reward for obedience and love is that He will show Himself to you. Jesus set an example for you in His life. He said, "The world must learn that I love the Father and that I do exactly what my Father has commanded me" (John 14:31). Jesus was obedient to every command of the Father. He demonstrated His love for the Father by obedience.

How can you demonstrate your love for God?

_____

A love relationship with God requires that you demonstrate your love by obedience. This is not just a following of the "letter" of the law, but it is a following of the "spirit" of the command as well. If you have an obedience problem, you have a love problem. Focus your attention on God's love.

God's Nature

God's nature is love. God can never function contrary to His own nature. Never in your life will God ever express His will toward you except that it is not an expression of perfect love. He can't! He can never give you second best. His nature will not let Him. He will bring discipline, judgment, and wrath on those who continue in sin and rebellion. His disciplines, however, always are based on love (Heb. 12:6). Because His nature is love, I am always confident that however He expresses Himself to me is always best. Two verses describe His love toward us:

• John 3:16—"God so loved the world that he gave his one and only Son."
• 1 John 3:16—"This is how we know what love is: Jesus Christ laid down his life for us."

If I love Him, I will obey Him!

"Whoever has my commands and obeys them, he is the one who loves me. He who loves me will be loved by my Father, and I too will love him and show myself to him." —John 14:21

Love?

Obey!

God is love.

His will is always best.

"God is love" (1 John 4:16). Your trust in the love nature of God is crucial. This has been a powerful influence in my own life. I never look on circumstances without seeing them on the backdrop of the cross. My relationship to God determines everything I do.

Fill in the two blanks in the statements below.

God is _____. His will is always _____.

Your relationship with God right now reveals what you believe about Him. It is spiritually impossible for you to believe one way and practice another. If you really believe that God is *love*, you will also accept the fact that His will is always *best*.

God is all-knowing.

His directions are always right.

By nature God is omniscient—all-knowing. He has all knowledge—past, present, and future. Nothing is outside the knowledge of God. Whenever God expresses Himself to you, therefore, His directions are always right.

Have you ever asked God to give you several alternatives, so you can choose the one that is best for you? How many options does God have to give you so you will have the right one? God always gets it right the first time!

Fill in the two blanks in the statements below.

God is all _____. His directions are always _____.

Whenever God gives you a directive, it is always right. God's will is always best. You never have to question whether His will is best or right. It always is best and right. This is true because He loves you and knows all. Because He loves you perfectly, you can trust Him and obey Him completely.

God is all-powerful.

He can enable you to do His will.

God is omnipotent—all-powerful. He was able to create the world out of nothing. He can accomplish anything He purposes to do. If He ever asks you to do something, He Himself will enable you to do it. We will look at this fact more closely during day 5.

Fill in the two blanks in the statements below.

God is all _____. He can _____ me to do His will.

Match the fact about the nature of God on the left with the correct statement of application on the right. Write the correct letters in the blanks.

_____1. God is love.   A. God's directions are right.

_____2. God is all-knowing.   B. God can enable me to do His will.

_____3. God is all-powerful.   C. God's will is best.

When your life is in the middle of God's activity, He will start rearranging a lot of your thinking. God's ways and thoughts are so different from yours and mine they will often sound wrong or crazy. You need a readiness to believe God and trust Him completely. You need to believe that what He is doing is best for you. Don't try to second-guess Him. Just let Him be God. Answers are: 1-C; 2-A; 3-B.

God will start to make Himself known to you very simply as He would to a child. As you respond to Him in a simple child-like trust, you will find a whole new way of looking at life begin to unfold for you. Your life will be fulfilling. You will never have to sense an emptiness or lack of purpose. He always fills your life with Himself. When you have Him, you have everything there is.

When you hear words like *commands*, *judgments*, *statutes*, or *laws*, is your first impression negative or positive?   Negative ❑   Positive ❑

God's Commands

God's commands are expressions of His nature of love. In Deuteronomy 10:12-13 He says the commands are for our own good:

> What does the Lord your God ask of you but to fear the Lord your God,
> to walk in all his ways, to love him, to serve the Lord your God with all
> your heart and with all your soul, and to observe the Lord's commands
> and decrees that I am giving you today for your own good?

Read Deuteronomy 32:46-47 in the margin. How important are God's words to you?

_____

"He said to them, 'Take to heart all the words I have solemnly declared to you this day, so that you may command your children to obey carefully all the words of this law. They are not just idle words for you—they are your life. By them you will live long in the land you are crossing the Jordan to possess.'"
—Deuteronomy 32:46-47

The foundation of these passages is the love relationship. When you come to know God by experience, you will be convinced of His love. When you are convinced of His love you can believe Him and trust Him. When you trust Him you can obey Him. When you love Him, you have no problem obeying Him. "This is love for God: to obey his commands. And his commands are not burdensome" (1 John 5:3).

God loves you deeply and profoundly. Because He loves you, He has given you guidelines for living lest you miss the full dimensions of the love relationship. Life also has some land mines that can destroy you or wreck your life. God does not want to see you miss out on His best, and He does not want to see your life wrecked.

Suppose you had to cross a field full of land mines. A person who knew exactly where every one of them was buried offered to take you through it. Would you say to him, "I don't want you to tell me what to do. I don't want you to impose your ways on me"?

I don't know about you, but I would stay as close to that person as I could. I certainly would not go wandering off. His directions to me would be to preserve my life. He would say, "Don't go that way, because that way will kill you. Go this way and you will live."

That is the purpose of God's commands. He wants you to have life and have it abundantly. When the Lord gives you a command, He is trying to protect and preserve the best He has for you. He does not want you to lose it. When God gives a commandment, He is not restricting you. He is freeing you.

Read Deuteronomy 6:20-25 at right and then describe the purpose of the commandments, decrees, stipulations, and laws of God.

What is the purpose of the commands? _____

_____

"In the future, when your son asks you, 'What is the meaning of the stipulations, decrees and laws the Lord our God has commanded you?' tell him:. . . . 'The Lord commanded us to obey all these decrees and to fear the Lord our God, so that we might always prosper and be kept alive, as is the case today. And if we are careful to obey all this law before the Lord our God, as he has commanded us, that will be our righteousness.' "
—Deuteronomy 6:20-25

He has given His commands so you may prosper and live life to its fullest measure. Let me give you an example. Suppose the Lord says, "Let me tell you where a beautiful, wonderful expression of love is. I will provide you with a spouse—a husband or a wife. Your relationship with this person will bring out the very best in you. It will give you an opportunity to experience some of the deepest and most meaningful expressions of human love. That individual will release in you some wonderful things, affirm some things in you, and will be there to strengthen you when you lose heart. In that relationship that person will love you, believe in you, and trust you. Out of that relationship I will give you some children, and those children will sit on your knee and say, "Daddy, I love you."

So you may prosper and live life to its fullest measure.

But, He says, "Do not commit adultery" (Matt. 5:27). Is that command to limit or restrict you? No! It is to protect and free you to experience love at its human best. What happens if you break the command and commit adultery? The love relationship is ruptured between husband and wife. Trust is gone. Hurt sets in. Guilt and bitterness creep in. Even the children begin to respond differently. Scars may severely limit the future dimensions of love you could have experienced together.

God's commands are designed to guide you to life's very best. You will not obey Him, however, if you do not believe Him and trust Him. You cannot believe Him if you do not love Him. You cannot love Him unless you know Him.

Know Him

Love Him

If, however, you really come to know Him as He reveals Himself to you, you will love Him. If you love Him, You will believe and trust Him. If you believe and trust Him, you will obey Him.

Believe Him

Trust Him

Obey Him

God is love. Because of His love, His will for you is always best. He is all knowing, so His directions are always right. He has given His commands so you may prosper and live life to its fullest measure. If you love Him, you will obey Him! If you do not obey Him, you do not really love Him (John 14:24).

Review today's lesson. Pray and ask God to identify one or more statements or Scriptures that He wants you to understand, learn, or practice. Underline it (them). Then respond to the following:

What was the most meaningful statement or Scripture you read today?

_____

_____

Reword the statement or Scripture into a prayer of response to God.

_____

_____

What does God want you to do in response to today's study?

_____

_____

Practice quoting your Scripture memory verses aloud or write them on separate paper.

SUMMARY STATEMENTS

- Obedience is the outward expression of my love of God.
- If I have an obedience problem, I have a love problem.
- God is love. His will is always best.
- God is all-knowing. His directions are always right.
- God is all-powerful. He can enable me to do His will.
- All of God's commands are expressions of His nature of love.
- When God gives a commandment, He is not restricting me. He is freeing me.
- If I love Him, I will obey Him!

DAY 4   GOD INVITES YOU TO JOIN HIM

When you see the Father at work around you, that is your invitation to adjust your life to Him and join Him in that work.

The Bible is the record of God's activity in the world. In it He reveals Himself (His nature), His purposes and plans, and His ways. The Bible is not primarily a book about individual persons and their relationship with God (Abraham, Moses, or Paul), but rather the activity of God and His relationship with individuals. The focus is on God and His activity.

Review the first four realities we have been looking at in this course. Fill in the blanks below with the correct words. If you need help, look on the inside back cover.

1. _____ is always at work around you.
2. God pursues a continuing love _____ with you that is real and _____.
3. God invites you to become _____ with Him in His _____.
4. God speaks by the _____ _____ through the Bible, _____, circumstances, and the _____ to reveal Himself, His _____, and His ways.

God Works Through People

God is at work in the world.

The Bible reveals that God always has been involved in the world. He has never been absent from it or what is taking place in history. When we read the Bible, we are reading the redemptive activity of God in our world. We see that He chooses to take the initiative and involve His people with Him. He chooses to work *through* them to accomplish His purposes.
- When God was ready to judge the world, He came to Noah. He was about to do something, and He was going to do it through Noah.
- When God was ready to build a nation for Himself, He came to Abraham. God was going to accomplish His will through Abraham.
- When God heard the cry of the children of Israel and decided to deliver them, He appeared to Moses. God came to Moses because of His purpose. He planned to deliver Israel through Moses.

This is true all through the Old Testament and New Testament. When God's fullness of time had come to redeem a lost world through His Son, He gave 12 men to His Son to prepare them to accomplish His purposes.

When He is about to do something, He takes the initiative and comes to one or more of His servants. He lets them know what He is about to do. He invites them to adjust their lives to Him, so He can accomplish His work through them. The prophet Amos indicated that, "The Sovereign Lord does nothing without revealing his plan to his servants the prophets" (Amos 3:7).

God takes the initiative to involve people in His work.

✳ **Mark the following statements as T (true) or F (false).**

_____ 1. God created the world and then left it alone to function on its own.

_____ 2. God is not absent. He is actively at work in the world.

_____ 3. People do God's work by deciding on their own what they think would be good to do and then doing it.

_____ 4. God involves people in His work.

_____ 5. God always takes the initiative to involve people in His work.

I hope this is "review" material for you by now. Statements 2, 4, and 5 are true. The others are false.

God's Revelation Is Your Invitation

You may be asking, "How does God invite me to be involved with Him?" Let's review Jesus' example from John 5:17, 19-20. (See Unit 1, p. 14.)

Jesus' Example

1. The Father has been working right up until now.
2. Now God has Me working.
3. I do nothing on My own initiative.
4. I watch to see what the Father is doing.
5. I do what I see the Father is already doing.
6. You see, the Father loves Me.
7. He shows Me everything that He, Himself, is doing.

✳ **How did Jesus know what to do in His Father's work?**

_____

How did Jesus respond? _____

_____

"My Father is always at his work to this very day, and I, too, am working. . . . I tell you the truth, the Son can do nothing by himself; he can do only what he sees his Father doing, because whatever the Father does the Son also does. For the Father loves the Son and shows him all he does."
—John 5:17, 19-20

To experience God personally, remember God has been at work in our world from the very beginning, and He still is at work. Jesus indicated this in His life. He announced that He had come, not to do His own will, but the will of the Father who had sent Him (John 4:34; 5:30; 6:38; 8:29; 17:4). To know the Father's will, Jesus said He watched to see what the Father was doing. Then Jesus joined Him in that work.

The Father loved the Son, and took the initiative to come to Him and reveal what He (the Father) was doing, or was about to do. The Son kept on looking for the Father's activity around Him, so He could unite His life with the Father's activity.

✳ **In the preceding box listing Jesus' example, circle the key word in statement #4 that tells what Jesus did to know the Father's invitation to join Him.**

As God's *obedient* child, you are in a love relationship with Him. Because He loves you and wants to involve you in His work, He will show you where He is working so you can join Him. The key word in statement #4 is *watch*. Jesus watched to see where the Father was at work. When He *saw*, He did what He saw the Father doing. For Jesus the revelation of where the Father was working was His invitation to join in the work. When you see the Father at work around you, that is your invitation to adjust your life to Him and join Him in that work.

God's revelation is your invitation to join Him.

Elisha's servant

Is it possible for God to be working around you and you not see it? Yes. Elisha and his servant were in the city of Dothan surrounded by an army. The servant was terrified, but Elisha was calm. "Elisha prayed, 'O Lord, open his eyes so he may see.' Then the Lord opened the servant's eyes, and he looked and saw the hills full of horses and chariots of fire all around Elisha" (2 Kings 6:17). Only when the Lord opened the servant's eyes did he see God's activity all around him.

Jerusalem's leaders

Jesus wept over Jerusalem and its leaders as He prophesied the destruction that would take place in A.D. 70. He said, "If you, even you, had only known on this day what would bring you peace—but now it is hidden from your eyes" (Luke 19:42). Here was God in their midst performing wonderful signs and miracles, and they did not recognize Him.

Two factors

Two factors are important for you to recognize the activity of God around you.
1. You must be living in an intimate love relationship with God.
2. God must take the initiative to open your spiritual eyes, so you can see what He is doing.

Fill in the blank:
God's revelation to me of His activity is my _____ to join Him.

What are two factors important to your recognizing the activity of God around you?

1. _____

2. _____

Unless God allows you to see where He is working, you will not see it. When God reveals to you what He is doing around you, that is your invitation to join Him. Recognizing God's activity is dependent on your love relationship with Him and His taking the initiative to open your spiritual eyes to see it.

Working Where God Is at Work

Church planting

Our church sensed that God wanted us to help start new churches all across Central and Western Canada. We had hundreds of towns and villages that had no evangelical church.

If you were in that situation, how would you decide which towns to choose?

_____

Some churches would start with a population study or survey. Then they would apply human logic to decide where the most promising and productive places might be. By now you know that we would take a different approach. We tried to find out what God already was doing around us. We believed that He would show us where He was at work, and that revelation would be our invitation to join Him. We began praying and watching to see what God would do next in answer to our prayers.

Allan

Allan was a small town 40 miles from Saskatoon. It had never had a Protestant church. One of our members felt led to conduct a Vacation Bible School for the children in Allan. We said, "Let's find out if God is at work here."

So we conducted the Vacation Bible School. At the end of the week, we held a parents' night. We said to the group, "We believe God may want us to establish a Baptist church in this town. If any of you would like to begin a regular Bible study group and maybe be a part of a new church, would you just come forward."

"I have prayed for 30 years . . ."

From the back of the hall came a lady. She was weeping. She said, "I have prayed for 30 years that there would be a Baptist church in this town, and you are the first people to respond."

"I promised God . . . I would pray four to five hours every day until God brought us a Baptist church in our town."

Right behind her came an elderly man. He too was deeply moved and weeping. He said, "For years I was active in a Baptist church. Then I went into alcohol. Four and a half years ago I came back to the Lord. I promised God then that I would pray four to five hours every day until God brought us a Baptist church in our town. You are the first people to respond."

We didn't have to take a survey. God had just shown us where He was at work! That was our invitation to join Him. We went back and joyfully shared with our church what God was doing. The church immediately voted to start a new church in Allan. As of today, that church in Allan has started one church and two mission churches.

God hasn't told us to go away and do some work for Him. He has told us that He is already at work trying to bring a lost world to Himself. If we will adjust our lives to Him in a love relationship, He will show us where He is at work. That revelation is His invitation to us to get involved in His work. Then, when we join Him, He completes His work through us.

Work where God is at work.

☼ **Review today's lesson. Pray and ask God to identify one or more statements or Scriptures that He wants you to understand, learn, or practice. Underline it (them). Then respond to the following:**

What was the most meaningful statement or Scripture you read today?

_____

_____

Reword the statement or Scripture into a prayer of response to God.

_____

_____

What does God want you to do in response to today's study?

_____

_____

SUMMARY STATEMENTS

- God is at work in the world.
- God takes the initiative to involve me in His work.
- God must take the initiative to open my spiritual eyes, so I can see what He is doing.
- When I see the Father at work around me, that is my invitation to adjust my life to Him and join Him in that work.
- God's revelation is my invitation to join Him.

KNOWING WHERE GOD IS AT WORK

DAY 5

There are some things only God can do.

God has tried, at times, to get our attention by revealing where He is at work. We see it, but we do not immediately identify it as God's work. We say to ourselves, *Well, I don't know if God wants me to get involved here, or not. I had better pray about it.* By the time we leave that situation and pray, the opportunity to join God is gone. A tender and sensitive heart will be ready to respond to God at the slightest prompting. God makes your heart tender and sensitive in the love relationship we already have talked about.

If you are going to join God in His work, you need to know where God is working. The Scriptures tell us of some things only God can do. You need to learn to identify these. Then, when something happens around you that only God can do, you can know it is God's activity. This does not deny God's initiative. Unless God opens your spiritual eyes, you will not know it is Him at work.

Things Only God Can Do

☼ **I gave an illustration about something only God can do at the beginning of unit 2, page 26. Review "College Campus Bible Studies" and write something only God can do.**

_____

_____

_____

The Scriptures say that no one can come to Christ except the Father draws him (John 6:44). No one will seek God or pursue spiritual things unless the Spirit of God is at work in his life. Suppose a neighbor, a friend, or one of your children begins to inquire after spiritual things. You do not have to question whether that is God drawing him or her. He is the only one who can do that. No one will ever seek after God unless God is at work in his life.

Zacchaeus

For example, as Jesus passed through a crowd, He was always looking for where the Father was at work. The crowd was not the harvest field. The harvest field was within that crowd. Jesus saw Zacchaeus in a tree. Jesus may have said to Himself, "Nobody can seek after Me with that kind of earnestness unless My Father is at work in his heart." So Jesus pulled away from the crowd and said, "Zacchaeus come down immediately. I must stay at your house today" (Luke 19:5). What happened? Salvation came to that household that night. Jesus always looked for the activity of the Father and joined Him. Salvation came as a result of Jesus' joining His life to the activity of God.

Read the following Scriptures and answer the questions that follow.

> **John 14:15-17**—"If you love me, you will obey what I command. And I will ask the Father, and he will give you another Counselor to be with you forever—the Spirit of truth. . . . You know him, for he lives with you and will be in you."

1. If you love and obey Christ, whom will the Father give you? List two of His names.

   _____

2. Where will this Person live? _____

   > **John 14:26**—"The Counselor, the Holy Spirit, whom the Father will send in my name, will teach you all things and will remind you of everything I have said to you."

3. What are two things the Holy Spirit will do for Jesus' disciples?

   _____

   _____

   > **John 16:8**—"When he comes, he will convict the world of guilt in regard to sin and righteousness and judgment."

4. What are three more things the Holy Spirit does?

   _____

   _____

When you are saved, you enter a love relationship with Jesus Christ—God Himself. At that point the Counselor, the Spirit of truth, comes to take up residence in your life. He is ever present to teach you. The Holy Spirit also convicts people of guilt regarding sin. He convicts the world of righteousness and judgment. Here is a summary of some things only God can do:

Things Only God Can Do
1. God draws people to Himself.
2. God causes people to seek after Him.
3. God reveals spiritual truth.
4. God convicts the world of guilt regarding sin.
5. God convicts the world of righteousness.
6. God convicts the world of judgment.

When you see one of these things happening you can know God is at work. God is at work when you see someone coming to Christ, asking about spiritual matters, coming to understand spiritual truth, experiencing conviction of sin, being convinced of the righteousness of Christ, being convinced of judgment.

What is God doing . . .

where you work?
in your home?
in your church?

When I was speaking in a series of meetings, Bill, a plant manager, said, "You know, I have not been looking on the job to see the activity of God." He mentioned Christian people in key positions in his plant. He wondered if God had not placed them in those positions for a purpose. He decided to get these coworkers together and say, "Let's see if God wants us to take this entire plant for Jesus Christ." Does that sound like something God might want to do? Yes!

☀ **Suppose you were in Bill's place. You plan to bring these Christians together. How would you find out what to do next?**

_____

_____

You start by praying. Only the Father knows what He has purposed. He knows the best way to get it done. He even knows why He brought these individuals together in this plant and why He gave Bill the burden to bring them together. After you pray, get up off your knees and watch to see what God does next. Watch to see what people are saying when they come to you. Suppose someone in the plant comes to Bill and says, "My family is really having a tough time financially. I am having an especially tough time with my teenager."

Pray and watch to see what God does next.

Bill had just prayed, "Oh, God, show me where You are at work." He needs to make the connection between his prayers and what happens next. If you do not connect what happens next, you may miss God's answer to your prayer. Always connect what happens next. Then what should Bill do?

Make the connection.

Find out what God is already doing.

Ask the kind of questions that will reveal what is happening in that person's life. Learn to ask questions of people who cross your path to find out what God is doing in their lives. For instance:
- How can I pray for you?
- What can I pray for you?
- Do you want to talk?
- What do you see as the greatest challenge in your life?
- What is the most significant thing happening in your life right now?
- Would you tell me what God is doing in your life?
- What is God bringing to the surface in your life?
- What particular burden has God given you?

Ask probing questions.

The person responds, "I really don't have a relationship with God. But in the last little while with this problem with my teenager, I sure have been thinking about it." Or "When I was a kid I used to go to Sunday School. My mother and dad made me go. I got away from it, but the financial problems we are under has really caused me to think about this." Those statements sound like God is at work in the person's life. He may be drawing the person to Himself, causing the person to seek after God, or bringing conviction of sin.

Listen.

☀ **Answer the following questions:**

A. What are some actions described in the previous paragraphs that will help you see if God is at work in a situation?

_____

_____

_____

_____

B. Look back at the box listing "Things Only God Can Do." What would you watch for as you look for the activity of God in the lives of people around you? List at least three.

I would watch for someone who . . .

1. _____

2. _____

3. _____

C. List in the margin the names of people around you who are experiencing any of these activities of God in their lives.

When you want to know what God is doing around you, pray. Watch to see what happens next. Make the connection between your prayer and what happens. Find out what God is doing by asking probing questions. Then listen. Be ready to make whatever adjustments are required to join God in what He is doing.

A Visitor Came by "Accident"

We had a man visit our church by accident. He saw on the bottom of the bulletin, "Pray for our mission in Kyle; pray for our mission in Prince Albert; pray for our mission in Love; pray for our mission in Regina; pray for our mission in Blaine Lake" and others. He asked what it meant.

"If God ever shows us where someone desires a Bible study or a church, we will respond."

"I explained that our church had made a commitment. If God ever shows us where someone desires a Bible study or a church, we will respond. He asked, "You mean to say, that if I were to ask you to come and help us start a Baptist church in our town, you would respond?" I told him that we would, and he started to cry. He was a construction worker in Leroy, 75 miles east of us. He said that he had been pleading with people to start a Baptist church in Leroy for 24 years. Nobody had wanted to help. He asked if we would come.

We established a church in Leroy. We bought two lots on the main street. This man was so excited he bought a school building and moved it to the site. He is now functioning as a lay pastor in a work beyond Leroy. Both of his sons have responded to the call to the gospel ministry.

As a church, we were already conditioned to seeing things that only God can do. When He let us see where He was working, we immediately saw that as our invitation to join Him. Frequently, the reason we do not join Him is we are not committed to join Him. We are wanting God to bless us, not to work through us. As a church, do not look for how God is going to bless you. Look for how God is going to reveal Himself by working through you and out beyond you to accomplish His purposes. The working of God in you will bring a blessing. The blessing is a by-product of your obedience and experience of God at work in your midst.

Who can tell what a solitary visit by a stranger can mean in your church? Ask some questions about what God is doing where that person is. Then you will know how to adjust your life to be an instrument of God, so that God can do what He wants to do. When you start to see God moving, adjust your life and respond.

Has this illustration given you any ideas about how you can begin to watch for the activity of God around you? in your family? in your work? in your church? Write down the ideas you have.

_____

_____

_____

The impressions you wrote down may be from God Himself. He may be inviting you to look for His activity. Don't miss the opportunity. Pray and watch to see what happens next.

Two More Points

We have spent two days focusing on the fact that God invites you to become involved in His work. You need to connect the following two points to this fact.

1. God speaks when He is about to accomplish His purposes.

1. God speaks when He is about to accomplish His purposes. When God reveals to you what He is doing is when you need to respond. He speaks when He is about to accomplish His purposes. That is true throughout Scripture. Now, keep in mind, the final completion may be a long time off. Abram's son was born 25 years after the promise from God. The time God comes to you, however, is the time for your response. You need to begin adjusting your life to Him. You may need to make some preparations for what He is about to do through you.

2. What God initiates, He completes.

2. What God initiates, He completes. Isaiah confirmed this when God said through him, "What I have said, that will I bring about; what I have planned, that will I do" (Isa. 46:11). Earlier he warned God's people, saying, "The Lord Almighty has sworn, 'Surely, as I have planned, so it will be, and as I have purposed, so it will stand. . . . For the Lord Almighty has purposed, and who can thwart him? His hand is stretched out, and who can turn it back?' " (Isa. 14:24, 27). God says that if He ever lets His people know what He is about to do, it is as good as done—He Himself will bring it to pass. (See also 1 Kings 8:56 and Phil. 1:6.)

What God speaks, He stands to guarantee that it will come to pass. This holds enormous implications to individual believers, churches, and denominations. When we come to God to know what He is about to do where we are, we also come with the assurance that what God indicates He is about to do is certain to come to pass.

☼ **Do you agree or disagree with the following statement? "What God initiates, He always completes." I Agree ❑   I Disagree ❑   Why? What is the reason for your response?**

_____

_____

_____

Some of you may have disagreed with the statement. Be sure you always base your understanding of God on Scripture, not on personal opinion or experience alone. Throughout history, people have said they have a word from the Lord and then it does not come to pass. You cannot look to these kinds of experiences to determine your understanding of God.

A strong word of caution comes to spiritual leaders. If you ever indicate to God's people that you "have a word from the Lord," you are obligated to stay at it until God brings it to pass. For God said that anyone who says, "I have a word from the Lord!", and it does not come to pass, that one is a false prophet (Deut. 18:18-22; Jer. 28:9; Ezek. 12:24, 25). The true prophet of God is one who has a word from the Lord, and it comes to pass. God's nature demands it! What God says comes to pass.

Spiritual leaders beware

☼ **Review today's lesson. Pray and ask God to identify one or more statements or Scriptures that He wants you to understand, learn, or practice. Underline it (them). Then respond to the following:**

What was the most meaningful statement or Scripture you read today?

_____

_____

_____

Reword the statement or Scripture into a prayer of response to God.

_____

_____

_____

What does God want you to do in response to today's study?

_____

_____

Review your Scripture memory verses and be prepared to recite them to a partner in your small-group session this week.

SUMMARY STATEMENTS

- A tender and sensitive heart will be ready to respond to God at the slightest prompting.
- Pray and watch to see what God does next.
- Make the connection. Ask probing questions. Listen.
- God speaks when He is about to accomplish His purposes.
- What God initiates, He completes.

God Speaks, Part 1

UNIT

5

When I accepted the call to go to Faith Baptist Church in Saskatoon, Saskatchewan, Canada, few people were left—about 10. They recently had held a meeting to decide whether to disband as a church. What could God do here? What did He want to do? We had a heart to wait before Him, and look around us to see what He was doing.

When I arrived on the field on a cold Saturday morning in 1970, a car with five men pulled up to join us for lunch. They came from Prince Albert, a city of 30,000 people 90 miles to the north. They had heard I was coming to Saskatoon. They began to pray, and they became convinced that I was to be their pastor, too. They had come to share their "word from the Lord."

Little did they know that almost 20 years earlier, as a teenager I had told the Lord, "If you ever call me into the ministry, and if there is ever a people anywhere within driving distance who want a Bible study or a church, I will go." When these people asked me to come, I could not say "no."

Faith Church had never sponsored a mission. I had never pastored a church that had sponsored a mission. We could not proceed on our own skill or experience. We had to depend entirely on the Lord's guidance. We were assured that the yearning in the hearts of God's people in Prince Albert was the activity of God. Since they were led to come to us, we realized that was God's way of indicating where we should serve Him.

God began to reveal His larger purposes for Prince Albert. God developed this church. They called a pastor, obtained property and a building. Then they began to multiply. They started new churches in Love, Smeaton, Melfort, Tisdale, and Leoville. They began an Indian mission in Prince Albert and churches at three Native Indian Reserves. They started significant ministries in Nipiwan, LaRonge, Deschambault, Cumberland House and other surrounding communities. They began an annual Indian Conference for Chiefs, Band Councils, and other Indian people from across the northern part of Saskatchewan. Truly, God did far more than we could have even asked for or imagined (Eph. 3:20-21).

Verse to Memorize
this Week

He who belongs to God hears what God says. The reason you do not hear is that you do not belong to God. **—JOHN 8:47**

One critical point to understanding and experiencing God is *knowing clearly when God is speaking*. If the Christian does not know when God is speaking, he is in trouble at the *heart* of his Christian life! We will focus our attention on how God speaks through the Holy Spirit to reveal Himself, His purposes, and His ways. We will examine ways God speaks through the Bible, prayer, circumstances, and the church or other believers.

If the Christian does not know when God is speaking, he is in trouble at the heart of his Christian life!

Many Different Ways

"In the past God spoke to our forefathers through the prophets at many times and in various ways" (Heb. 1:1). One truth that is evident throughout the Bible is that God speaks to His people. In the Old Testament, God spoke through:

- angels (Gen. 16)
- visions (Gen. 15)
- dreams (Gen. 28:10-19)
- the use of the Urim and Thummim (Ex. 28:30)
- symbolic actions (Jer. 18:1-10)
- a gentle whisper (1 Kings 19:12)
- miraculous signs (Ex. 8:20-25)
  and others.

In the Old Testament God spoke in many different ways.

How God spoke in the Old Testament is not the most important factor. *That* He spoke is the crucial point. Those He spoke to *knew* it was God, and they *knew* what He was saying.

☀ **Which of the following is most important? How God spoke ❑ or That God spoke ❑ When God spoke to a person in the Old Testament what two things did the person know? He knew . . .**

_____

Four Important Factors

That God spoke to people is far more important than *how* He spoke. When He spoke, the person knew God was speaking, and he knew what God was saying. I see four important factors each time God spoke in the Old Testament. The burning bush experience of Moses in Exodus 3 is an example.

That God spoke is the most important factor, not how He spoke.

1. **When God spoke, it was usually unique to that individual.** For instance, Moses had no precedent for a burning bush experience. He could not say, "Oh, this is my burning bush experience. My fathers, Abraham, Isaac, and Jacob had theirs, and this is mine." There were no other experiences of God speaking this way. It was unique, because God wants our experience with Him, and His voice, to be personal to us. He wants us to look to Him in a relationship rather than depend on some method or technique. If Moses had been around today, he would have been tempted to write a book about *My Burning Bush Experience*. Then people all over our land would be out trying to find *their* burning bush. The key is not *how* God spoke, but *that* He spoke. That has not changed. He will speak to His people today.

Unique to the individual

☀ **What is the first important factor in the way God spoke to individuals in the Old Testament?**

1. _____

2. **When God spoke, the person was sure God was speaking.** Because God spoke to Moses in a unique way, Moses had to be certain it was God. The Scripture testifies that Moses had no question that his encounter was with God—The "I AM THAT I AM" (Ex. 3:14). He trusted God, obeyed Him, and experienced God responding just as He said He would. Could Moses logically prove to someone else that he had heard from God? No, all Moses could do was testify to his encounter with God. Only God could cause His people to know that the word He gave Moses was a word from the God of their fathers.

Sure God was speaking

When someone like Gideon lacked assurance, God was very gracious to reveal Himself even more clearly. When Gideon first asked for a sign, he prepared a sacrifice. Then "the angel of the Lord touched the meat and the unleavened bread. Fire flared from the rock, consuming the meat and the bread. And the angel of the Lord disappeared. When Gideon realized that it was the angel of the Lord, he exclaimed, 'Ah, Sovereign Lord! I have seen the angel of the Lord face to face!'" (Judg. 6:21-22). Gideon was sure that God had spoken.

What is the second important factor in the way God spoke in the Old Testament?

2. _____

Knew what God said

3. When God spoke, the person knew what God said. Moses knew what God was telling him to do. He knew how God wanted to work through him. That is why Moses raised so many objections. He knew exactly what God was expecting. This was true for Moses; and it was true for Noah, Abraham, Joseph, David, Daniel, and others.

What is the third important factor in the way God spoke in the Old Testament?

3. _____

The encounter with God

4. When God spoke, that was the encounter with God. Moses would have been foolish to say, "This has been a wonderful experience with this burning bush. I hope this leads me to an encounter with God!" That *was* the encounter with God! When God reveals truth to you, by whatever means, that is an encounter with God. That is an experience of His presence in your life. God is the only One who can cause you to experience His presence.

What is the fourth important factor in the way God spoke in the Old Testament?

4. _____

Using the "hint" below, see if you can write the four factors you just read about.

1. Unique— _____

2. Sure— _____

3. What— _____

4. Encounter— _____

Check your answers.

This pattern of God speaking is found throughout the Old Testament. The **method** He used to speak was different from person to person. What is important is:
- God uniquely spoke to His people.
- They knew it was God.
- They knew what He said.

When God spoke, that was an encounter with God. When God speaks to you by the Holy Spirit through the Bible, prayer, circumstances, and the church, you will come to know it is God; and you will know what He is saying. When God speaks to you, that is an encounter with God.

A Wrong Pattern

I hear many people say something like this: "Lord, I really want to know your will. Stop me if I am wrong and bless me if I am right." Another version of this is: "Lord, I will proceed in this direction. Close the door if it is not your will." The only problem is I don't see this as a pattern anywhere in the Scripture.

You cannot allow yourself to be guided by experience alone. You cannot allow yourself to be guided by tradition, a method, or a formula. Often people trust in these ways because they are easy. People do as they please and put the whole burden of responsibility on God. If they are wrong, He must intervene and stop them. If they make a mistake, they blame Him.

If you want to know the will and voice of God, you must give the time and effort to cultivate a love relationship with Him. That is what He wants!

Which of the following is the scriptural pattern for knowing God's will? Check one.
❑ Look for open and closed doors.
❑ Ask God to stop you if you are wrong.
❑ Wait until you hear a clear word from God.

The Word of God is our guide. The pattern I see in Scripture is that God always gives a direction on the front end. He may not tell you all you want to know at the beginning, but

He will tell you what you need to know to make necessary adjustments and to take the first step of obedience. Your task is to wait until the Master gives you instructions. If you start "doing" before you have a direction from God, more than likely you will be wrong.

Specific Directions

A popular teaching says God does not give you clear directives. It says He just sets your life in motion. Then you try to figure out the directions using your God-given mind. This implies that a Christian always thinks correctly and according to God's will. This does not take into account that the old nature is constantly battling with the spiritual nature (Rom. 7). Our ways are not God's ways (Isa. 55:8). Only God can give you the kind of specific directions to accomplish His purposes *in His ways*.

After God spoke to Noah about building an ark, Noah knew the size, the type of materials, and how to put it together. When God spoke to Moses about building the tabernacle He was very specific about the details. When God became flesh in the Person of Jesus Christ, He gave specific directions to His disciples—where to go, what to do, how to respond.

What about when God called Abraham (Abram) and said, "Go to the land I will show you" (Gen. 12:1)? That was not very specific. That required faith. But God did say, "I will show you." God always will give you enough specific directions to do *now* what He wants you to do. When you need more directions, He gives you more in His timing. In Abraham's case, God later told him about the son to be born to him, the number of his descendants, the territory they would inhabit, that they would go into bondage and be brought out.

The Holy Spirit gives clear directives today. God is personal. He wants to be intimately involved in your life. He will give you clear guidance for living. You may say, "That has not been my experience." You need to:

> Base your understanding of God on Scripture not on experience.

☀ **Underline the suggestions in the following paragraph that will help you as you look to God for direction in your life.**

If you do not have clear instructions from God in a matter, pray and wait. Learn patience. Depend on God's timing. His timing is always right and best. Don't get in a hurry. He may be withholding directions to cause you to seek Him more intently. Don't try to skip over the relationship to get on with *doing*. God is more interested in a love relationship with you than He is in what you can do for Him.

☀ **In your own words summarize the directions you underlined.**

_____

_____

_____

Review today's lesson. Pray and ask God to identify one or more statements or Scriptures that He wants you to understand, learn, or practice. Underline it (them). Then respond to the following:

What was the most meaningful statement or Scripture you read today?

_____

_____

Reword the statement or Scripture into a prayer of response to God.

_____

_____

What does God want you to do in response to today's study?

_____

_____

Write your Scripture memory verse for this unit on the following lines and review your verses from other units. Remember, you may select a different verse if you want to.

_____

_____

_____

> ## SUMMARY STATEMENTS
>
> * If I do not know when God is speaking, I am in trouble at the heart of my Christian life!
> * God speaks to His people.
> * *That* God spoke to people is far more important than *how* He spoke.
> * When God spoke, it was usually unique to that individual.
> * When God spoke, the person was sure it was God.
> * When God spoke, the person knew what God said.
> * When God spoke, that was the encounter with God.
> * If I do not have clear instructions from God in a matter, I will pray and wait. I will not try to bypass the love relationship.

DAY 2   GOD SPEAKS BY THE HOLY SPIRIT

When I understand spiritual truth, it is because the Holy Spirit is working in my life.

Hebrews 1:1-2 says, "In the past God spoke to our forefathers through the prophets at many times and in various ways, but in these last days he has spoken to us by his Son."

In the Gospels . . .

God spoke by His Son.

In the Gospels God spoke through His Son—Jesus. The Gospel of John begins: "In the beginning was the Word, and the Word was with God, and the Word was God. . . . The Word became flesh and made his dwelling among us" (John 1:1, 14). God became flesh in the Person of Jesus Christ. (See also 1 John 1:1-4.)

The disciples would have been foolish to say, "It's wonderful knowing You, Jesus; but we really would like to know the Father."

Philip even said, "Lord, show us the Father and that will be enough for us" (John 14:8).

Jesus responded, "Don't you know me, Philip, even after I have been among you such a long time? Anyone who has seen me has seen the Father. How can you say, 'Show us the Father'? Don't you believe that I am in the Father, and that the Father is in me? The words I say to you are not just my own. Rather, it is the Father, living in me, who is doing his work" (John 14:9-10). When Jesus spoke, the Father was speaking through Him. When Jesus did a miracle, the Father was doing His work through Jesus.

Just as surely as Moses was face-to-face with God at the burning bush, the disciples were face-to-face with God in a personal relationship with Jesus. Their encounter with Jesus *was* an encounter with God. To hear from Jesus *was* to hear from God.

Write a summary statement of how God spoke during the life of Jesus. _____

_____

_____

In the Gospel accounts God was in Christ Jesus. God spoke by Jesus. When the disciples heard Jesus, they heard God. When Jesus spoke, that was an encounter with God.

In Acts and to the Present . . .

God speaks by the Holy Spirit.

When we move from the Gospels to Acts and to the present, we quite often change our whole mind-set. We live as if God quit speaking personally to His people. We fail to realize that an encounter with the Holy Spirit *is* an encounter with God. God clearly spoke to His people in Acts. He clearly speaks to us today. From Acts to the present, God has been speaking to His people by the Holy Spirit.

The Holy Spirit takes up residence in the life of a believer. "You yourselves are God's temple and . . . God's Spirit lives in you" (1 Cor. 3:16). "Your body is a temple of the Holy Spirit, who is in you, whom you have received from God" (1 Cor. 6:19). Because He is always present in a believer, He can speak to you clearly and at any time.

We have already studied about God's speaking to His people. Here are some of the key ideas we examined:

Review "God Speaks"

- In the Old Testament God spoke in many different ways.
- In the Gospels God spoke through His Son.
- In Acts and to the present He speaks by the Holy Spirit.
- God speaks by the Holy Spirit through the Bible, prayer, circumstances, and the church to reveal Himself, His purposes, and His ways.
- Knowing God's voice comes from an intimate love relationship with God.
- God speaks when He has a purpose in mind for your life.
- The moment God speaks to you is the very moment He wants you to respond to Him.
- The moment God speaks to you is God's timing.

Answer the following questions.

1. How did God speak in the Old Testament?

   _____

2. How did God speak in the Gospels?

   _____

3. How did God speak in Acts and to the present time?

   _____

4. How do you come to know God's voice?

   _____

5. How do you know God's timing?

   _____

Check your answers in the preceding review list.

Let's pull together several other things you studied in earlier units:
- Because of sin, "There is no one who understands, no one who seeks God. All have turned away, they have together become worthless; there is no one who does good, not even one" (Rom. 3:11, 12).
- The Holy Spirit is called the "Spirit of truth" (John 14:17; 15:26; 16:13).
- Spiritual truths can be revealed only by God: " 'No eye has seen, no ear has heard, no mind has conceived what God has prepared for those who love him'—but God has revealed it to us by his Spirit. The Spirit searches all things, even the deep things of God. . . . No one knows the thoughts of God except the Spirit of God. We have not received the spirit of the world but the Spirit who is from God, that we may understand what God has freely given us" (1 Cor. 2:9-12).
- Jesus said the Holy Spirit would "Teach you all things and will remind you of everything I have said to you" (John 14:26).
- The Holy Spirit will testify about Jesus (John 15:26).
- "He will guide you into all truth. He will not speak on his own; he will speak only what he hears, and he will tell you what is yet to come. He will bring glory to me by taking from what is mine and making it known to you" (John 16:13, 14).

Encountering God

When God spoke to Moses and others in the Old Testament, those events *were* encounters with God. An encounter with Jesus *was* an encounter with God for the disciples. In the same way an encounter with the Holy Spirit *is* an encounter with God for you.

Now that the Holy Spirit is given, He is the one who guides you into all truth and teaches you all things. You understand spiritual truth because the Holy Spirit is working in your

An encounter with the Holy Spirit is an encounter with God.

You never discover truth. Truth is revealed.

life. You cannot understand the Word of God unless the Spirit of God teaches you. When you come to the Word of God, the Author Himself is present to instruct you. You never *discover* truth; truth is *revealed*. When the Holy Spirit reveals truth to you, He is not leading you to an encounter with God. That *is* an encounter with God!

Has God been speaking to you during this course? Yes ❑   No ❑ As a review, look back through the end of the day activities in units 1-4.
- **Read through the statements or Scriptures that God called to your attention.**
- **Read and pray again the prayer responses.**
- **Review the things you sensed God wanted you to do in response to the lessons.**

Briefly summarize what you sense God has been saying to you this far in the course. Focus on the general themes or directions rather than specific details.

_____

_____

_____

_____

_____

Have you been responding to what God has been calling to your attention? How would you describe your response to His leading?

_____

_____

What do you sense is your greatest spiritual challenge right now?

_____

_____

Without looking, try to quote the first four statements of the realities of experiencing God. Use these hints: work, relationship, invitation, speaks. Check yourself using the inside back cover or quote them to another person and ask him to check your answers.

Immediately Respond

When God spoke to Moses, what he did next was crucial. After Jesus spoke to the disciples, what they did next was crucial. What you do next after the Spirit of God speaks to you through His Word is crucial. Our problem is that when the Spirit of God speaks to us, we go into a long discussion. Moses went into a long discussion with God (Ex. 3:11—4:13), and it limited him for the rest of his life. Moses had to speak to the people through his brother Aaron (Ex. 4:14-16).

I challenge you to review what you sense God has been saying to you on a regular basis. If God speaks and you hear but do not respond, a time could come when you will not hear His voice. Disobedience can lead to a "famine of hearing the words of the Lord" (Amos 8:11-12).

"The Lord was with Samuel as he grew up, and he let none of his words fall to the ground."
—1 Samuel 3:19

When Samuel was a young boy, God began to speak to him. The Scriptures say, "The Lord was with Samuel as he grew up, and he let none of his words fall to the ground" (1 Sam. 3:19). Be like Samuel. Don't let a single word from the Lord fail to bring adjustments in your life. Then God will do in you and through you everything He says to you.

In Luke 8:5-15, Jesus told the parable of the sower and the seeds. The seed that fell on the good soil represented one who heard the word of God, retained it, and produced fruit. Then Jesus said, "Consider carefully how you listen. Whoever has will be given more; whoever does not have, even what he thinks he has will be taken from him" (Luke 8:18). If you hear the Word of God and do not apply it to produce fruit in your life, even what you think you have will be taken away. Be careful how you listen to God! Make up your mind now that when the Spirit of God speaks to you, you are going to do what He says.

Review today's lesson. Pray and ask God to identify one or more statements or Scriptures that He wants you to understand, learn, or practice. Underline it (them). Then respond to the following:

What was the most meaningful statement or Scripture you read today?

_____

_____

Reword the statement or Scripture into a prayer of response to God.

_____

_____

What does God want you to do in response to today's study?

_____

_____

SUMMARY STATEMENTS

- An encounter with the Holy Spirit is an encounter with God.
- I understand spiritual truth because the Holy Spirit is working in my life.
- When I come to the Word of God, the Author Himself is present to instruct me.
- I never *discover* truth; truth is *revealed*.

GOD REVEALS

DAY 3

God's revelations are designed to bring you into a love relationship with Him.

God speaks to His people. When He speaks, what does He reveal? Throughout the Scriptures, when God speaks, it is to reveal something about Himself, His purposes, or His ways. God's revelations are designed to bring you into a love relationship with Him.

God Reveals Himself

When God speaks by the Holy Spirit to you, He often reveals to you something about Himself. He reveals His name. He reveals His nature and character.

Read these Scriptures. After each one, write what God revealed about Himself.

"When Abram was ninety-nine years old, the Lord appeared to him and said, "I am God Almighty" (Gen. 17:1).

_____

"The Lord said to Moses, 'Speak to the entire assembly of Israel and say to them: "Be holy because I, the Lord your God, am holy" ' " (Lev. 19:1-2).

_____

" 'I the Lord do not change. . . . Ever since the time of your forefathers you have turned away from my decrees and have not kept them. Return to me, and I will return to you,' says the Lord Almighty." (Mal. 3:6-7).

_____

Jesus said to the Jews, "I am the living bread that came down from heaven. If anyone eats of this bread, he will live forever" (John 6:51).

_____

God revealed Himself to Abram by His name—God Almighty. To Moses He revealed His holy nature. God spoke through Malachi to Israel and revealed that He is unchanging and forgiving. Jesus revealed Himself as "living bread" and the source of eternal life.

God speaks when He wants to involve a person in His work. He reveals Himself in order to help the person respond in faith. The person can better respond to God's instructions when he believes God is who He says He is, and when he believes God can do what He says He will do.

God reveals Himself to increase my faith.

☀ **Stop for a minute and meditate on why God revealed Himself as He did to each of the people in the Scriptures above. When you think you have an idea of why each revelation was given, read on.**

- Ninety-nine-year-old Abram needed to know God was almighty (all powerful—able to do anything) so He could *believe* that God could give Him a son in his old age.
- Through Moses, God said He was holy. His people had to believe He was holy, so they would respond by being holy themselves.
- Through Malachi, God revealed His forgiving nature so the people could believe that they would be forgiven if they would return to God.
- Jesus revealed that He was the source of eternal life so the Jews could believe and respond to Him and receive life.

☀ **Why does God reveal Himself (His name, His nature, His character)?**

_____

God reveals Himself to increase faith that leads to action. You will need to listen attentively to what God reveals to you about Himself. This will be critical when you come to the crisis of belief.

- You will have to **believe** God is who He says He is.
- You will have to **believe** God can do what He says He will do.
- You will have to **adjust** your thinking in light of this belief.
- Trusting that God will demonstrate Himself to be who He says He is, you then obey Him.
- When you **obey**, God does His work through you and demonstrates that He is who He says He is.
- Then you will **know** God by experience.
- You will **know** He is who He says He is.

For example, when did Abram know God was almighty? Well, he knew it in his mind as soon as God said it. But, he came to know God by experience as God Almighty when God did something in his life that only God could do. When God gave Abraham (100 years old) and Sarah (90 years old) a son, Abraham *knew* God was God Almighty.

☀ **When God speaks by the Holy Spirit, what is one thing He reveals?**

God speaks by the Holy Spirit to reveal _____, His purposes, and His ways.

God Reveals His Purposes

God reveals His purposes so I will do His work.

God reveals His purposes so you will know what *He* plans to do. If you are to join Him, you need to know what God is about to do. What you plan to do for God is not important. What He plans to do where you are is very important. God speaks with a purpose in mind. This point should be a review for you. (See pp. 38-41.)

Noah

When God came to Noah He did not ask, "What do you want to do for me?" He came to reveal what He was about to do. It was far more important to know what *God* was about to do. It really did not matter what Noah had planned to do for God. God was about to destroy the world. He wanted to work through Noah to accomplish *His* purposes of saving a remnant of people and animals to repopulate the earth.

Abram

Similarly, God came to Abram and spoke to him because He had a purpose in mind. He was preparing to build a nation for Himself. God was about to accomplish *His* purposes through Abram.

When God prepared to destroy Sodom and Gomorrah, He did not ask Abraham what he wanted to do, or was planning to do for Him. It was crucial for Abraham to know what *God* was about to do. God revealed His purposes.

"Surely the Sovereign Lord does nothing without revealing his plan to his servants the prophets." —Amos 3:7

This sequence is seen throughout the entire Bible: the Judges, David, the prophets, the disciples, and Paul. When God was about to do something, *He* took the initiative to come to His servants (Amos 3:7). He spoke to reveal His purposes and plans. Then He could involve them and accomplish *His* purposes through them.

In contrast, we set about to dream our dreams of what WE want to do for God. Then we tend to make long-range plans based on priorities of *our* choosing. What is important is what *God* plans to do where we are, and how He wants to accomplish it through us. Look what the Psalmist had to say about our plans and purposes:

The Lord foils the plans of the nations;
    he thwarts the purposes of the peoples.
But the plans of the Lord stand firm forever,
    the purposes of his heart through all generations.
                      —Psalm 33:10-11

Read Proverbs 19:21 (right) and Psalm 33:10-11 (above). Why does God reveal His purposes?

_____

_____

"Many are the plans in a man's heart, but it is the Lord's purpose that prevails."
          —Proverbs 19:21

Based on Psalm 33:10-11, answer the following questions.

1. What does the Lord do to the plans of the nations?

_____

2. What does the Lord do to the purposes of the peoples?

_____

3. What happens to the plans and purposes of the Lord?

_____

Do you see why you need to know God's plans and purposes? Your plans and purposes must be God's plans and purposes or you will not experience God working through you. God reveals His purposes so you will know what He plans to do. Then you can join Him. His plans and purposes will stand. They will be accomplished. The Lord foils and thwarts the plans of the nations and the purposes of the peoples.

Planning is a tool God may cause you to use, but it never can become a substitute for God. Your relationship with God is far more important to Him than any planning you will ever do. Our biggest problem with planning is that we plan and carry out things in our own wisdom that only God has a right to determine. We cannot know the when, or where, or how of God's will until He tells us.

God wants us to follow *Him* daily, not just follow a plan. If we try to spell out all the details of His will in a planning session, we have a tendency to think: "Now that we know where we are going and how to get there, *we* can get the job done." Then we forget about the need for the daily, intimate relationship with God. We may set about to accomplish our plans and forget the relationship. God created us for an eternal love relationship. Life is our opportunity to experience Him at work.

Planning is not all wrong. Just be very careful not to plan more than God intends for you to plan. Let God interrupt or redirect your plans any time He wants. Remain in a close relationship with Him so you can always hear His voice when He wants to speak to you.

God's purposes
versus
our plans

*For Review see
Unit 2 pp. 29-32.*

When God speaks by the Holy Spirit, what are two things He reveals?

God speaks by the Holy Spirit to reveal _____, His _____, and His ways.

God Reveals His Ways

Even the casual or uninformed reader of the Bible can see that God's ways and plans are so different from man's. God uses *Kingdom* principles to accomplish *Kingdom* purposes. God reveals His ways to us because they are the only way to accomplish *His* purposes.

His goal always is to reveal Himself to people to draw them into a love relationship with Himself. His ways are redemptive. He acts in such a way to reveal Himself and His Love. He does not simply wait around in order to help us achieve our goals for Him! He comes to accomplish His own goals through us—and in His own way.

God said, "My thoughts are not your thoughts, neither are your ways my ways" (Isa. 55:8). God does not work in man's ways. We will not accomplish God's work in our own ways. This is one of the basic sin problems people face: "We all, like sheep, have gone astray, each of us has turned to his own way" (Isa. 53:6).

*God reveals His ways so
I can accomplish
His purposes.*

"My thoughts are not your thoughts, neither are your ways my ways." —Isaiah 55:8

☀ **Why does God reveal His ways?** _____
_____

Our ways may seem good to us. We may accomplish some moderate successes. When we try to do the work of God in our own ways, however, we will never see the mighty power of God in what we do. God reveals His ways because that is the only way to accomplish His purposes. When God accomplishes His purposes in His ways through us, people will come to know God. They will recognize that what has happened can only be explained by God. He will get glory to Himself!

Using Kingdom ways, Jesus fed 5,000. (Matt. 14:13-21)

Using Kingdom ways is seen in the life of the disciples. Jesus asked them to feed the multitudes. Their response was, "Send them home!" Jesus, using *Kingdom* principles, sat them down, fed them, and had baskets full of leftovers. They saw the Father work a miracle. What a contrast! The disciples would have sent the people home empty and hungry. God displayed to a watching world His love, His nature, and His power. This kind of display would draw people to Himself through His Son Jesus. This kind of mighty display happened many times in the lives of the disciples. They had to learn to function according to *Kingdom* principles to do *Kingdom* work.

God gets the glory

God's purposes accomplished in His ways bring glory to Him. You must learn to do Kingdom work in Kingdom ways. "Come, let us go up to the mountain of the Lord . . . . He will teach us his ways, so that we may walk in his paths" (Mic. 4:2).

☀ **When God speaks by the Holy Spirit, what are three things He reveals?**

God speaks by the Holy Spirit to reveal _____, His _____, and His _____.

Match the things God reveals with the correct reason. Write the correct letters in the blanks.

God reveals ...	Because ...
_____1. Himself	A. He wants me to know how to accomplish things only He can do.
_____2. His purposes	B. He wants me to know what He is about to do so I can join Him.
_____3. His ways	C. He wants me to have faith to believe He can do what He says.

Answers to the matching activity are: 1-C, 2-B, 3-A.

When I was first learning how to walk with God, I depended too much on other people. I would run to other people and say, "Do you think this is really God? Here is what I think. What do you think?" I would unconsciously, or consciously, depend on them rather than on the relationship I had with God.

Finally I had to say, "I am going to go to the Lord and clarify what I am absolutely convinced He is saying to me. Then, I am going to proceed and watch to see how God affirms it." I began that process over a period of time in many areas of my life. My love relationship with God became all important. I began to discover a clear personal way in which God was making known His ways to me. God revealed His ways to me through His Word. Tomorrow we will look at how God speaks through His Word. In future lessons we will look at how God speaks through prayer, circumstances, and the church to confirm His will to us.

☀ **Review today's lesson. Pray and ask God to identify one or more statements or Scriptures that He wants you to understand, learn, or practice. Underline it (them). Then respond to the following:**

What was the most meaningful statement or Scripture you read today?

_____
_____
_____

Reword the statement or Scripture into a prayer of response to God.

_____

_____

What does God want you to do in response to today's study?

_____

_____

Practice quoting your Scripture memory verses aloud.

GOD SPEAKS THROUGH THE BIBLE

God speaks to you by the Holy Spirit to reveal Himself, His purposes, and His ways. Perhaps the questions people ask most about God's speaking are:
- How does God speak to me?
- How can I know when God is speaking?
- How can God be more real and personal to me?

God speaks uniquely to individuals, and He can do it in any way He pleases. As you walk in an intimate love relationship with God, you will come to recognize His voice. You will know when God is speaking to you.

Jesus compared the relationship He has with His followers to the relationship a shepherd has with his sheep. He said, "The man who enters by the gate is the shepherd of his sheep. . . . The sheep listen to his voice. . . . His sheep follow him because they know his voice" (John 10:2-4). In just this way, when God speaks to you, you will recognize His voice and follow Him.

God speaks through a variety of means. In the present God primarily speaks by the Holy Spirit through the Bible, prayer, circumstances, and the church. These four means are difficult to separate. God uses prayer and the Bible together. Often circumstances and the church, or other believers, will help confirm what God is saying to you. Frequently, God uses circumstances and the church to help you know His timing. We will talk more about that in the next unit. Today, I want us to look at how God speaks through the Bible. Tomorrow we will look at the subject of prayer.

Mark the following statements as T (true) or F (false).

_____ 1. God can uniquely speak to individuals any way He chooses.

_____ 2. In the present God primarily speaks through dreams and visions.

_____ 3. When rightly related to God, His people will hear and recognize His voice.

_____ 4. God frequently speaks by the Holy Spirit through the Bible and prayer.

God is sovereign. He can do whatever He chooses to do. With the Scripture as our guide, we know God can speak in unique ways to individuals. His people will hear and recognize His voice. In the present time, He primarily speaks by the Holy Spirit through the Bible, prayer, circumstances, and the church. Only item 2 is false. The others are true.

The Spirit of Truth

The Bible is God's Word. It describes God's complete revelation of Himself to humanity. God speaks to you through the Bible. As you have already learned, however, a person

When the Spirit directs my attention to a truth, I write it down, meditate on it, and adjust my life to it. I alert myself to watch for ways God may be that way in my life during the day.

"His sheep . . . know his voice."

cannot understand spiritual truth unless the Spirit of God reveals it. The Holy Spirit is "the Spirit of truth" (John 14:17). The following diagram should help you visualize how the Holy Spirit speaks to you through God's Word.

THE BIBLE

This is a diagram of an encounter with God. When the Holy Spirit reveals a spiritual truth from the Word of God, He is personally relating to your life. That is an encounter with God. The sequence is this:

1. You read the Word of God—the Bible.
2. The Spirit of Truth takes the Word of God and reveals truth.
3. You adjust your life to the truth of God.
4. You obey Him.
5. God works in and through you to accomplish His purposes.

Using the description and the diagram, write a summary of how God speaks through the Bible.

_____

_____

_____

Write the following key words in the correct sequence: *adjust, reveals, obey, read.*

1. I _____ the Word of God—the Bible.

2. The Spirit of Truth takes the Word of God and _____ a truth.

3. I _____ my life to the truth of God.

4. I _____ Him.
5. God works in and through me to accomplish His purposes.

Check your work.

The Spirit uses the Word of God (the sword of the Spirit—Eph. 6:17) to reveal God and His purposes. The Spirit uses the Word of God to instruct us in the ways of God. On our own we cannot understand the truths of God. Unaided by the Spirit of God, it will be foolishness to us (1 Cor. 2:14). Aided by the Spirit, we can understand all things (1 Cor. 2:15).

Respond to the following:

God probably has used a particular verse of Scripture to speak to you at some time during this course. Look back through units 1-5 and find one passage of Scripture that God seems to have called to your attention. What is the verse (reference)?

_____

"The man without the Spirit does not accept the things that come from the Spirit of God, for they are foolishness to him, and he cannot understand them, because they are spiritually discerned. The spiritual man makes judgments about all things."

—1 Corinthians 2:14-15

1. What does that verse reveal to you about God, His purposes, or His ways?

_____

_____

2. Meditate on this verse and pray. Ask God to continue speaking to you about the truth in this passage. Keep in mind that He is more interested in what you become than what you do.

3. What does God want to do or be in and through your life?

_____

_____

_____

4. What adjustments would you have to make to align your life with this truth

in your personal life? _____

your family life? _____

your church life? _____

your work life? _____

5. Write a prayer response to God concerning this truth and its application to your life.

_____

_____

6. Since you first came to understand this truth, has God done anything in your life that required you to apply the truth or share it with someone else? Yes ❏   No ❏ If so, what?

_____

_____

Understanding spiritual truth does not lead you *to* an encounter with God, it *is* the encounter with God. You cannot understand the purposes and ways of God, unless the Spirit of God teaches you. If God has revealed spiritual truth to you through this passage of Scripture, you have encountered God Himself working in you!

Understanding spiritual truth does not lead you to an encounter with God, it is the encounter with God.

Responding to Truth

Reading the Scripture is an exciting time of anticipation for me. The Spirit of God knows the mind of God. He knows what God is ready to do in my life. The Spirit of God then begins to open my understanding about God and His purposes and His ways. I take that very seriously. Here is how I respond when God reveals truth to me in His Word.

I write down the passage of Scripture. Then I meditate on it. I try to immerse myself in the meaning of that verse or passage. I adjust my life to the truth and, thus, to God. I agree with God and take any actions necessary to allow God to work in the way He has revealed. Then I alert myself to watch for ways God may use that truth in my life during the day. You may want to follow this same process as God reveals truth to you.

When God leads you to a fresh understanding of Himself or His ways through Scripture:

• Write down the verse(s) in a spiritual journal or diary.
• Meditate on the verse.
• Study it to immerse yourself in the meaning of the verse. What is God revealing about Himself, His purpose, or His ways?
• Identify the adjustments you need to make in your personal life, your family, your church, and your work so God can work that way with you.
• Write a prayer response to God.
• Make the necessary adjustments to God.
• Watch to see how God may use that truth about Himself in your life during the day.

Here is an illustration of the way God may use His Word to speak to you. Suppose you are reading your daily Bible reading from Psalm 37. You have read this Psalm many times before. You come to verse 21 and read: "The wicked borrow and do not repay." You are "drawn" back to that verse. You read it again. Then you remember a debt you have failed to repay. You realize that this Scripture applies to you.

The Holy Spirit has just spoken to you through that verse. You have encountered truth. Now you understand that those who borrow and do not repay are sinning in God's sight. The Holy Spirit has called your attention to a specific instance where this verse applies to you. He is convicting you of sin. He is the only One who can do that. God has just spoken to you by the working of the Holy Spirit and through His Word. God wants you to have no hindrances to a love relationship with Him in your life.

※ **If you were in this situation, what should you do next? Following the sequence in the diagram on page 84, what do you do after the Holy Spirit reveals an understanding of truth to you?**

_____

_____

Adjust

Once God has spoken to you through His Word, how you respond is crucial. You must adjust your life to the truth. In this case the adjustment is this:

- You must *agree* with the truth—those who borrow and do not repay are wicked in God's sight.
- You must *agree* that the truth applies to you in the particular instance brought to your memory. This is confession of sin. You *agree* with God about your sin.

In this way you have adjusted your understanding about borrowing and repaying to agree with God's will in this matter. To agree with God you must change your understanding to agree with His. This requires an adjustment. Is that all you must do? No! Agreeing with God is not enough. Until you repay the debt, you will continue to be seen as sinning in God's sight. This is where obedience comes in. You obey God's will by repaying the debt.

Obey

Now you are free to experience a more complete relationship with God. Always tie a revealed truth to your understanding of God and your relationship with Him.

※ **Review today's lesson. Pray and ask God to identify one or more statements or Scriptures that He wants you to understand, learn, or practice. Underline it (them). Then respond to the following:**

What was the most meaningful statement or Scripture you read today?

_____

_____

_____

Reword the statement or Scripture into a prayer of response to God.

_____

_____

_____

What does God want you to do in response to today's study?

_____

_____

_____

SUMMARY STATEMENTS

- God speaks uniquely to individuals, and He can do it in any way He pleases.
- When God speaks to me, I will recognize His voice and follow Him.
- I cannot understand spiritual truth unless the Spirit of God reveals it.
- He is more interested in what I become than what I do.

If you are not keeping a spiritual journal[1] or diary, you need to. If the God of the universe tells you something, you should write it down. When God speaks to you in your quiet time, immediately write down what He said before you have time to forget. Then record your prayer response. I write down the verse of Scripture He uses and what God has said to me about Himself from that verse. I write down the prayer response I am making; so I have in place the encounter with God, what God said, and how I responded to Him. I also write out what I need to do to adjust my life to God, so I can begin to experience Him relating to me in this way.

Truth Is a Person

☀ **Carefully read the following paragraphs and fill in the blanks in the key statements that follow.**

The Holy Spirit reveals truth. Truth is not just some concept to be studied. Truth is a Person. Jesus did not say, "I will teach you the truth." He said, "I am . . . the truth" (John 14:6).

When God gives you eternal life, He gives you Himself (John 17:3). When the Holy Spirit reveals Truth, He is not teaching you a concept to be thought about. He is leading you to a relationship with a Person. *He* is your life! When God gives you eternal life, He gives you a Person. When you became a Christian, Jesus didn't give you some *thing*; He gave you Himself.

☀ **Fill in the blanks with the correct words from the previous paragraphs.**

    1. The Holy Spirit reveals _____.

    2. Truth is not just some _____ to be studied.

    3. Truth is a _____.

    4. The Holy Spirit is leading you to a _____ with a Person.

Here is a summary of how I have tried to live out my relationship to God:
- God creates in me the desire to participate in His mission to reconcile a lost world to Himself.
- I respond and come to God seeking to know His will.
- When God reveals a truth to me, I know He is trying to alert me to what He is doing in my life.

When God reveals truth to me through His Word, that doesn't lead me to an encounter with God, that *is* the encounter with God. When He does reveal truth to me, I sit in the presence of a living Person. He is the Author of the Scriptures. The Author is telling me what He is doing in my life, and He uses His Word to do it.

The Spirit of God knows the mind of God. He will make the will of God known to me through the Word of God. I must then take that truth and immediately adjust my life to Him. I do not adjust my life to a concept or a philosophy but to a Person.

Have you ever read a Scripture you have read many times before, but suddenly you see something in it for the first time? That truth is not a concept for you to figure out how to work into your life. God is introducing you to Himself and alerting you that He is wanting to apply this truth to your life right now. When God is ready to do something in your life, the Spirit of God uses the Word to make that known to you. Then you can adjust your life to Him and what He has just revealed of Himself, His purposes, or His ways.

Prayer Is a Relationship

Prayer is two-way fellowship and communication with God. You speak to God and He speaks to you. It is not a one-way conversation. Your personal prayer life may primarily be one-way communication—you talking to God. Prayer is more than that. Prayer includes listening as well. In fact, what God says in prayer is far more important than what you say.

Prayer is a relationship, not just a religious activity. Prayer is designed more to adjust you to God than to adjust God to you. God doesn't need your prayers, but He wants you to pray. You need to pray because of what God wants to do in and through your life during

Prayer is a relationship, not just a religious activity.

"I am the truth."
—Jesus

My relationship to God

The Author is telling me what He is doing in my life.

Prayer is a relationship, not just a religious activity.

your praying. God speaks to His people by the Holy Spirit through prayer. Here is a diagram of how God speaks through prayer.

PRAYER

This diagram illustrates an encounter with God. When the Holy Spirit reveals a spiritual truth to you in prayer, He is present and working actively in your life. Genuine prayer does not lead *to* an encounter with God. It *is* an encounter with God. What happens as you seek God's will in prayer? The sequence is this:

1. God takes the initiative by causing you to want to pray.
2. The Holy Spirit takes the Word of God and reveals to you the will of God.
3. In the Spirit you pray in agreement with the will of God.
4. You adjust your life to the truth (to God).
5. You look and listen for confirmation or further direction from the Bible, circumstances, and the church (other believers).
6. You obey.
7. God works in you and through you to accomplish His purposes.
8. You experience Him just as the Spirit revealed as you prayed.

Read back through the previous list and circle a key word or phrase in each statement.

I believe the Spirit of God uses the Word of God when you pray. I find that when I pray about something, Scripture often comes to my mind. I don't see it as a distraction. I believe He is trying to guide me through the Scripture. I have found that, as I pray about a particular matter, the Spirit of God takes the Word of God and applies it to my heart and my mind to reveal the truth. I immediately stop my praying and open the Word of God to the passage I believe the Spirit of God brought to my mind.

Praying in the Spirit

The Spirit of God will take the Word of God to guide you in the area of your praying.

Read the passage at the left and answer the following questions.

   1. Why do we need the help of the Holy Spirit when we pray? (v. 26)

   _____

   2. What advantage does the Holy Spirit have that we do not have? (v. 27)

   _____

   3. What does the Holy Spirit do for us? _____

   _____

26"The Spirit helps us in our weakness. We do not know what we ought to pray for, but the Spirit himself intercedes for us with groans that words cannot express. 27And he who searches our hearts knows the mind of the Spirit, because the Spirit intercedes for the saints in accordance with God's will."
—Romans 8:26-27

We are weak and do not know how we ought to pray. The Holy Spirit has an advantage over us—He already knows the will of God. When He prays for us, He is praying absolutely in agreement with the will of God. He then helps us know the will of God as we pray.

For his sixth birthday, my oldest son Richard was old enough to have a bicycle. I looked all around for a bicycle. I found a blue Schwinn. I bought it and hid it in the garage. Then I had a task—to convince Richard that he needed a blue Schwinn bike. For the next little while, we began to work with Richard. Richard decided that what he really wanted for his birthday was a blue Schwinn bike. Do you know what Richard got? Well, the bike was already in the garage. I just had to convince him to ask for it. He asked for it, and he got it!

A bicycle for Richard's birthday

What happens when you pray? The Holy Spirit knows what God has "in the garage." It is already there. The Holy Spirit's task is to get you to want it—to get you to ask for it. What will happen when you ask for things God already wants to give or do? You will always receive it. Why? Because you have asked *according to the will of God*. When God answers your prayer, He gets the glory and your faith is increased.

Is it important to know when the Holy Spirit is speaking to you? Yes! How do you know what the Holy Spirit is saying? I cannot give you a formula. I can tell you that you will know His voice when He speaks (John 10:4). You must decide, however, that you only want His will. You must dismiss any selfish or fleshly desires of your own. Then, as you start to pray, the Spirit of God starts to touch your heart and cause you to pray in the direction of God's will (Phil. 2:13).

"It is God who works in you to will and to act according to his good purpose."
—Philippians 2:13

When you pray, anticipate that the Holy Spirit already knows what God has ready for your life. He does not guide you on His own initiative; He tells you only what He hears from the Father. He guides you when you pray.

"He will not speak on his own; he will speak only what he hears, and he will tell you what is yet to come."
—John 16:13

I always write down what God is saying to me when I pray and as I read His Word. I write down what I sense He is leading me to pray. As I begin to see what God is telling me about Himself, His purposes, and His ways, I often see a pattern begin to develop. As I watch the direction the Spirit is leading me to pray, I begin to get a clear indication of what God is saying to me. This process calls for spiritual concentration!

Write down what God is saying.

You may be asking the question: But how do I know that the directions I am praying are the Spirit's leading and not my own selfish desires? Do you remember what George Mueller said he does first in seeking God's directions?

Look back at item #1 on page 34. What did he do in the beginning?

_____

Deny self first. In all honesty with yourself and before God, come to the place where you are sure that your only desire is to know God's will alone. Then check to see what the Holy Spirit is saying in other ways. Ask yourself:
- What is He saying to me in His Word?
- What is He saying to me in prayer?
- Is He confirming it through circumstances?
- Is He confirming it through the counsel of other believers?

Deny self

God never will lead you in opposition to His written Word. If what you sense in prayer runs contrary to Scriptures, it is wrong. For instance, God will never, never lead you to commit adultery. He always is opposed to that. Watch for God to use the written Word to confirm what you are sensing in prayer. Don't play games with God, though. Don't just look for a Scripture that seems to say what *you* selfishly want to do, and then claim it is God's will. That is very dangerous. Don't do it.

Look back at the diagram and try to summarize what it illustrates. Write a summary of how God speaks through prayer.

_____

_____

_____

Write the following key words in the correct sequence: *adjust, confirmation, Word, initiative, agreement, obey*. If you need help look at the list following the diagram.

1. God takes the _____ by causing me to want to pray or need to pray.

2. The Holy Spirit takes the _____ of God and reveals to me the will of God.

3. I pray in the Spirit in _____ with the will of God.

4. I _____ my life to the truth.

5. I look and listen for _____ or further direction from the Bible, circumstances, and the church (other believers).

6. I _____ .

7. God works in me and through me to accomplish His purposes.

Has God spoken to you by the Holy Spirit through prayer during this course? Yes ❑   No ❑ If He has, describe below what you sensed He was saying in one of the times He has spoken. If you do not think He has, ask Him to reveal to you the reason.

_____

_____

_____

Has He given you any confirmation through the Bible, circumstances, or the church (other believers) ? Yes ❑   No ❑ If so, what did you sense He was saying?

_____

_____

Review today's lesson. Pray and ask God to identify one or more statements or Scriptures that He wants you to understand, learn, or practice. Underline it (them). Then respond to the following:

What was the most meaningful statement or Scripture you read today?

_____

Reword the statement or Scripture into a prayer of response to God.

_____

_____

_____

What does God want you to do in response to today's study?

_____

_____

Review your Scripture memory verses and be prepared to recite them to a partner in your small-group session this week.

SUMMARY STATEMENTS

- When the God of the universe tells me something important, I should write it down.
- Truth is a Person.
- Prayer is two-way communication with God.
- Prayer is a relationship, not just a religious activity.
- I need to make sure that my only desire is to know God's will.

---

[1]If you are not keeping a spiritual diary, you may want to use *MasterLife Day by Day: Personal Devotional Guide* by Avery T. Willis, Jr. It gives brief instructions on how to cultivate a daily quiet time, how to memorize Scripture, how to take sermon notes, and how to use various kinds of prayers. It provides a day by day record of your spiritual life. Orders or order inquiries may be sent to Customer Service Center, 127 Ninth Avenue, North, Nashville, TN 37234, or call 1-800-458-2772. Order Item #7785-15.

GOD SPEAKS, PART 2

Have you ever prayed for one thing and got another? I have. Then some dear soul would say, "God is trying to get you to persist. Keep on praying until you get what you want." During one of those times I kept asking God in one direction, and I kept getting something else.

In the middle of that experience, I started reading from the second chapter of Mark in my quiet time. That is the story of the four men who brought their crippled friend to Jesus to be healed. Because of the crowd, they opened a hole in the roof and let the man down in front of Jesus. Jesus said, "Son, your sins are forgiven" (Mark 2:5).

I started to read on, but I sensed that the Spirit of God said, "Henry, did you see that?" I went back and began to meditate on that Scripture. Under the guiding, teaching ministry of the Holy Spirit, I began to see a wonderful truth. The four men were asking Jesus to heal the man, but Jesus forgave the man's sins. Why? They asked for one thing, and Jesus gave another! This man and his friends asked for a particular gift, but Jesus wanted to make the man a child of God so he could inherit everything!

I found myself weeping before God and saying: Oh, God, if I ever give You a request and You have more to give me than I am asking, cancel my request!

UNIT

6

Jesus gave them this answer: "I tell you the truth, the Son can do nothing by himself; he can do only what he sees his Father doing, because whatever the Father does the Son also does."

—JOHN 5:19

Verse to Memorize
This Week

Only the Spirit of God knows what God is doing or purposing in my life.

"The Spirit searches all things, even the deep things of God. For who among men knows the thoughts of a man except the man's spirit within him? In the same way no one knows the thoughts of God except the Spirit of God. We have not received the spirit of the world but the Spirit who is from God, that we may understand what God has freely given us."
—1 Corinthians 2:10-12

If I start asking God for one thing and something different happens, I always respond to what begins happening. I have found that God always has far more to give me than I can even ask or think. Paul said, "Now to him who is able to do immeasurably more than all we ask or imagine, according to his power that is at work within us, to him be glory in the church and in Christ Jesus throughout all generations, for ever and ever!" (Eph. 3:20-21).

You can't even think a prayer that comes close to what God wants to give you. Only the Spirit of God knows what God is doing or purposing in your life. Let God give you all that He wants to give. (See 1 Cor. 2:10-12.)

If God wants to give you more than you are asking, would you rather have what you are asking or what God wants to give?

I would rather have _____

Who alone can instruct you in the activity of God in your life?

_____

Suppose you wanted to start a mission church in a particular area of town. You have taken a survey to identify the needs. You have made all your long-range plans. You have asked God to bless and guide your work. Then God begins to bring to your church a group of ethnic people who don't live in the target area. What would you do? Check your response.

❏ 1. I would "keep on keeping on" in my praying until God helps us start the mission church we have planned.
❏ 2. I would get frustrated and quit.
❏ 3. I would start asking questions to see if we should start an ethnic mission church instead of or in addition to the other one.

❏ 4. Other _____

Do you know what I would do with that? I would immediately go before God and clarify what He is saying. If I have been working and praying in one direction and I see God working in a different direction, I adjust my life to what God is doing. In this kind of situation, you have to decide whether you are going to do what you want and ask God to bless it, or go to work where He is working.

You have to decide whether you are going to do what you want and ask God to bless it, or go to work where He is working.

We started a special emphasis to reach university students in Vancouver. We began with 30 students in the fall. By the end of the spring semester, we had about 250 attending. Two-thirds of these were international students. We could have said, "We didn't plan for a ministry to internationals. Please go somewhere else, and may God bless you." Of course we didn't do that. We adjusted our plans to what God began to do around us.

Spiritual Concentration

Our problem is that we pray and then never relate anything that happens to our praying.

Our problem is that we pray and then never relate anything that happens to our praying. After you pray, the greatest single thing you need to do is turn on your spiritual concentration. When you pray in a direction, immediately anticipate the activity of God in answer to your prayer. I find this all the way through the Scripture, when God's people prayed, He responded.

Here's what happens if you pray and then forget about what you have prayed. Things start to happen during the day that are not normal for your day. You see them all as distractions, and try to get rid of them. You fail to connect them with what you have just prayed.

Watch to see what happens next.

When I pray, I immediately begin to watch for what happens next. I prepare to make adjustments to what begins to happen in my life. When I pray, it never crosses my mind that God is not going to answer. Expect God to answer your prayers, but stick around for the answer. His timing is always right and best.

Expect an answer.

Respond to the following:

1. Have you ever prayed persistently for something and not received it or gotten something different? Yes ❏   No ❏ Briefly describe one or more such times.

_____

_____

_____

_____

2. Review what you have just written and make a list of things you can do in response to times like these.

_____

_____

_____

_____

3. Are you praying for anything right now that God is not granting? Yes ❑   No ❑ If so, what are you praying for?

_____

If you answered yes to #3, pause right now and ask God to help you understand what He is doing in your life. Then watch to see what happens next, or pay attention to what He begins to reveal to you through His Word.

The Silences of God

I went through a lengthy time when God was silent. You probably have had that experience, too. I had been praying over many days, and there seemed to be total silence from God. I sensed that heaven was shut up. I didn't understand what was happening. Some folk have told me that if God does not hear my prayer, I have sin in my life. They gave me a "sin checklist" to work through. I prayed through the sin checklist on this occasion. As far as I could tell, I was okay. I could not understand the silence of God.

Do you remember a biblical person who had a problem like this? Job did. His counselors told him that all his problems were because of sin. Job kept saying, "As best I know, God and I are on the right terms." Job did not know all that God was doing during that time, but his counselors were wrong. There was another reason for what God was doing.

Job

If you have experienced the silences of God, briefly describe one such time below.

_____

_____

The only thing I knew to do was go back to God. I believe that the God who is in a love relationship with me will let me know what is going on in my life when and if I need to know. So I prayed, "Heavenly Father, I don't understand this silence. You are going to have to tell me what You are doing in my life." He did! —from His Word. This became one of the most meaningful experiences in my life.

I did not frantically go searching for an answer. I continued the daily reading of the Word of God. I was convinced that, as I was reading the Word of God, the Spirit of God (who knew the mind of God for me) was in the process of helping me understand what God was doing in my life. God will let you know what He is doing in your life when and if you need to know.

God will let you know what He is doing in your life when and if you need to know.

One morning I was reading the story of the death of Lazarus (John 11:1-45). Let me go through the sequence of what happened as I read. John reported that Jesus loved Lazarus, Mary, and Martha. Having received word that Lazarus was sick unto death, Jesus delayed going until Lazarus died. In other words, Mary and Martha asked Jesus to come help their brother, and there was silence. All the way through the final sickness and death of Lazarus, Jesus did not respond. They received no response from the One who *said* He loved Lazarus. Jesus even said He loved Mary and Martha. Yet, there was still no response.

Lazarus

Lazarus died. They went through the entire funeral process. They fixed his body, put him in the grave, and covered it with a stone. Still they experienced silence from God. Then Jesus said to His disciples, "Let's go."

When Jesus arrived, Lazarus had been dead four days. Martha said to Jesus, "Lord, if you had been here, my brother would not have died" (v. 32).

Then the Spirit of God began to help me understand something. It seemed to me as if Jesus had said to Mary and Martha:

> "You are exactly right. If I had come, your brother would not have died. You know that I could have healed him, because you have seen me heal many, many times. If I had come when you asked me to, I would have healed him. But, you would have never known any more about Me than you already know. I knew that you were ready for a greater revelation of Me than you have ever known in your life. I wanted you to come to know that I am the resurrection and the life. My refusal and My silence were not rejection. It was an opportunity for Me to disclose to you more of Me than you have ever known."

When that began to dawn on me, I almost jumped straight out of my chair. I said, "That's what's happening in my life! That's what's happening! The silence of God means that He is ready to bring into my life a greater revelation of Himself than I have ever known." I immediately changed the whole attitude of my life toward God. With great anticipation, I began to watch for what God was going to teach me about Himself. I then had some things happen in my life that I might never have responded to without that kind of readiness and anticipation.

What are two possible reasons for the silence of God when you pray?

_____

_____

Now, when I pray and there is a silence from God, I still pray through my sin checklist. Sometimes God's silences are due to sin in my life. If there is unconfessed sin in my life, I confess it and make it right. If, after that, there is still a silence with God, I get ready for a new experience with God that I have never known before. Sometimes God is silent as He prepares to bring you into a deeper understanding of Himself. Whenever a silence comes, continue doing the last thing God told you and watch and wait for a fresh encounter with Him.

You can respond to the silence of God in two ways. One response is for you to go into depression, a sense of guilt, and self-condemnation. The other response is for you to have an expectation that God is about to bring you to a deeper knowledge of Himself. These responses are as different as night and day.

Truth set me free!

. . . and Truth is a Person!

Do you know what set me free? Truth. And, Truth is a *Person* who is actively involved in my life. The moment that I understood what God might have been doing, I made an adjustment of my life to God. I put away the attitude of depression and guilt. I quit feeling that maybe I was of no use to God and that He wouldn't hear me anymore. I made the major adjustment in my life to an attitude of expectation, faith, and trust. The moment I did that, God began to show me how I could respond to Him in such a way that I would know Him in a greater way.

Review today's lesson. Pray and ask God to identify one or more statements or Scriptures that He wants you to understand, learn, or practice. Underline it (them). Then respond to the following:

What was the most meaningful statement or Scripture you read today?

_____

_____

Reword the statement or Scripture into a prayer of response to God.

_____

_____

What does God want you to do in response to today's study?

_____

_____

Write your Scripture memory verse for this unit on the following lines and review your verses from other units. Remember, you may select a different verse if you want to.

_____

_____

_____

GOD SPEAKS THROUGH CIRCUMSTANCES

DAY 2

To understand your bad or difficult circumstances, God's perspective is vital.

The Holy Spirit uses the Bible, prayer, and circumstances to speak to us, or show us the Father's will. This third way—circumstances—is seen in the way Jesus knew what the Father wanted Him to do. This is how Jesus knew the Father's will for His life and daily activity. Jesus described the process in John 5:17, 19-20.

Verse 19 is your memory verse this week. Write it below.

_____

_____

_____

_____

Jesus said that He did not take the initiative in what to do for the Father (v. 19). Only the Father has the right to take the initiative. The Father had been working right up until Jesus' earthly time, and He was still working (v. 17). The Father would let the Son know what He was doing (v. 20). When the Son saw the _Father's_ activity, that was the Father's invitation for the Son to join Him.

"Jesus said to them, 'My Father is always at his work to this very day, and I, too, am working.'"

—_John 5:17_

We have looked at Jesus' example twice already. By way of review, see if you can fill in the blanks in the following sequence using the key words in the right margin.

1. The _____ has been working right up until now.

2. Now God has Me _____.

3. I do nothing on My own _____.

4. I _____ to see what the Father is doing.

5. I do what I see the Father is already _____.

6. You see, the Father _____ Me.

7. He shows Me _____ that He, Himself, is doing.

working

everything

watch

Father

doing

initiative

loves

nothing

Check your answers with the sequence on page 15.

God used circumstances to reveal to Jesus what He was to do. The circumstances were the things Jesus saw the Father doing. There are some things that only the Father can do.

Turn to page 68 and review the list of some things only God can do.

Jesus always was looking for where the Father was at work, and joined Him. The Father loved the Son, and showed Him everything He was doing. Jesus did not have to guess what to do. Jesus did not have to dream up what He could do for the Father. He watched to see what the Father was doing around His life, and Jesus put His life there. The Father then could accomplish *His* purposes through Jesus.

This is exactly what Jesus wants us to do with *His* lordship in our lives. We see what *He* is doing, and adjust our lives, our plans, and our goals to *Him*. We are to place our lives at His disposal—where *He* is working—so He can accomplish His purposes through us.

Check your memory. Without looking at the illustration on the back of the book, see if you can write the seven realities in your own words. Use the key words below as hints.

1. work— _____

2. relationship— _____

3. invitation— _____

4. speaks— _____

_____

5. crisis— _____

_____

6. adjust— _____

_____

7. obey— _____

_____

Check your work with the diagram on the inside back cover of the book.

The example of Jesus is a positive way God speaks through circumstances. Sometimes circumstances appear to be "bad." Maybe you have found yourself in the middle of a "bad" circumstance and you wanted to ask God, "Why is this happening to me?" You are not alone.

God's Perspective Is Vital

Job

Job had a bad experience like that. He did not know what was happening when everything he owned was destroyed, when his children were killed, and when he developed sores all over his body (Job 1—2). Job wrestled with understanding his circumstances. He did not know what was happening from God's perspective (Job 1:6-12; 2:1-7). Neither did He know the last chapter (Job 42:12-17) where God would restore his property, his family, and his health.

Job's friends thought they had God's perspective and told Job to confess his sin. Job could not find any unrighteousness in his life to confess. If you didn't have that last chapter and didn't know God's perspective, whose side do you think you would be on? God's or Job's? You probably would be with Job, saying, "I want to ask God what is going on. Why is He allowing this to happen?" You would think God was being cruel to Job.

To understand your bad or difficult circumstances, God's perspective is vital. When you face difficult or confusing circumstances, they can overwhelm you. If you put yourself in the middle of the circumstances and try to look at God, you will always have a distorted understanding of God. For instance you might say, "God doesn't love me" or "God is not fair." Both of those statements about God are false.

Have you ever been in the middle of a tragic or confusing circumstance where, in your prayers, you began to accuse God of some things that you know are not really true of God? Yes ❏   No ❏ If so, describe one of those circumstances.

_____

_____

Perhaps you began to question God's love or His wisdom. Maybe you were afraid to say that He was wrong, but you sort of said, "God you deceived me in letting me believe that this was the right thing to do. Why didn't you stop me?" A whole lot of wrong things can happen if you try to look at God from the middle of circumstances.

What do you do? First, go to God and ask Him to show you His perspective on your circumstance. Look *back* at your circumstances from the heart of God. When you face difficult or confusing circumstances, the Spirit of God again will take the Word of God and help you understand your circumstances from God's perspective. He will reveal to you the truth of the circumstance.

Go to God and ask Him to show you His perspective on your circumstance.

Carrie's Cancer

I told you at the beginning of unit 3 about our daughter Carrie's bout with cancer. That was a difficult circumstance for our whole family. The doctors prepared us for six or eight months of chemotherapy plus radiation. We knew God loved us, so we went to Him in prayer and asked for understanding about what He was doing or going to do in our lives. We wanted to be rightly adjusted to Him through this time. We prayed, "What are you purposing to do in this experience that we need to adjust ourselves to?"

"What are you purposing to do in this experience that we need to adjust ourselves to?"

As we prayed, a Scripture promise came that we believed was from God. Not only did we receive the promise, but we received letters and calls from many people who quoted this same Scripture promise to us. They also sensed this verse was from God for our circumstance. The verse reads, "This sickness will not end in death. No, it is for God's glory so that God's Son may be glorified through it" (John 11:4). Our sense that God was speaking to us grew stronger as the Bible, prayer, and the testimony of other believers began to line up and say the same thing. We then adjusted our lives to the truth and began to watch for ways God would use this situation for His glory.

During this time, people from many places in Canada, Europe, and the United States began praying for Carrie. Individuals, college student groups, and churches called to tell us of their prayers. One thing surfaced in conversations with many of these people. Many said something like this: "Our prayer life (prayer ministry) has become so dry and cold. We haven't seen any special answers to prayer in a long time. But, when we heard about Carrie, we put her on our prayer list."

After *three* months of treatments, the doctors ran more tests. They said, "We don't understand this, but all the tests are negative. We cannot find any trace of the cancer." I immediately began to communicate this answer to prayer with those who had committed to pray for Carrie. In instance after instance people said that this answer to prayer was what God used to totally renew their prayer life. Church prayer ministries were revitalized. Student prayer groups found new life.

Then I began to see what God had in mind for this circumstance. Through this experience God was glorified in the eyes of His people. Many, many people sensed a fresh call to prayer. They personally began to experience anew the presence of Truth—and Truth as a Person. Some of Carrie's closest friends began to pray fervently at this time. Some students even came to know the Lord after observing what God had done in and through Carrie. God did bring glory to Himself through this sickness.

Do you see what happened? We faced a trying situation. We could have looked back at God from the middle of that and gotten a very distorted understanding of God. Instead we went to Him. We sought His perspective. The Holy Spirit took the Word of God and revealed to us God's perspective on the end result of that circumstance. We believed God and adjusted our lives to Him and to what He was doing. We then went through the circumstance looking for ways His purposes would be accomplished in ways that would bring Him glory. So, when the answer to prayer came, I knew immediately my job was to "declare the wonderful works of the Lord" to His people. In the process we came to know God in a new way because of the compassion He showed us by revealing His perspective on our situation.

Let me summarize how you can respond when circumstances are difficult or confusing:

When Circumstances Are Confusing

1. Settle in your own mind that God has forever demonstrated His absolute love for you on the cross. That love will never change.
2. Do not try to understand what God is like from the middle of your circumstances.
3. Go to God and ask Him to help you see His perspective on your situation.
4. Wait on the Holy Spirit. He may take the Word of God and help you understand your circumstances.
5. Adjust your life to God and what you see Him doing in your circumstances.
6. Do all He tells you to do.
7. Experience God working in and through you to accomplish His purposes.

Read back through the previous list and circle a key word or phrase in each statement.

In your own words, summarize what you need to do when you find yourself in circumstances that are confusing.

_____
_____

You do need to remember that God is sovereign. You may face a situation like Job experienced where God does not tell you what He is doing. In those instances acknowledge God's love and sovereignty and depend on His sustaining grace to see you through the situation.

Review today's lesson. Pray and ask God to identify one or more statements or Scriptures that He wants you to understand, learn, or practice. Underline it (them). Then respond to the following:

What was the most meaningful statement or Scripture you read today?

_____
_____

Reword the statement or Scripture into a prayer of response to God.

_____
_____

What does God want you to do in response to today's study?

_____
_____

SUMMARY STATEMENTS

- God used circumstances to reveal to Jesus what He was to do.
- Jesus watched circumstances to know where the Father wanted to involve Him in His work.
- To understand my bad or difficult circumstances, God's perspective is vital.

DAY 3   THE TRUTH OF YOUR CIRCUMSTANCE

You cannot know the truth of your circumstance, until you have heard from God.

You cannot know the truth of your circumstance, until you have heard from God. In Exodus 5—6 Moses did as he was told and asked Pharaoh to let Israel go. Pharaoh refused and multiplied the hardship on the Israelites. The Israelites turned to Moses and criticized him for causing so much trouble.

What would you have done if you had been in Moses' place? Check one or more responses:

❏ 1. I would have gotten mad at Israel and gone back to tending sheep.
❏ 2. I would have gotten mad at God and told Him to get somebody else.
❏ 3. I would have decided that I misunderstood God's will.
❏ 4. I would have patiently gone back to God and asked Him to give me His perspective on this "bad" circumstance.

Moses' story really encourages me. The first three responses above are more like the way we usually respond. If you haven't read Exodus 5—6, you may have the idea from what I have said that Moses would have picked response #4. He didn't! He blamed God and accused Him of failing to do what He promised. Moses said, "O Lord, why have you brought trouble upon this people? Is this why you sent me? Ever since I went to Pharaoh to speak in your name, he has brought trouble upon this people, and you have not rescued your people at all" (Ex. 5:22-23). Moses was so discouraged he was ready to quit (Ex. 6:12).

God is patient.

I'm glad God is patient with us, too! God took time to explain to Moses His perspective. God explained that He *wanted* Pharaoh to resist so the people could see God's mighty hand of deliverance. He wanted the people to come to know Him (by experience) as the great "I AM." Learn from Moses' example. When you face confusing circumstances, don't start blaming God. Don't just give up following Him. Go to God. Ask Him to reveal the truth of your circumstances. Ask Him to show you His perspective. Then wait on the Lord.

You need to have your life radically oriented to God. The most difficult thing you will ever have to do is deny self, take up the will of God, and follow after Him. The most difficult part of your relationship to God is being God-centered. If you were to record a whole day in your life you might find that your prayers, your attitudes, your thoughts, everything about that day is radically self-centered. You may not be seeing things from God's perspective. You may try to explain to God what your perspective is. When He becomes the Lord of your life, He alone has the right to be…
—the Focus in your life
—the Initiator in your life
—the Director of your life.
That is what it means for Him to be Lord.

Hearing from Truth

When the Holy Spirit talks to you, He is going to reveal Truth to you. He is going to talk to you about a Person. He is going to talk to you about Jesus. Truth is a Person! (See John 14:6.)

"I am . . . the truth."
—John 14:6

The disciples were in a boat in a storm. Jesus was asleep in the back of the boat. If you were to have gone to those disciples in the middle of that storm, and said to them, "What is the truth of this situation?" what would they have said? "We perish!" Was that the truth? No, Truth was asleep at the back of the boat. Truth is a person. In just a moment Truth Himself would stand up, and He would still the storm. Then they knew the Truth of their circumstance. Truth is a person who is always present in your life. You cannot know the truth of your circumstance until you have heard from God. He is the Truth! And the Truth is present and active in your life!

The disciples in a storm

Read Luke 7:11-17 at the right and answer the following questions.

1. Suppose you were attending this funeral. Before Jesus came, how do you think the widow of Nain would have responded to this question: "What is the truth of this situation?"

She would have said… _____

2. When Truth (Jesus) was present, what difference did He make?

_____

3. When Truth (Jesus) revealed Himself to that crowd, how did they respond?

_____

If you had asked the widow who was in the funeral procession of her only son, "What's the truth of this situation?" she might have replied, "My husband died at a young age. I had one son, and I had anticipated that we would spend wonderful days together. He would care for me, and we would have fellowship together. Now my son is dead, and I must live the rest of my life alone." Was that the truth?

"Jesus went to a town called Nain, and his disciples and a large crowd went along with him. As he approached the town gate, a dead person was being carried out—the only son of his mother, and she was a widow. And a large crowd from the town was with her. When the Lord saw her, his heart went out to her and he said, 'Don't cry.'
Then he went up and touched the coffin, and those carrying it stood still. He said, 'Young man, I say to you, get up!' The dead man sat up and began to talk, and Jesus gave him back to his mother.
They were all filled with awe and praised God. 'A great prophet has appeared among us,' they said. 'God has come to help his people.' This news about Jesus spread throughout Judea and the surrounding country." —Luke 7:11-17

No, Truth was standing there! When Truth reached out and touched her son and restored him, all was changed. You never know the truth of any situation until you have heard from Jesus. When Jesus was allowed to reveal Himself in this circumstance, the people "were all filled with awe and praised God. 'A great prophet has appeared among us,' they said. 'God has come to help his people.' This news about Jesus spread throughout Judea and the surrounding country" (Luke 7:16-17). Never, ever determine the truth of a situation by looking at the circumstances. Don't evaluate your situation until you have heard from Jesus. He is the Truth.

You never know the truth of any situation until you have heard from Jesus.

Read John 6:1-15 and answer the following questions.

1. Five thousand hungry people came to Jesus. He wanted to feed them. If you were to have asked the disciples what the truth of the situation was, how do you think they would have responded?

_____

2. Why did Jesus ask Philip where they could buy bread? (vv. 5-6)

_____

_____

3. When Truth (Jesus) was present what difference did it make?

_____

_____

4. When Truth (Jesus) revealed Himself to that crowd, how did they respond? (v. 14)

_____

I wonder if God ever tests our faith like He did Philip's. Does He say, "Feed the multitudes" and our church responds, "Our budget couldn't do it"? If you had asked the disciples at that moment about the truth of the situation, they may have said, "We can't do it. Lord, the truth of the situation is that it is impossible." Was that true? No. We know the other half of the story. Wouldn't we be better off if we trusted God with the other half of the story in our lives? Truth Himself fed 5,000 men plus their families, and had 12 baskets full of leftovers!

Can you trust Him with the other half of the story?

Suppose God says to your church, "Take the Gospel to the whole world!" and the group says, "We can't." Truth stands in the middle of that church, as the Head of that church to say, "Believe Me. I will never give you an order that I will not Myself release My power to enable it to happen. Trust Me and obey Me and it will happen."

Review today's lesson. Pray and ask God to identify one or more statements or Scriptures that He wants you to understand, learn, or practice. Underline it (them). Then respond to the following:

What was the most meaningful statement or Scripture you read today?

_____

_____

Reword the statement or Scripture into a prayer of response to God.

_____

_____

What does God want you to do in response to today's study?

_____

_____

SUMMARY STATEMENTS

- Never, ever determine the truth of a situation by looking at the circumstances.
- I cannot know the truth of my circumstance until I have heard from God.
- The Holy Spirit takes the Word of God and reveals God's perspective on the circumstance.

The diagram I used for circumstances may imply that the circumstance is a "bad" situation. That is not always the case. Sometimes the circumstance is a decision-making situation. In a decision-making time your greatest difficulty may not be choosing between good and bad, but choosing between good and best. You often may have several options that all appear to be good. At a time like this, the place to start is to say with all of your heart:

> "Lord, whatever I know to be Your will, I will do it. Regardless of the cost and regardless of the adjustment, as best I know my heart, I commit myself to follow Your will ahead of time. Lord, no matter what that will looks like, I will do it!"

You need to say that at the beginning of seeking God's will. Otherwise you do not mean, "Thy will be done." You would be saying, "Thy will be done as long as it does not conflict with my will." Two words in the Christian's language cannot go together: No, Lord. If you say, "No," He is not Lord. If He really is your Lord, your answer must always be "Yes." In decision making, always begin here. Do not proceed until you can honestly say, "Whatever you want of me, Lord, I will do it."

Physical Markers of Spiritual Encounters

When Israel crossed the Jordan River into the promised land, God gave Joshua the following instructions: "Choose twelve men from among the people, one from each tribe, and tell them to take up twelve stones from the middle of the Jordan from right where the priests stood and to carry them over with you and put them down at the place where you stay tonight" (Josh. 4:2-3). These stones were to serve as a sign to the Israelites. Joshua explained, "In the future, when your children ask you, 'What do these stones mean?' tell them that the flow of the Jordan was cut off before the ark of the covenant of the Lord. When it crossed the Jordan, the waters of the Jordan were cut off. These stones are to be a memorial to the people of Israel forever" (Josh. 4:6-7).

The stones were to be a reminder of a mighty act of God in behalf of His people. On many other occasions men built altars or set up stones as a reminder of a significant encounter with God.

Select ONE of the following persons. Check the box beside the person you choose to study. Read about his encounter with God. Then answer the questions that follow.

❏ **Noah**—Genesis 6—8   ❏ **Moses**—Exodus 17:8-16 or 24:1-11
❏ **Abram**—Genesis 12:1-8 or 13:1-18 ❏ **Joshua**—Joshua 3:5—4:9
❏ **Isaac**—Genesis 26:17-25   ❏ **Gideon**—Judges 6:11-24
❏ **Jacob**—Genesis 28:10-22 and 35:1-7 ❏ **Samuel**—1 Samuel 7:1-13

1. Briefly describe the encounter between this person and God. What did God do?

_____

_____

2. Why do you think the person built an altar or set up the stone marker?

_____

3. What, if any, special names of God or of the stone/altar are given in the text?

_____

Often men in the Old Testament set up a stone marker or altar as a reminder of their encounters with God. Places like Bethel ("house of God") and Rehoboth ("room") became reminders of God's great activity in the midst of His people. Moses named an altar "The Lord is my Banner" and Samuel named a stone "Ebenezer" saying, "Thus far has the Lord helped us" (1 Sam. 7:12). These altars and stones became physical markers of great spiri-

When God gets ready for you to take a new step or direction in His activity, it will always be in sequence with what He has already been doing in your life.

"Yes, Lord!"

These stones will serve as a sign to you.

These altars and stones became physical markers of great spiritual encounters with God.

God gave perspective on what He was doing.

tual encounters with God. They provided an opportunity for people to teach their children about the activity of God in behalf of His people.

Seeing God's Perspective

God works in sequence to accomplish His divine purposes. What He did in the past was done with a Kingdom purpose in mind. What He is doing in the present is in sequence with the past and with the same Kingdom purpose in mind. Every act of God builds on the past with a view toward the future.

When God called Abraham (Gen. 12), He began to develop a people for Himself. When He came to Isaac, Isaac saw God's perspective when God reminded Isaac of His relationship with Isaac's father Abraham (Gen. 26:24). To Jacob God identified Himself as the God of Abraham and Isaac (Gen. 28:13). When God came to Moses, He helped Moses see His perspective of what He was doing through history. He said He was the God of Abraham, Isaac, and Jacob (Ex. 3:6-10). At each new step in His divine plan, God involved a person. Often in the call, God rehearsed His activity so the individual could see God's perspective on what was happening.

Moses gave perspective on what God was doing.

Israel needed to see that the new direction was in line with all that God had been doing.

Throughout Deuteronomy, Moses reviewed all that God had done for Israel. God was getting ready to move the people into the promised land. God wanted the people to have the perspective of history as they took this new step. In Deuteronomy 29 Moses gave a brief summary of the nation's history. At this time of covenant renewal, Moses wanted to remind the people to be faithful in following God. They were getting ready to change leaders (from Moses to Joshua) and move into the promised land. They needed to see this new direction from God's perspective. Israel needed to see that the new direction was in line with all that God had been doing.

In the diagram we have been using on the inside back cover, God's purposes are illustrated by the arrow at the top of the diagram.

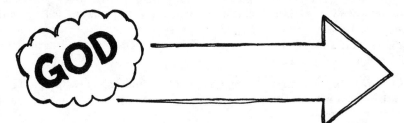

Moses

Look at the perspective God gave Moses when He called him into service at the burning bush in Exodus 3. In the lines that follow:
* **Write PAST beside items that speak of God's past activity with His people.**
* **Write PRESENT beside those items that speak of what God was doing at the time He spoke to Moses.**
* **Write FUTURE beside those items that speak of what God was going to do.**

_____1. "I am the God of your father, the God of Abraham, the God of Isaac and the God of Jacob" (v. 6).

_____2. "I have indeed seen the misery of my people in Egypt. I have heard them crying out because of their slave drivers" (v. 7).

_____3. "I am concerned about their suffering. So I have come down to rescue them from the hand of the Egyptians" (vv. 7-8).

_____4. "So now, go. I am sending you to Pharaoh to bring my people the Israelites out of Egypt" (v. 10).

_____5. "I will be with you. And this will be the sign to you that it is I who have sent you: When you have brought the people out of Egypt, you will worship God on this mountain" (v. 12).

_____6. "I have promised to bring you up out of your misery in Egypt into the land of the Canaanites . . . —a land flowing with milk and honey" (v. 17).

_____7. "I will make the Egyptians favorably disposed toward this people, so that when you leave you will not go empty-handed. . . . And so you will plunder the Egyptians" (vv. 21-22).

Do you see what God was doing with Moses? He was helping Moses see his call from God's perspective.

- God had been working with Abraham, Isaac, Jacob, and even Moses' father to build a nation.
- God had promised Abraham that He would bring the people out of bondage and give them the promised land.
- God had been watching over them in Egypt.
- Now He was ready to respond to their suffering.
- God had chosen to involve Moses in His divine purpose for Israel. He was going to use Moses to deliver the Israelites out of Egypt and plunder the Egyptians at the same time.
- After Moses obeyed, God would bring them to this very mountain to worship. This worship service on the mountain would be Moses' sign that God had sent him.

Items 1, 2, and 6 are past. Items 3 and 4 are present. Items 5 and 7 are future.

God wants to involve you in His purposes. God has been working in the world all along (John 5:17). He has been working in your life since your birth. He was working out His purposes for your life prior to your birth. God said to Jeremiah the prophet, "Before I formed you in the womb I knew you, before you were born I set you apart; I appointed you as a prophet to the nations" (Jer. 1:5). When God gets ready for you to take a new step or direction in His activity, it will always be in sequence with what He already has been doing in your life. He does not go off on tangents or take meaningless detours. He builds your character in an orderly fashion with a divine purpose in mind.

A Spiritual Inventory

One thing I have found helpful is to identify "spiritual markers" in my life. Each time I have encountered God's call or directions for my life, I have mentally built a spiritual marker at that point. A spiritual marker identifies a time of transition, decision, or direction when I clearly know that God has guided me. Over time I can look back at these spiritual markers and see how God has faithfully directed my life according to His divine purpose.

When I face a decision about God's direction, I rehearse those spiritual markers. I don't take the next step without the context of the full activity of God in my life. This helps me see God's perspective for my past and present. Then I look at the options that are before me. I look to see which one of the options seems to be most consistent with what God has been doing in my life. Often one of these directions will be most consistent with what God already has been doing. If none of the directions seem consistent, I continue to pray and wait on the Lord's guidance. When circumstances do not align with what God is saying in the Bible and in prayer, I assume that the timing may be wrong. I then wait for God to reveal His timing.

In your own words write a definition of "spiritual markers."

_____

_____

Using the previous paragraph, describe in your own words how you could use spiritual markers to help you discern God's direction at a time of decision.

_____

_____

_____

Why do you think "spiritual markers" are helpful? What do they help you do?

_____

_____

When I was approached about coming to the Home Mission Board to direct the emphasis on prayer and spiritual awakening, I had never had such a job in my life. Only God could reveal whether this was part of His divine purpose. I recalled the spiritual markers in my life to see this decision from God's perspective.

My heritage goes back to England where a number of my family were graduates of Spurgeon's College at a time when Spurgeon was trying to win England to Christ. I grew up in a town in Canada where there was no evangelical witness to Christ. My father served as a

A spiritual marker identifies a time of transition, decision, or direction when I clearly know that God has guided me.

Using spiritual markers

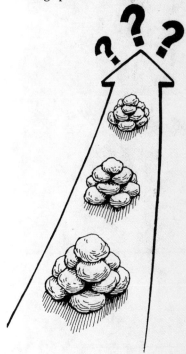

My call to the Home Mission Board

lay pastor to help start a mission in that town. Way back in my teen years I began to sense a deep burden for communities all across Canada that did not have an evangelical church. In 1958 when I was in seminary, God assured me that He loved my nation enough to want to bring a great movement of His Spirit across our land. When I accepted God's call to go to Saskatoon as a pastor, God used the prospect of a spiritual awakening there to affirm my call. As you will read in unit 11, a spiritual awakening that started there spread all across Canada in the early 1970's.

In 1988 Bob Hamblin from the Home Mission Board called me. He said, "Henry, we have prayed much about filling a position in prayer for spiritual awakening. We have been seeking a person for over two years to fill this position. Would you consider coming and directing Southern Baptists in the area of spiritual awakening?"

"Spiritual awakening has been a deep current through my life."

As I reviewed God's activity in my life (my spiritual markers), I saw that an emphasis on spiritual awakening was an important element throughout my ministry. I said to Bob, "You could have asked me to do anything in the world, and I would not have even prayed about leaving Canada—except spiritual awakening. That has been a deep current that has run through my life since the time I was an older teenager, and more particularly since 1958." After much prayer and confirmation in the Word and by other believers, I accepted the position at the Home Mission Board. God didn't shift me, He focused me in something He had already been doing down the course of my life.

Prepare a spiritual inventory of your life. Identify your own spiritual markers. These may begin with your heritage, your salvation experience, times you made significant decisions regarding your future, and so forth. What are some of the times of transition, decision, or direction in your life when you knew clearly that God guided you? Using a separate sheet of paper or a notebook, start preparing a list. Start this list today, but don't feel like you have to have a comprehensive list. Add to it as you reflect and pray about God's activity in your life.

You will have opportunity to share some of your spiritual markers in this week's small-group session.

Review today's lesson. Pray and ask God to identify one or more statements or Scriptures that He wants you to understand, learn, or practice. Underline it (them). Then respond to the following:

What was the most meaningful statement or Scripture you read today?

_____

_____

Reword the statement or Scripture into a prayer of response to God.

_____

_____

_____

What does God want you to do in response to today's study?

_____

_____

SUMMARY STATEMENTS

- In a decision-making time my greatest difficulty may not be choosing between good and bad, but choosing between good and best.
- Two words in the Christian's language cannot go together: No, Lord.
- God works in sequence to accomplish His divine purposes.
- When God gets ready for me to take a new step or direction in His activity, it will be in sequence with what He has already been doing in my life.
- A spiritual marker identifies a time of transition, decision, or direction when I clearly know that God has guided me.

GOD SPEAKS THROUGH THE CHURCH

The Holy Spirit speaks to us through God's people, the local church. Later in this course we are going to spend a whole unit on how a church hears and understands God's will. Today we will look at some ways that will help you understand God's will through the church.

Let's review for a moment. Answer the following questions.

1. How did God speak in the Old Testament?

_____

2. How did God speak in the Gospels?

_____

3. How does God speak from Acts through the present?

_____

4. What are four ways through which the Holy Spirit speaks?

_____

_____

The Body of Christ

One of the problems many evangelical churches face today is that they have so emphasized the doctrine of the priesthood of believers they have lost their sense of corporate identity. What does that mean in simple words? Christians think they stand alone before God and that they are not accountable to the church. Christians do have direct access to God. They only need to go through Christ as their Mediator. God, however, created the church as His redemptive agent in the world. He has a purpose for the church. God places every member in a church to accomplish His redemptive purposes through that church.

A church is a body. It is the body of Christ (1 Cor. 12:27)! Jesus Christ is present as Head of a local church (Eph. 4:15), and every member is placed in the body as it pleases God (1 Cor. 12:18). The Holy Spirit manifests Himself to every person for the common good (1 Cor. 12:7). The whole body is fitted together by the Father. Members are enabled and equipped by the Holy Spirit to function where the Father has placed them in the body. The body then functions to build itself up into the Head, until *every member* comes to the measure of the stature of the fullness of Christ (Eph. 4:13). God made us mutually interdependent. We need each other. What one lacks, others in the body can and will supply. What those "suppliers" lack, another member can supply.

Therefore, what God is doing in and through the body is essential to my knowing how to respond to Him. Where I see Him working in the body, I adjust and put my life. In the church, I let God use me in any way He chooses to complete His work in each member. This was Paul's goal when he said, "We proclaim him, admonishing and teaching everyone with all wisdom, so that we may present everyone perfect in Christ" (Col. 1:28). Paul was constantly requesting the believers to become vitally involved with his life and ministry. The effectiveness of Paul's ministry rested on them (Col. 4:3; 2 Thess. 3:1, 2; Eph. 6:19).

Read 1 Corinthians 12:7-31 and answer the following questions.

1. Paul was addressing the Christians of a local church, the church of Corinth. What is a local church? (v. 27)

_____

2. Based on verse 12, circle one of the following pictures that best illustrates a church.

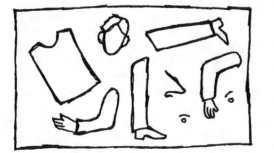 

As I function in relationship to the church, I depend on others in the church to help me understand God's will.

"Instead, speaking the truth in love, we will in all things grow up into him who is the Head, that is, Christ. From him the whole body, joined and held together by every supporting ligament, grows and builds itself up in love, as each part does its work."
—Ephesians 4:15-16

3. What does verse 25 say should be true of the church? Is this true of your church?

_____

4. Based on verses 14-24, mark the following statements as True (T) or False (F). For the statements that are false, rewrite the statement on the following line so that it is stated correctly.

_____ a. The body is made up of one part.

_____

_____ b. The foot is still a part of the body even though it is not a hand.

_____

_____ c. The ear is not part of the body because it is not an eye.

_____

_____ d. Members of the body decide how they should be arranged.

_____

_____ e. All the members need every other member of the body.

_____

Answers: (1) A local church is the body of Christ. All believers worldwide are united in the kingdom of God under the rule of the King! But the local church is to function like a body. It is not *part* of a body. It *is* a body. (2) Picture A may better represent the way some churches function. However, God has always intended for the church to function as a unit, not just as individual parts. (3) The church should have no division in the body. If your church does have division, it is a sick body of Christ. The Great Physician, Christ Himself, can bring about healing of the body, if your church will let Him. (4) Statements a, c, and d are false. The others are true.

Apart from the body, you cannot fully know God's will for your relationship to the body. Without the eye the hand does not know where to touch. Without the ear the rest of the body may not know when or how to respond. Every member needs to be listening to what the other members are saying. If the members are not talking about what they sense God is doing, the whole body is in trouble.

As I function in relationship to the church, I depend on others in the church to help me understand God's will. Let me illustrate this for you. Then, in unit 10 I will give more time to help you understand how members function as part of a body.

Allow God to Speak Through the Church

While I was in seminary, I was involved in a local church. The first year I taught teenage boys. I did that with a willing heart. The next year I was asked to be music and education director. I had never done that in my life. I had sung in a choir, but I had never led a bit of music. I didn't know anything about directing the educational program of this church. Here is how I approached this decision.

The people of God at this church had a need for a leader. As they prayed they sensed that God put me there purposely to meet that need. I, too, saw the need and realized God could use me there. As a servant of Jesus Christ, I did not have an option to say no. I believed that the Head—Jesus Christ—could speak through the rest of the body to guide me to know how I should function in the body. I said I would do the best I knew to do.

For two years I served as Music and Education Director. Then the church voted to call me to be their pastor. I hadn't preached three sermons in my life. I had not come to the seminary because I felt called to be a pastor. I did, however, go to the seminary because I felt called of God into a *relationship* with Him for *whatever* He had in mind. I sensed that I needed to put the seminary training in place so that I would have some tools for God to work with. I didn't say, "I am going into foreign missions or home missions." I didn't say music, or education, or preaching. I said, "Lord, whatever You direct me to do in relation to your body, that is what I will do. I am your servant for your purposes." So, I agreed to be their pastor.

In the church, the need does not constitute the call. The need, however, is not to be ignored. Don't ever be afraid to let the body of believers assist you in knowing God's will. Keep in mind, also, that one individual is not the church. In the final analysis, you are going to have to take all the counsel of people and go to God for the clear direction. What you will find is that a number of things begin to line up. What you are hearing from the Bible and prayer and circumstances and the church will begin to say the same thing. Then you can proceed with confidence.

You may say to me, "Henry, you don't know my church. I can't depend on them to help me know God's will." Be careful. When you say that, you have said more about what you believe about God than what you believe about your church. You are saying, "Henry, not even God can work through these people. He just is not powerful enough." You don't believe that in your mind, I don't think. But what you do says more about what you believe about God than what you say.

"Henry, you don't know my church."

This is the point where we need to focus on the *crisis of belief*. Watch out! Next week may be a real challenge to you.

Review today's lesson. Pray and ask God to identify one or more statements or Scriptures that He wants you to understand, learn, or practice. Underline it (them). Then respond to the following:

What was the most meaningful statement or Scripture you read today?

_____

_____

Reword the statement or Scripture into a prayer of response to God.

_____

_____

_____

_____

What does God want you to do in response to today's study?

_____

_____

_____

_____

Write your Scripture memory verse (John 5:19) on the following lines.

_____

_____

_____

_____

Review your other Scripture memory verses and be prepared to recite them to a partner in your small-group session this week.

If you have not completed your list of spiritual markers (day 4), try to finish before your group session this week. Bring the paper or notebook with you to the session.

SUMMARY STATEMENTS

- A church is a body. It is the body of Christ!
- Jesus Christ is present as Head of a local church.
- Every member is placed in the body as it pleases God.
- God made us mutually interdependent. We need each other.
- Apart from the body, I cannot fully know God's will for my relationship to the body.
- Every member needs to be listening to what the other members are saying.
- As I function in relationship to the church, I depend on others in the church to help me understand God's will.

THE CRISIS OF BELIEF

A Faith Budget For Our Church

UNIT

7

One year the people on our finance committee said, "Pastor, you have taught us to walk by faith in every area of the life of our church except in the budget." I asked them to explain. They said, "Well, when we set the budget, we set the budget on the basis of what we believe we can do. It does not reflect that we expect God to do anything."

"Hummm," I said. "Then how do you feel we ought to set the budget?"

They said, "First, we ought to determine all that God wants to do through us. Second, we need to put down what that will cost. Then we need to divide the budget goal into three categories: (1) what we plan to do through our tithes, (2) what others have promised to do, and (3) what we must depend on God to do."

As a church we prayed and decided God wanted us to use this approach to budgeting. We did not try to dream our own dreams for God. We had to be absolutely sure God was leading us to do the things we put in the budget. Then we listed what that would cost. We listed what we thought our people would give and what others (denominational board, partnership churches, and individuals) had said they would give. The difference between what we could reasonably expect to receive and the total was what we would ask God to provide.

The big question was: What is our operating budget? Well, by faith we adopted the grand total as our operating budget. At this point we reached a crisis of belief. Did we really believe that the God who led us to do these things also would provide the resources to bring them to pass? Anytime God leads you to do something that has God-sized dimensions, you will face a crisis of belief. When you face a crisis of belief, what you do next reveals what you really believe about God.

The budget of our church normally would have been $74,000. The budget we set was $164,000. We pledged to pray daily that God would meet our needs. Any money that came in that we did not anticipate we credited to God. At the end of that year we had received $172,000. God taught our church a lesson in faith that radically changed us all.

Verse to Memorize this Week

Without faith it is impossible to please God, because anyone who comes to him must believe that he exists and that he rewards those who earnestly seek him.   —HEBREWS 11:6

A Turning Point

This unit focuses on a turning point in your following God's will. When God invites you to join Him in His work, He has a God-sized assignment for you. You will realize that you cannot do it on your own. If God doesn't help you, you will fail. This is the crisis point where many decide not to follow what they sense God is leading them to do. Then they wonder why they do not experience God's presence and activity the way other Christians do.

When God tells me what He wants to do through me, I will face a crisis of belief.

Let's spend a few minutes reviewing in order to see the relationship between the crisis of belief and what you have already studied.

Review

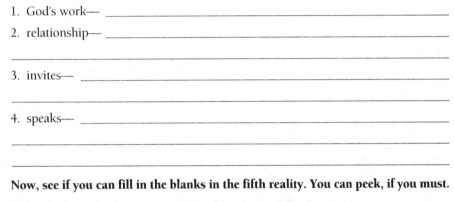

We have been studying seven realities of the sequence in which God works with His people. Using the following hints, see if you can write the first four in your own words. Then check yourself on the inside back cover of the book.

1. God's work— _____

2. relationship— _____

   _____

3. invites— _____

   _____

4. speaks— _____

   _____

   _____

Now, see if you can fill in the blanks in the fifth reality. You can peek, if you must.

5. God's invitation for you to work with Him always leads you to a

   _____ of _____ that requires

   _____ and _____

Crisis

The word *crisis* comes from a word that means "decision." The same Greek word is often translated judgment. The crisis of belief is a turning point where you must make a decision. You must decide what you believe about God. How you respond at this turning point will determine whether you go on to be involved with God in something God-sized that only He can do, or whether you will continue to go your own way and miss what God has purposed for your life. This is not a one-time experience. It is a daily experience. How you live your life is a testimony of what you believe about God.

How I live my life is a testimony of what I believe about God.

You read about our church budget process at the beginning of this unit. In that experience what was the crisis of belief? Check your response.
- ❏ 1. When the committee decided to change the way we developed the budget.
- ❏ 2. When the church had to decide what God was leading us to do in the coming year.
- ❏ 3. When the committee had to decide to recommend the grand total as the operating budget or to recommend what they knew the church could do.

In a way every one of these could have been checked. In each case we had to decide what we believed about God. The greatest crisis came when we decided to operate on the grand total rather than what we knew we could do. Operating on the $74,000 amount would not take much faith. We were sure we could do that much. Operating on a budget of $164,000 required faith. We could not see any way to get that much money unless God provided it. Do you see the turning point—the crisis of belief? We could have decided on the lesser budget and never known anything more about God. People in the community watching our church would have only seen what people can do. They would not have seen God and what He can do.

Another crisis of belief came in the middle of our church's building program. We had a unique opportunity to buy a building on Main Street in Allan, Saskatchewan, Canada for use as a church building for our mission. Len Koster, our mission pastor, talked with the owner. He said, "I bought this for $15,000 and I put $7,000 into it. But, we will sell this building to you and the property on Main Street for $15,000." He asked us for $9,000 down, and said he would give us a loan of $6,000 at eight percent interest.

Len said, "Give us two weeks, and we will get back to you."

We were a small group of people ourselves, and we were sponsoring four missions. At that point, we were $100,000 short in our own building program. God had called us to start the mission, but we didn't have nine cents, let alone $9,000. We went to the church family and said, "What do you suppose God wants us to do?"

"Let's pray earnestly that
God will provide for
our mission."

With one heart, the church said, "Let's pray earnestly that God will provide for our mission." We began to pray. We decided that any unexpected money that came in during the next two weeks would be God's provision for Allan in answer to prayer.

Almost a week later, I received a phone call from a church in Halfway, Texas. The caller said, "Someone came by our church and told us that you are doing mission work. Would you describe it to us over the phone?" I did. He said, "We are thinking of sending you $5,000 and then $200 a month for two years to support a mission pastor. Do you know where that might be used?"

"Oh, yes," I said. "We would use it at Allan. We are now praying for Allan."

The very next day I got a phone call from another pastor in Texas who said, "Someone has told our church about the mission work you are doing. We have a lady whose husband was an evangelist. He died, and she would like to give a thousand dollars to mission work. Do you know a place where you are that could use the money?"

And I said, "Oh, yes! We are praying for our mission in Allan." Now, we had $6,000 for the building and $200 for a pastor. We kept praying. At the end of the two weeks we were short $3,000. Len went back to see the owner.

Before Len could say anything, this man said, "By the way, since you were last here I did some thinking about income tax. It would be a lot better for me if you put $6,000 down, and I will carry the $9,000 at eight percent. How would that be?"

"Oh," Len said. "That is exactly what I was going to suggest." We got the clear deed to the property and built that church. That church has since bought other property and built another building. They have two missions out from their own congregation.

When God tells me what He
wants to do through me, I
will face a crisis of belief.

If we had looked at what we had in the bank, would we have proceeded? Not at all. If we had looked at all of the circumstances, would we have proceeded? No. But, what you believe about God will determine what you do. When God tells you what He wants to do through you, you will face a crisis of belief. What you do shows what you believe.

A. In your own words, define "crisis of belief."

_____

_____

B. Read each of the following passages of Scripture and describe the crisis of belief you see in each case.

Joshua 6:1-5 _____

_____

Judges 6:33; 7:1-8 _____

_____

1 Chronicles 14:8-16 _____

_____

Matthew 17:24-27 _____

_____

C. Have you or your church ever sensed that God wanted you to do something big and

you faced a crisis of belief? Yes ❏   No ❏ If so, briefly describe one situation and how you (or your church) responded.

_____

_____

D. What did your response demonstrate about your belief in God? Did it show faith or lack of faith?

_____

Would you tell a whole army to follow you in walking around a city expecting the walls to fall down when you blow some trumpets? That was a crisis of belief for Joshua and for all Israel as well. They had to decide if they believed God could do what He said. Though this group had just seen God dam up the Jordan River for them to cross, this next step required faith. In fact, every assignment God gave Israel required a new measure of faith.

Joshua and the walls of Jericho

Gideon must have really struggled with his crisis. Joint forces of the Midianites, Amalekites, and other eastern peoples were prepared to attack. Gideon started with 32,000 men, but God had Gideon send 31,700 of them home. He was going to give victory with 300. Do you see what a difference it made from God's perspective? When the battle was won, everyone knew God did it!

Gideon and his 300 men

David was a faithful servant of the Lord's. David refused to rely on human wisdom for guidance. He asked for God's direction. Was this a crisis of belief since God said He would give David victory over the Philistines? Yes! David still had to decide what He believed about God. He had to trust God to do what He said He would do.

David and the Philistines

Did you notice that David stayed in a close relationship with God. He didn't rely on yesterday's guidance for today. David didn't use human wisdom to decide whether to attack this second time. This is a good example of how God wants you to depend on Him—not a method or a program. What worked yesterday, or in some other church, may not be what God wants to use today. Only He has a right to tell you what to do next!

Peter was a fisherman. Never before had he found coins in the mouth of a fish. Great faith was required to go and catch one fish to find the exact amount for the tax! He acted on his faith and God provided.

Peter, a fish, and taxes

As we continue our study of the crisis of belief, we will examine four principles. These are:

The Crisis of Belief

1. An encounter with God requires faith.
2. Encounters with God are God-sized.
3. What you do in response to God's revelation (invitation) reveals what you believe about God.
4. True faith requires action.

In the previous list, underline a key word or phrase in each principle.

Review today's lesson. Pray and ask God to identify one or more statements or Scriptures that He wants you to understand, learn, or practice. Underline it (them). Then respond to the following:

What was the most meaningful statement or Scripture you read today?

_____

_____

Reword the statement or Scripture into a prayer of response to God.

_____

_____

_____

What does God want you to do in response to today's study?

_____

_____

Write your Scripture memory verse for this unit on the following lines and review your verses from other units.

_____

_____

_____

_____

SUMMARY STATEMENTS

- When God invites me to join Him in His work, He has a God-sized assignment for me.
- How I live my life is a testimony of what I believe about God.
- When God tells me what He wants to do through me, I will face a crisis of belief.

DAY 2   ENCOUNTERS WITH GOD REQUIRE FAITH

Faith is confidence that what God has promised or said will come to pass.

When God speaks, your response requires faith. All through Scripture when God revealed Himself, His purposes, and His ways, the response to Him required faith.

Read the following Scriptures and respond to the questions.

1. "Faith is being sure of what we hope for and certain of what we do not see" (Heb. 11:1). **What is "faith"?**

_____

2. "We live by faith, not by sight" (2 Cor. 5:7). **What is an opposite of faith?**

_____

3. "A prophet who presumes to speak in my name anything I have not commanded him to say . . . must be put to death. . . . If what a prophet proclaims in the name of the Lord does not take place or come true, that is a message the Lord has not spoken. That prophet has spoken presumptuously" (Deut. 18:20, 22). **How important is it for your faith to be in God and what He says rather than what you or someone else decides would be a nice thing to have happen?**

_____

_____

4. Jesus said, "Anyone who has faith in me will do what I have been doing. He will do even greater things than these, because I am going to the Father" (John 14:12). **What is the potential of faith?**

_____

5. " 'I tell you the truth, if you have faith as small as a mustard seed, you can say to this mountain, "Move from here to there" and it will move. Nothing will be impossible for you' " (Matt. 17:20-21). **How much faith is required for God to do through you what is humanly impossible?**

_____

6. Paul said, "My message and my preaching were not with wise and persuasive words, but with a demonstration of the Spirit's power, so that your faith might not rest on men's wisdom, but on God's power" (1 Cor. 2:4-5). **On what should we base our faith? On what should we NOT base our faith?**

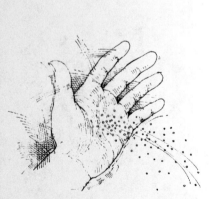

Mustard Seed

Base our faith on..._____

Not..._____

7. "If you do not stand firm in your faith, you will not stand at all" (Isa. 7:9). **What is one danger of lack of faith?**

_____

Faith is confidence that what God has promised or said will come to pass. Sight is an opposite of faith. If you can see clearly how something can be accomplished, more than likely faith is not required. Remember the illustration about our church budget? If we had chosen to operate on what we knew we could do, faith would not have been necessary.

> Faith was believing that the God who called us to the assignments was the One who would provide for their accomplishment.

Your faith does not rest in a concept or an idea. Faith must be in a PERSON—God Himself. If you or someone else decides something would be nice to have happen and then leads people to "believe" or "have faith," you are in a dangerous position. Faith is only valid in God and what He says He is purposing to do. If the thing you expect to happen is from you and not God, then you must depend on what you can do. Before you call yourself, your family, or your church to exercise faith, be sure you have heard a word from God.

Faith is in a Person.

With only a mustard-seed (very small) size faith in God, nothing is impossible. Jesus said His followers would do even greater things than He had done. Our faith, however, must be based on God's power and not human wisdom. Without a firm faith, you will stumble and fall.

Something Only God Can Do

Moses could not deliver the children of Israel from Pharaoh's army, cross the Red Sea on dry land, provide water from a rock, or provide bread and meat for food. Moses had to have faith that the God who called him would do the things He said He would do. Joshua could not take the Israelites across the Jordan River on dry land, bring down walled cities, defeat enemies, or make the sun stand still. Only God could have done these things. Joshua had to have faith in God.

Moses

Joshua

In the New Testament this also was true for the disciples. On their own, they could not feed the multitudes, heal the sick, still a storm, or raise the dead. Only God could do these things. But God called servants to let Him do these things through them.

The disciples

When God lets you know what He wants to do through you, it will be something only God can do. What you believe about Him will determine what you do. If you have faith in the God who called you, you will obey Him; and He will bring to pass what He has purposed to do. If you lack faith, you will not do what He wants. That is disobedience. Jesus questioned those around Him, "Why do you call me, 'Lord, Lord,' and do not do what I say?" (Luke 6:46). Jesus frequently rebuked His disciples for their lack of faith and unbelief. Their unbelief revealed that they really had not come to know who He was. Thus, they did not know what He could do.

Answer the following questions:

1. What are some things God wanted to do through Moses that only God could do?

_____

_____

2. What are some things Jesus wanted to do through the disciples that only God could do?

_____

_____

3. When God asks a person to join Him in doing something only He can do, what is required for the person to respond?

_____

4. If the person disobeys, what does that indicate?

_____

5. If the person obeys, what does that indicate?

_____

6. Your memory verse (Heb. 11:6) tells why faith is important. Write it here:

_____

_____

_____

_____

Obedience shows faith

Major problem: self-centeredness

God speaks to reveal what He is going to do through us.

"Jesus looked at them and said, 'With man this is impossible, but not with God; all things are possible with God.' "
—Mark 10:27

Faith was required of Moses and the disciples. When God calls a person to join Him in a God-sized task, faith is always required. Obedience indicates faith in God. Disobedience often indicates a lack of faith. Without faith, a person cannot please God. Without faith, a church cannot please God.

We face the same crisis Bible characters faced. When God speaks, what He asks of us requires faith. Our major problem, however, is our self-centeredness. We think we have to accomplish the assignment on our own power and with our current resources. We think, "I can't do that. That is not possible."

We forget that when God speaks He always reveals what *He* is going to do—not what He wants us to do for Him. We join Him so He can do His work through us. We don't have to be able to accomplish the task within our limited ability or resources. With faith, we can proceed confidently to obey Him; because we know that *He* is going to bring to pass what *He* purposes. Jesus indicated that what is impossible with man is possible with God (Mark 10:27). The Scriptures bear witness that this is true.

Faith required

Len Koster and mission churches

"The God who has called me will help me."

In the Saskatoon church we sensed that we needed to be of use to God in reaching people for Christ throughout Saskatchewan. The province contained over two hundred cities, towns, and villages. This meant we would have to start new (mission) churches. To do that we felt God was leading us to call Len Koster to become a minister of mission outreach. He would equip the church to start churches.

For 14 years Len and Ruth had pastored small churches. Len was so committed to the Lord that he worked as a service station attendant for 14 years in order to pastor bivocationally. Without a part-time pastor these churches would have had no pastor at all. In that time Len and Ruth had saved $7,000, hoping that one day they would have enough money to buy their own home. When Len felt absolutely convinced that he ought to come help us start churches, I said, "Len we have no money to move you and no money to pay you."

He said, "Henry, the God who has called me will help me. We will take the money from our savings, and we will move." Later, Len came into my office and said, "Henry, my wife and I prayed and talked all night. I have worked bivocationally for 14 years, and I have no problem of working to provide for my family. But, the need here is so great, and the direction of God is such that I feel I need to be full-time. My wife and I realized last night that the $7,000 we have in the bank is God's, and He wants us to use that to live off. When we have finished that, He will show us how to live. So," he said, "Henry, don't worry about my support."

When Len went out of that room, I fell on my face. I wept and wept before the Father. I said, "Father, I don't understand why such a faithful couple should have to make this kind of a sacrifice." I saw in Len and Ruth a great faith that was demonstrated by their actions.

Two days later I received a letter from a Presbyterian layman in Kamloops, British Columbia. It was a very short letter that simply said, "I understand a man by the name of Len Koster has come to work with you. God has laid it on my heart that I am to help support his ministry. Enclosed find a check for $7,000 to be used for his support." When I opened that letter, I went back on my knees and wept before the Father. This time, I asked Him to forgive me for not trusting Him when He told me I could.

I called Len and said, "Len, you have placed your life savings on the altar of sacrifice, but God has something else in the bushes. The God who says, 'I am your Provider' has just provided!" Then I told him. Do you know what that did in Len's life? Do you know what it did in our church's life? We all grew in our faith to believe God. After that, we stepped out in faith to do things time and time again. We watched God do wonderful things. We never could have come to experience God that way had we not stepped out in faith to call Len. That experience helped us learn how to trust God.

When you encounter God, it will bring a crisis of belief. That crisis will require faith. Without that faith you will not be able to please God.

Describe a time in your life that required faith, and you did not respond because you lacked faith.

_____

_____

Describe a time in your life that required faith in God and you responded in faith. This would be a time when you could see no way to accomplish the task unless God did it through you or in you. (If, after some thought, you cannot think of a time, do not make one up just for the sake of a response.)

_____

_____

_____

What do you know God is wanting you to do that you are not doing?

_____

Why do you think you are hesitating?

_____

Have you ever wanted to pray like the disciples when they asked the Lord, "Increase our faith" (Luke 17:5)? Yes ❑   No ❑

Take a few moments to pray right now about your FAITH and what God is wanting to do through your life.

Review today's lesson. Pray and ask God to identify one or more statements or Scriptures that He wants you to understand, learn, or practice. Underline it (them). Then respond to the following:

What was the most meaningful statement or Scripture you read today?

_____

_____

_____

Reword the statement or Scripture into a prayer of response to God.

_____

_____

_____

What does God want you to do in response to today's study?

_____

_____

_____

DAY 3   ENCOUNTERS WITH GOD ARE GOD-SIZED

God is interested in the world's coming to know Him.

God is interested in the world's coming to know Him. The only way people will know what God is like is when they see Him at work. They know His nature when they see His nature expressed in His activity. Whenever God involves you in His activity, the assignment will have God-like dimensions to it.

God-sized Assignments

The kind of assignments God gives are God-sized.

Some people say, "God will never ask me to do something I can't do." I have come to the place in my life that, if the assignment I sense God is giving me is something that I know I can handle, I know it probably is *not* from God. The kind of assignments God gives in the Bible are always God-sized. They are always beyond what people can do, because He wants to demonstrate His nature, His strength, His provision, and His kindness to His people and to a watching world. That is the only way the world will come to know Him.

☀ **From memory, list some assignments God (either the Father or Jesus) gave to people in the Bible that were "God-sized" assignments—things that were humanly impossible.**

_____

_____

_____

_____

You could name many God-sized assignments in Scripture. He told Abraham to father a nation when Abraham had no son and Sarah was past the age to bear children. He told Moses to deliver the children of Israel, to cross the Red Sea, and to provide water from a rock. He told Gideon to defeat the giant Midianite army with 300 men. Jesus told the disciples to feed the multitudes and to make disciples of all the nations. None of these things were humanly possible. When God's people and the world see something happen that only God can do, they come to know God.

People Come to Know God

☀ **Read the following biblical accounts of God's activity through His servants. Underline statements that indicate how people responded to God's activity when they observed it. I have underlined one for you.**

Moses and the Red Sea

God had Moses lead the Israelites to camp beside the Red Sea. God knew He was going to deliver them by dividing the sea and letting them cross on dry ground. God said, "I will gain glory for myself through Pharaoh and all his army, and the Egyptians will know that I am the Lord" (Ex. 14:4). What was the result? "When the Israelites saw the great power the Lord displayed against the Egyptians, the <u>people feared the Lord and put their trust in him</u>" (Ex. 14:31).

Joshua and the Jordan River

God commanded Joshua to lead the Israelites across the Jordan River at flood stage. Why? "He did this so that all the peoples of the earth might know that the hand of the Lord is powerful and so that you [Israel] might always fear the Lord your God" (Josh. 4:24).

A vast army came to make war against Israel. King Jehoshaphat proclaimed a fast and led the people to seek God's counsel. He prayed, "O our God . . . . we have no power to face this vast army that is attacking us. We do not know what to do, but our eyes are upon you" (2 Chron. 20:12).

King Jehoshaphat and Israel against a vast army

God responded, "Do not be afraid or discouraged because of this vast army. For the battle is not yours, but God's. . . . You will not have to fight this battle. Take up your positions; stand firm and see the deliverance the Lord will give you" (2 Chron. 20:15, 17). Jehoshaphat sent a choir in front of the army singing praise to God for His enduring love. God destroyed the invading army before Jehoshaphat and Israel got to the battlefield. Then: "The fear of God came upon all the kingdoms of the countries when they heard how the Lord had fought against the enemies of Israel" (2 Chron. 20:29).

Shadrach, Meshach, and Abednego chose to obey God rather than King Nebuchadnezzar. Before being thrown into a blazing furnace, they said, "The God we serve is able to save us from it, and he will rescue us from your hand" (Dan. 3:17). The bystanding soldiers died, but God delivered these three faithful men.

Shadrach, Meshach, and Abednego

King Nebuchadnezzar said, "Praise be to the God of Shadrach, Meshach and Abednego, who has sent his angel and rescued his servants . . . . Therefore I decree that the people of any nation or language who say anything against the God of Shadrach, Meshach and Abednego be cut into pieces and their houses be turned into piles of rubble, for no other god can save in this way" (Dan. 3:28-29). This pagan king wrote to the whole nation, "It is my pleasure to tell you about the miraculous signs and wonders that the Most High God has performed for me. How great are his signs, how mighty his wonders!" (Dan. 4:2-3).

Christians in the early church followed the directions of the Holy Spirit. Here is the testimony of the impact God had on their world:

The early church

The disciples were filled with the Holy Spirit and spoke in foreign languages they had not learned. Then Peter preached and "Those who accepted his message were baptized, and about three thousand were added to their number that day" (Acts 2:41).

God used Peter and John to heal a crippled beggar in the name of Jesus. They preached, and "many who heard the message believed, and the number of men grew to about five thousand" (Acts 4:4).

God used Peter to raise Dorcas from the dead. "This became known all over Joppa, and many people believed in the Lord" (Acts 9:42).

Answer the following questions.

1. When people saw God at work through His servants, who got the credit—God or the servants?

   _____

2. What difference or impact do you see in the lives of people who saw or heard about God's activity?

   _____

3. How would you describe the response of the people in your community to the gospel of Jesus Christ?

   _____

   _____

What our world often is seeing in our day is a devoted, committed Christian serving God. But, they are not seeing God. They comment on what we are doing, "Well, there's a wonderful, dedicated, committed group of people serving God." They, however, do not see anything happening that can only be explained in terms of the activity of God. Why? Because, we are not attempting anything that only God can do.

Our world is not seeing God, because we are not attempting anything that only God can do.

Our world is not attracted to the Christ we serve, because they cannot see Him at work. They see us doing good things for God and say, "That is wonderful, but that is not my thing." The world is passing us by, because they do not want to get involved in what they see. They are not having an opportunity to see God. Let the world see God at work and He will attract people to Himself. Let Christ be lifted up—not in words, but in life. Let them see the difference that a living Christ makes in a life, a family, or a church; that will make a

Let the world see God at work and that will attract people!

difference in how they respond. When the world sees things happening through God's people that cannot be explained except that God Himself has done them, then the world will be drawn to the God they see.

Answer the following questions.

1. How will the world come to know God?

_____

2. Why are people in our world not being attracted to Christ and His church?

_____

3. What kind of assignments does God give His people?

_____

4. Why does God give God-sized assignments that the individual or church cannot do on their own?

_____

5. What are you attempting to do that only will happen if God brings it to pass?

_____

_____

6. What is your church attempting to do that only will happen if God brings it to pass?

_____

_____

7. Which of the following *best* describes the things you listed in questions 5 and 6? Check your response.
   ❏ a. They are things God led me/us to attempt.
   ❏ b. They are things I/we decided would be challenging to ask God to do.
8. What connection do you see between their response and the kinds of things you attempt that are God-sized?
   ❏ a. We are not attempting many God-sized tasks and few people are responding to the gospel.
   ❏ b. We are not attempting many God-sized tasks but many are responding to the gospel.
   ❏ c. We are seeing God do great things in and through our church but few people are responding to the gospel.
   ❏ d. We are seeing God do great things in and through our church and many people are responding to the gospel.

The world comes to know God when they see God's nature expressed through His activity. When God starts to work, He accomplishes something that only He can do. When God does that, both God's people and the world come to know Him in ways they have never known Him before. That is why God gives God-sized assignments to His people. The reason much of the world is not being attracted to Christ and His church is that God's people lack the faith to attempt those things that only God can do. If you or your church are not responding to God and attempting things that only He can accomplish, then you are not exercising faith. "Without faith it is impossible to please God" (Heb. 11:6). If people in your community are not responding to the gospel like you see in the New Testament, one possible reason is that they are not seeing God in what you are doing as a church.

You will rejoice that you have experienced Him.

God is far more interested in your having an experience with Him, than He is interested in getting a job done. You can complete a job and never experience God at all. He is not interested just in getting a job done. He can get the job done any time He wants. What is He interested in? You and the world—knowing Him and experiencing Him. So, God will come to you and give you a God-sized assignment. When you start to do what He tells you to do, He brings to pass what He has purposed. Then, you and all the people with you will rejoice that you have experienced Him. You and the people around you will know more of Him than you have ever known before.

A God-sized Assignment

Our church in Saskatoon was growing and needed more space. We sensed God leading us to start a building program even though we had only $749 in the building fund. The building was going to cost $220,000. We didn't have the foggiest notion how to do it.

We did much of the work to save on labor costs. Still, half way through that building program, we were $100,000 short. Those dear, dear people looked to their pastor to see if I believed that God would do what He called us to do. God put a confidence in my heart that the God who was leading us would show us how to do it.

God began providing the necessary funds. We were about $60,000 short toward the end. We had been expecting some money from a Texas foundation. Delay after delay came that we could not understand. One day, for two hours the currency exchange rate for the Canadian dollar hit the lowest point ever in its history. That was exactly the time the Texas foundation wired the money to Canada. You know what that did? It gave us $60,000 more than we would have gotten otherwise. Then the dollar went back up.

Does the heavenly Father look after the economy in order to help His children? Nobody in the world would believe that God did that for one single church, but I can show you a church that believes God did it! When that happened, I magnified what the Lord had done in the eyes of the people. I made sure we gave the credit to Him. God revealed Himself to us, and we came to know Him in a new way through that experience.

I magnified what the Lord had done.

☀ **Review today's lesson. Pray and ask God to identify one or more statements or Scriptures that He wants you to understand, learn, or practice. Underline it (them). Then respond to the following:**

What was the most meaningful statement or Scripture you read today?

_____

_____

Reword the statement or Scripture into a prayer of response to God.

_____

_____

What does God want you to do in response to today's study?

_____

_____

> ### SUMMARY STATEMENTS
>
> - The kind of assignments God gives are God-sized.
> - When God's people and the world see something only God can do, they come to know God.
> - Let people see the difference that a living Christ makes in a life, a family, or a church; that will make a difference in how they respond to the gospel.

WHAT YOU DO TELLS WHAT YOU BELIEVE

When God speaks to a person, revealing His plans and purpose, it will always cause a crisis of belief.

What you do reveals what you believe about God, regardless of what you say.

☀ **As a review, complete the first two statements about this crisis of belief.**

    1. An encounter with God requires _____.

    2. Encounters with God are _____.

3. What you do in response to God's revelation (invitation) reveals what you believe about God.
4. True faith requires action.

In each of the last two statements circle one or two key words that might help you remember the points.

What you believe about God will determine what you do and how you live.

What you do reveals what you believe about God, regardless of what you say. When God reveals what He has purposed to do, you face a crisis—a decision time. God and the world can tell from your response what you really believe about God.

David's Faith Demonstrated

In the following paragraphs, underline what David seems to have believed about God based on what he said. I have underlined one for you.

David

In 1 Samuel 16:12-13 God chose David and had Samuel anoint him to become the next king over Israel. In 1 Samuel 17 God brought David into the middle of His activity. While Saul was still king, the Israelites were at war with the Philistines. Still a young boy, David was sent by his father to visit his brothers in the army. When David arrived, Goliath (a giant soldier nine feet tall) challenged Israel to send one man to fight him. The losing nation would become the slaves of the winner. Israel's army was terrified. David asked in amazement, "Who is this uncircumcised Philistine that he should defy the armies of the <u>living God?</u>" (v. 26). David faced a crisis of belief. He may have realized that God had brought him to the battlefield and had prepared him for this assignment.

David said he would fight this giant. He stated his belief, "The Lord who delivered me from the paw of the lion and the paw of the bear will deliver me from the hand of this Philistine" (v. 37). David refused to take the normal weapons of war. Instead he took a sling and five smooth stones. He said to Goliath, "You come against me with sword and spear and javelin, but I come against you in the name of the Lord Almighty, the God of the armies of Israel, whom you have defied. This day the Lord will hand you over to me . . . and the whole world will know that there is a God in Israel. All those gathered here will know that it is not by sword or spear that the Lord saves; for the battle is the Lord's, and he will give all of you into our hands" (vv. 45-47). David killed Goliath, and Israel went on to victory.

What did David say he believed about God?

_____

_____

Based on David's response to Goliath, what do you think David believed about God?

_____

_____

By his actions, David revealed what he believed about God.

David's statements indicate that he believed God was the living God and that He was Deliverer. He said that God was Almighty and that God would defend Israel's armies. David's actions verify that he really did believe these things about God. Many thought David was a foolish young boy, and even Goliath laughed at him. God delivered the Israelites, however. He gave a mighty victory through David, so that the whole world would know that there was a God in Israel!

Sarai's Lack of Faith

Sarai

God called Abram and promised to make his offspring as numerous as the stars. Abram questioned God about this promise, since he remained childless into his old age. God reaffirmed, "A son coming from your own body will be your heir. . . . Abram believed the Lord, and he credited it to him as righteousness" (Gen. 15:4, 6).

Abram's wife Sarai was in her mid 70s at this time. She knew she was past childbearing years, so she decided she would have to "build a family" in a different way. She gave her maid to Abram as a wife and asked for a child through her. Ishmael was born to Haggar a year later. Sarai's actions indicated what she believed about God.

 Which of the following more closely indicates what Sarai seemed to *believe* about God? Check your response.

❏ a. Sarai believed God was Almighty and could do anything—including give her a child of her own, even though she was 77 years old.

❏ b. Sarai believed God could not possibly give her a child of her own at 77, and He needed her help in finding a way for Abram to become a father.

Do you see how Sarai's actions told what she really believed about God? She did not have the faith to believe that God could do the impossible and give her a child at 77. Her belief about God was limited by her own human reason. This act of unbelief was very costly. Ishmael caused Abram and Sarai much grief in their old age. Ishmael and his descendants have lived in hostility toward Isaac and the Jews from that time until today. What you do in response to God's invitation really does indicate what you believe about God.

Unbelief is very costly.

Read the following case studies. Evaluate the response of the individuals and churches to determine what they really believe about God. Check your response or write your own to each situation.

1. **Bill and Kathy** have just heard a missionary speaker. They believe God wants them to go as missionaries to Africa. Kathy reminds Bill that her parents would never agree to let them move so far away with her parents' only grandchildren. They decide not to pursue that sense of calling to be missionaries. What do you think Bill and Kathy really believe about God?

    ❏ a. God is Sovereign Lord and has a right to do anything in their lives that He pleases.

    ❏ b. God is able to convince Kathy's parents that this is His purpose, so they will be understanding.

    ❏ c. God may have been able to convince Pharaoh to let Israel go, but He would never be able to convince Kathy's parents to let Kathy, Bill, and the children go to Africa. After all, times have changed.

    ❏ d. Other _____

2. **Levona** privately has been praying that God would lead her to a place of service in the church. The Sunday School Director has been praying for an adult teacher. He believes that God is leading him to ask Levona to serve in that position. Levona responds, "I cannot accept that job. I don't have the abilities required. Besides, I have never done that before." What do you think Levona believes about God?

    ❏ a. The Holy Spirit will equip and enable me to do anything He calls me to do.

    ❏ b. God can't do anything through me that I am not able to do myself.

    ❏ c. Other _____

3. A group of adults has been meeting together for six months and praying that God would provide a church for their town. There are no evangelical churches in the town. As they pray, they sense that God wants them to approach Calvary Church with an urgent plea to come and start the new church. Calvary's members say, "We are still paying off a debt on our building. We can't afford to sponsor a new church right now. Why don't you try First Church downtown." What do you think Calvary believes about God?

    ❏ a. God's resources for work through our church are limited to what our people already give.

    ❏ b. God owns everything in the world. He can provide resources to do whatever He purposes to do.

    ❏ c. Other _____

4. **First Church's** budget committee prayed together for a month prior to talking with leaders about next year's budget. They had asked the leaders to pray as well. They develop a challenging budget based on what they believe God wants their church to do this next year. The church prayerfully considered the budget and voted unani-

mously to adopt it. The deacons led a pledge campaign that came up with 10% less than the adopted budget. The church required the budget committee to trim the budget by 10% so they would not overspend their income. What do you think First Church believes about God?

❏ a. God is faithful. He will provide for all that He leads our church to do.
❏ b. God is mean. He leads us to agree to do many things, but then He won't give us what we need to get the job done.
❏ c. God can't do anything that we as a church can't afford.
❏ d. Other _____

Bill, Kathy, Levona, Calvary Church, and First Church may have been dealing with many other variables. The answers to choose from in this activity may not have reflected what they really believe about God, but one thing is sure: Actions do indicate what we believe and do not believe about God.

When Bill and Kathy made a decision at their crisis of belief, they said far more about their belief in God than about Kathy's parents. Levona said far more about her belief in God's abilities than she did about her abilities. Calvary Church and First Church said far more about what they believed about God than they did about their own resources.

Actions Speak

When God invites you to join Him and you face a crisis of belief, what you do next tells what you believe about God. Your actions really do speak louder than words.

Read the following Scriptures and answer the questions.

Matthew 8:5-13. What did the centurion do to demonstrate his faith?

_____

What do you think the centurion believed about Jesus' authority and healing power?

_____

Matthew 8:23-27. What did the disciples do to demonstrate their "little faith" in the middle of this storm?

_____

Matthew 9:20-22. What did the woman do to demonstrate her faith?

_____

What do you think the woman believed about Jesus' power to heal?

_____

Matthew 9:27-31. What trait of God (Jesus) were these two blind men appealing to? (v. 27)

_____

On what basis did Jesus heal these two men? (v. 29)

_____

Complete the third statement on the crisis of belief in your own words.

1. An encounter with God requires faith.
2. Encounters with God are God-sized.
3. What I do in response to God's revelation (invitation)…

_____

4. True faith requires action.

When the two blind men demonstrated that they believed Jesus was merciful and that He was the Messiah (Son of David), Jesus healed them according to their faith. The woman believed that just a touch of Jesus' garment would allow His healing power to flow to her. She was willing to risk public ridicule in order to experience His healing power. When the storms of life overtake us like this storm overtook the disciples, we often respond as if God does not exist or does not care. Jesus rebuked them, not for their human tendency to fear, but for their failure to recognize His presence, protection, and power. "Just say the word, and my servant will be healed," the centurion claimed. Jesus commended the centurion's faith in His authority and power. What each of these people did indicated to Jesus what kind of faith they had.

☀ **Review today's lesson. Pray and ask God to identify one or more statements or Scriptures that He wants you to understand, learn, or practice. Underline it (them). Then respond to the following:**

What was the most meaningful statement or Scripture you read today?

_____

_____

_____

Reword the statement or Scripture into a prayer of response to God.

_____

_____

_____

_____

What does God want you to do in response to today's study?

_____

_____

Practice quoting your Scripture memory verses aloud or write them on separate paper.

SUMMARY STATEMENTS

- What I do reveals what I believe about God, regardless of what I say.
- What I believe about God will determine what I do and how I live.

TRUE FAITH REQUIRES ACTION

DAY 5

James 2:26, "As the body without the spirit is dead, so faith without deeds is dead." When you face a crisis of belief, what you do demonstrates what you believe. Faith without action is dead!

Faith without action is dead!

☀ **Take a moment to review this unit by filling in the blanks in the following four statements.**

1. An encounter with God requires _____.

2. Encounters with God are God-_____.

3. What I do in response to God's _____ (invitation) reveals what

   I _____ about God.

4. True faith requires _____.

Hebrews 11 is sometimes called "The Roll Call of Faith." Let's take a look at the actions of these individuals who demonstrated their faith.

☀ **Turn to Hebrews 11. The following list on the left includes people commended for their faith in Hebrews 11. The verses of the chapter are in parentheses under the name. Match the person on the left with the action on the right that demonstrated his faith. Write the correct letters in the blanks. Some of the names will have more than one letter.**

____ 1. Abel (v. 4)	A. Chose to be mistreated along with God's people
____ 2. Enoch (vv. 5-6)	B. Offered a righteous sacrifice to God
____ 3. Noah (v. 7)	C. Left Egypt
____ 4. Abraham (vv. 8-19)	D. Made his home in a foreign country
____ 5. Joseph (v. 22)	E. Marched around the walls of Jericho
____ 6. Moses (vv. 24-28)	F. Pleased God by earnestly seeking Him
____ 7. Israelites (vv. 29-30)	G. Gave instructions to bury his bones in the promised land
____ 8. Rahab (v. 31)	H. Followed God without knowing where he was going
	I. Kept the Passover
	J. Passed through the Red Sea on dry ground
	K. Welcomed and hid the Israelite spies
	L. Considered God faithful to keep His promise
	M. Built an ark to save his family
	N. Offered Isaac as a sacrifice

In the previous list of actions, circle the word (verb) in each lettered item that indicates an action taken as a demonstration of faith.

Based on Hebrews 11, is the following statement true or false? Circle one.

True or False?   Genuine faith is demonstrated by action.

Answers are: 1-B; 2-F; 3-M; 4-DHLN; 5-G; 6-ACI; 7-EJ; 8-K and true.

While you are studying Hebrews 11, you may notice that a faithful life does not always bring the same results in human terms.

The outcomes of a faithful life

Read Hebrews 11:32-38. Based on your own evaluation, list the "good" outcomes of a faithful life on the left and the "bad" outcomes on the right. I have listed two to get you started.

"Good" Outcomes	"Bad" Outcomes
Routed Enemies	*Stoned To Death*

Verses 33-35a describe the victory and deliverance some people of faith experienced. Verses 35b-38 describe the torture, mockery, and death other people of faith experienced. Were some more faithful than the others? No. "These were all commended for their faith" (Heb. 11:39). They decided a "Well done!" from their Master was more important than life itself. Verse 40 explains that God has planned something far better for people of faith than the world had to offer. Therefore:

> Since we are surrounded by such a great cloud of witnesses, let us throw off everything that hinders and the sin that so easily entangles, and let us run with perseverance the race marked out for us. Let us fix our eyes on Jesus, the author and perfecter of our faith, who for the joy set before him endured the cross, scorning its shame, and sat down at the right hand of the throne of God. Consider him who endured such opposition from sinful men, so that you will not grow weary and lose heart (Heb. 12:1-3).

Outward appearances of success do not always indicate faith, and outward appearances of failure do not always indicate lack of faith. A faithful servant is one that does what his Master tells him, whatever the outcome may be. Just like Jesus—He endured the cross, but now He is seated near the very throne of God! What a reward for faithfulness! Don't grow weary in being faithful. A reward is awaiting faithful servants.

Write your Scripture memory verse for this unit.

_____

_____

_____

_____

_____

I pray that you are trying to please God by earnestly seeking Him (Heb. 11:6). In the next unit we will look more carefully at the cost factors in following God's will. Part of the action required to demonstrate your faith will be the adjustment you must make to God. Following God's will always requires adjustments that are costly to you and even those around you.

Coming up next

Take some time to review some of your responses at the end of each day in units 1-7. Has God led you to do something that you did not do because you lacked faith? Yes ❏   No ❏ If yes, describe what you may need to do to demonstrate your faith in Him, His purposes, and His ways.

_____

_____

Spend some time praying about your faithfulness. Ask God to increase your faith.

Review today's lesson. Pray and ask God to identify one or more statements or Scriptures that He wants you to understand, learn, or practice. Underline it (them). Then respond to the following:

What was the most meaningful statement or Scripture you read today?

_____

_____

Reword the statement or Scripture into a prayer of response to God.

_____

_____

_____

What does God want you to do in response to today's study?

_____

_____

_____

Review your Scripture memory verses and be prepared to recite them to a partner in your small-group session this week.

SUMMARY STATEMENTS

- Faith without action is dead!
- Genuine faith is demonstrated by action.
- God has planned something far better for people of faith.
- Don't grow weary in being faithful. A reward awaits faithful servants.

ADJUSTING YOUR LIFE TO GOD

UNIT

8

A need arose in one of our mission points that was 40 miles away. I asked the church to pray that God would call someone to move to that community and be a lay pastor of the mission. A young couple responded. He was attending the university, and they had very little financially.

If they took up residence in the mission community, he would have to commute 80 miles a day to the university. I knew they couldn't afford to do it. I said, "No, I can't let you do that." I went through all the reasons why that would not be fair.

This young couple was deeply grateful that God had saved them. The young man looked at me and said, "Pastor, don't deny me the opportunity to sacrifice for my Lord." That statement crushed me. How could I refuse? Yet, I knew that this couple would have to pay a high price because our church had been obedient to start new missions.

We prayed for God to call out a lay pastor. I needed to have been open to God's answering our prayers in an unexpected way. When this couple responded with such a deep sense of commitment and personal sacrifice, the body (our church) affirmed their sense of call; and God provided for their needs!

Verse to Memorize
This Week

Any of you who does not give up everything he has cannot be my disciple.   —LUKE 14:33

Many of us want God to speak to us and give us an assignment. However, we are not interested in making any major adjustments in our lives. Biblically, that is impossible. Every time God spoke to people in the Scripture about something He wanted to do through them, major adjustments were necessary. They had to adjust their lives to God. Once the adjustments were made, God accomplished His purposes through those He called.

A Second Critical Turning Point

Adjusting your life to God is the second critical turning point in your knowing and doing the will of God. The first turning point was the crisis of belief—you must believe God is who He says He is and that He will do what He says He will do. Without faith in God, you will make the wrong decision at this first turning point. Making the adjustment of your life to God also is a turning point. If you choose to make the adjustment, you can go on to obedience. If you refuse to make the adjustment, you could miss what God had in store for your life.

☀ **If you have faith at the crisis of belief, what else is required as a demonstration of that faith? Fill in the blank below.**

(Reality 5) God's invitation for you to work with Him always leads you to a crisis of belief that requires faith and _____.

Once you have come to believe God, you demonstrate your faith by what you DO. Some action is required. This action is one of the major adjustments we are going to focus on in this unit. Your obedience also will be a part of the action required. Your adjustments and obedience will be costly to you and those around you.

> *Faith → Action*
> *Action = Adjustments + Obedience*

☀ **In you own words, summarize what you see stated in the preceding box.**

_____

_____

_____

_____

Adjustments to God

When God speaks to you, revealing what He is about to do, that revelation is your invitation to adjust your life to Him. Once you have adjusted your life to Him, His purposes, and His ways, you are in a position to obey. Adjustments prepare you for obedience. You cannot continue life as usual or stay where you are, and go with God at the same time. That is true throughout Scripture.

- **Noah** could not continue life as usual and build an ark at the same time (Gen. 6).
- **Abram** could not stay in Ur or Haran and father a nation in Canaan (Gen. 12:1-8).
- **Moses** could not stay on the back side of the desert herding sheep and stand before Pharaoh at the same time (Ex. 3).
- **David** had to leave his sheep to become king (1 Sam. 16:1-13).
- **Amos** had to leave the sycamore trees in order to preach in Israel (Amos 7:14-15).
- **Jonah** had to leave his home and overcome a major prejudice in order to preach in Nineveh (Jonah 1:1-2; 3:1-2; 4:1-11).
- **Peter, Andrew, James,** and **John** had to leave their fishing businesses in order to follow Jesus (Matt. 4:18-22).
- **Matthew** had to leave his tax collector's booth to follow Jesus (Matt. 9:9).
- **Saul** (later Paul) had to completely change directions in his life in order to be used of God to preach the gospel to the Gentiles (Acts 9:1-19).

You cannot stay where you are and go with God.

1. Crisis of Belief

2. Major Adjustments

God's revelation is your invitation to adjust your life to Him.

Enormous changes and adjustments had to be made! Some had to leave family and country. Others had to drop prejudices and change preferences. Others had to leave behind life goals, ideals, and desires. Everything had to be yielded to God and the entire life adjusted to Him. The moment the necessary adjustments were made God began to accomplish His purposes through them. Each one, however, learned that adjusting one's life to God is well worth the cost.

☀ **Your Scripture memory verse for this unit speaks of a major adjustment that must be made to be a disciple of Jesus. Write the verse here:**

_____

_____

Have you come to a place in your life where you are willing to yield "everything" to Him in order to follow Him? Yes ❑   No ❑

In the last unit you studied the fifth reality in the sequence of God's working through His people. In this unit we will look together at the sixth reality. To review and preview, fill in the blanks in the realities below.

5. God's invitation for you to work with Him always leads you to a

_____ of _____ that requires

_____ and _____

6. You must make major _____ in your life to join God in what He is doing.

You may be thinking: "But, God will not ask ME to make major adjustments." If you look to Scripture for your understanding of God, you will see that God most certainly will require adjustments of His people. He even required major adjustments of His own Son: "You know the grace of our Lord Jesus Christ, that though he was rich, yet for your sakes he became poor, so that you through his poverty might become rich" (2 Cor. 8:9). Jesus emptied Himself of position and wealth in heaven in order to join the Father in providing redemption through His death on the cross—that was a major adjustment!

Even Jesus had to make major adjustments.

If you want to be a disciple—a follower—of Jesus, you have no choice. You will have to make major adjustments in your life to follow God. Following your Master requires adjustments in your life. Until you are ready to make any adjustment necessary to follow and obey what God has said, you will be of little use to God. Your greatest single difficulty in following God may come at the point of the adjustment.

Your greatest single difficulty in following God may come at the point of the adjustment.

Our tendency is to want to skip the adjustment and go from believing God to obedience. If you want to follow Him, you don't have that choice. His ways are so different than yours (Isa. 55:9) that the only way to follow Him will require an adjustment of your life to His ways.

"As the heavens are higher than the earth, so are my ways higher than your ways and my thoughts than your thoughts."
—Isaiah 55:9

☀ **Elisha and the Rich Young Ruler were given invitations to join God. Read about them and answer the following questions.**

Elisha—1 Kings 19:15-21   Rich Young Ruler—Luke 18:18-27

1. What adjustment was required of each?
   Elisha: _____

   Rich Young Ruler: _____

2. What was the response of each?
   Elisha: _____

   Rich Young Ruler: _____

Rich Young Ruler

The rich ruler wanted eternal life, but he didn't want to make the necessary adjustment to Jesus. His money and wealth were more important. Jesus knew that. Jesus knew that man could not love God completely and love his money at the same time (Matt. 6:24). Jesus asked him to put away the thing that had become his god—his wealth. The young ruler refused to make the necessary adjustment, and he missed out on experiencing eternal life.

✸ What is "eternal life" according to John 17:3?

_____

_____

"Now this is eternal life: that they may know you, the only true God, and Jesus Christ, whom you have sent."
—John 17:3

The rich young ruler's love of money and his greed made him an idolater (Eph. 5:5). He missed coming to know the True God and Jesus Christ whom God had sent. He wanted eternal life, but he refused to make the necessary adjustment of his life to the True God.

Elisha

Elisha responded much differently. He had to leave family and career (farming) in order to follow God's call. You have heard the phrase about "burning your bridges behind you." Well, Elisha burned his farm equipment and killed his 24 oxen. He cooked the meat and fed the people of the community. He was not about to turn back! When he made the necessary adjustments, he was in a position to obey God. As a result, God worked through Elisha to perform some of the greatest signs and miracles recorded in the Old Testament (2 Kings 2—13). Elisha had to make the adjustments on the front end of his call. Not until he made the adjustments, was God able to work through him to accomplish the miracles.

No one can sum up all God is able to accomplish through one solitary life, wholly yielded, adjusted, and obedient to Him!

✸ **Do you want to be one who is wholly yielded, adjusted, and obedient to God? Yes ❑ No ❑**

As you come to know and do the will of God, in what order do the following responses come? Number them in the correct order. (Refer to the seven realities on the inside back cover if you need help.)

_____ obedience

_____ adjustments

_____ faith

When God invites you to join Him, the task will have such God-sized dimensions you will face a crisis of belief. Your response will first require faith. Faith will be demonstrated by action. The first action will involve the adjustment of your life to God. The second action will be your obedience to what God asks you to do. You cannot go on to obedience without first making the adjustments. So the order is faith—adjustment—obedience.

✸ **Review today's lesson. Pray and ask God to identify one or more statements or Scriptures that He wants you to understand, learn, or practice. Underline it (them). Then respond to the following:**

What was the most meaningful statement or Scripture you read today?

_____

_____

_____

Reword the statement or Scripture into a prayer of response to God.

_____

_____

_____

_____

What does God want you to do in response to today's study?

_____

_____

Write your Scripture memory verse for this unit and review your other verses.

_____

_____

DAY 2   KINDS OF ADJUSTMENTS

God is interested in absolute surrender.

What kind of adjustments are required? Trying to answer that question is like trying to list all the things God might ask you to do. The list could be endless. I can, however, point you to some examples and give you some general categories of adjustments that may be required.

Adjustments

Adjustments may be required in one or more of the following areas:
- **In your circumstances** (like job, home, finances, and others)
- **In your relationships** (family, friends, business associates, and others)
- **In your thinking** (prejudices, methods, your potential, and others)
- **In your commitments** (to family, church, job, plans, tradition, and others)
- **In your actions** (how you pray, give, serve, and others)
- **In your beliefs** (about God, His purposes, His ways, your relationship to Him, and others)

The list could go on and on. The major adjustment will come at the point of acting on your faith. When you face the crisis of belief, you must decide what you believe about God. That mental decision may be the easy part. The hard part is adjusting your life to God and taking an action that *demonstrates* your faith. You may be called to attempt things that only *God* can do, where formerly you may have attempted only that which you knew *you* could do.

✴ **Read each of the following Scriptures. What kind of adjustment was (or is) required in each? Match the Scripture on the left with the correct adjustment required on the right. Some may call for more than one type of adjustment. Write a letter or letters in each blank.**

Scriptures	Adjustments
_____ 1. Matthew 4:18-22	A. In circumstances
_____ 2. Matthew 5:43-48	B. In relationships
_____ 3. Matthew 6:5-8	C. In thinking
_____ 4. Matthew 20:20-28	D. In commitments
_____ 5. Acts 10:1-20	E. In actions
	F. In beliefs

Sometimes an adjustment may involve several of these areas at once. For instance, Peter's experience with Cornelius probably required adjustments in Peter's relationships with Gentiles, his thinking and beliefs about what is clean and unclean, his commitments to the traditions of the Jews, and his actions regarding fellowship with Gentiles. Being able to place a title on an adjustment is not as important as your identifying what change God wants you to make to Him, His purposes, or His ways. The primary adjustments I see in the Scriptures above are: 1—A; 2—B or C; 3—E; 4—B, C, or E; 5—C or F. You may have seen others and that is okay.

✳ **List at least four areas in which God may ask you to make an adjustment of your life to Him. I have given you one.**

1. _beliefs_ _____
2. _____
3. _____
4. _____

Now go back and give one example for each area. For instance, an adjustment in circumstances may require that you leave your hometown or change your job.

Absolute Surrender

God frequently requires adjustments in areas you have never considered or been open to in the past. You may have heard someone say something like this: "Don't ever tell God something you will NOT do. That is what He will ask you to do." God is not looking for ways to make you "squirm." He does, however, want to be Lord of your life. Whenever you identify a place where you refuse to allow His lordship, that is a place He will go to work. He is interested in absolute surrender. God may or may not require you to do that very thing you identified, but He will keep working until you are willing for Him to be Lord of all. Remember, because God loves you, His will is always best for you! Any adjustment God expects you to make is for your good. As you follow Him, the time may come that your life and future may depend on your adjusting quickly to God's directives.

God is interested in absolute surrender.

The adjusting is always to a Person. You adjust your life to God. You adjust your viewpoints to be like His viewpoints. You adjust your ways to be like His ways. After you make the necessary adjustments, He will tell you what to do next to obey Him. When you obey Him, you will experience Him doing through you something only God can do.

You adjust to a Person.

First: adjust

Then: obey

✳ **Describe at least one adjustment you have had to make in your *thinking* as you have studied this course. (One person might respond: "I had to accept the fact that I cannot do anything of Kingdom value apart from God. Instead of doing things for God, I now am watching and praying to see what God wants to do through me.")**

_____
_____
_____

Has God ever asked you to make a major adjustment to Him? Yes ❑   No ❑ If so, briefly describe the adjustment that was required and your response.

_____
_____
_____

Read these statements made by godly men. Under each statement *describe the kind of adjustment* this person had made or was willing to make. In the first quote, for example, one adjustment David Livingstone was willing to make was to live in poverty as a missionary (in Africa) rather than to have riches as a physician in his homeland.

David Livingstone (medical missionary to Africa)—*"Forbid that we should ever consider the holding of a commission from the King of Kings a sacrifice, so long as other men esteem the service of an earthly government as an honor. I am a missionary, heart and soul. God Himself had an only Son, and He was a missionary and a physician. A poor, poor imitation I am, or wish to be, but in this service I hope to live. In it I wish to die. I still prefer poverty and missions service to riches and ease. This is my choice."[1]*

Adjustment(s) _____

Jim Elliot (missionary to Quichua Indians in South America)—*"He is no fool who gives what he cannot keep to gain what he cannot lose."[2]*

Adjustment(s) _____

Bob Pierce (established World Vision and Samaritan's Purse)—*"Let my heart be broken by the things that break the heart of God."*[3]

Adjustment(s) _____

Oswald J. Smith (missionary statesman of Canada)—*"I want Thy plan, O God, for my life. May I be happy and contented whether in the homeland or on the foreign field; whether married or alone, in happiness or sorrow, health or sickness, prosperity or adversity—I want Thy plan, O God, for my life. I want it; oh, I want it!"*[4]

Adjustment(s) _____

C. T. Studd (missionary to China, India, and Africa)—*"If Jesus Christ be God and died for me, then no sacrifice is too great for me to give for Him."*[5]

Adjustment(s) _____

Some adjustments these men made or were willing to make include:
- Livingstone considered the work of a missionary to Africa as a high honor, not a sacrifice.
- Jim Elliot was willing to give up earthly things for heavenly reward. He was killed by South American Indians as he sought to spread the gospel to those who had never heard about Jesus.
- Bob Pierce was willing to be broken hearted so he could be like the Father.
- Oswald Smith so wanted God's plan for his life, that he was willing to be content with any pleasure or adversity.
- C. T. Studd was willing to make any sacrifice for Jesus' sake.

Draw a star in the margin beside the quote that is the most meaningful to you.

Think about the level of commitment that is reflected in that quote. If you are willing to make a similar commitment to the lordship of Christ, spend a few moments in prayer expressing your willingness to adjust your life to Him.

You cannot stay where you are and go with God!

I have tried to help you understand that you cannot stay where you are and go with God in obedience to His will. Adjustments must come first. Then you can follow in obedience. Keep in mind—the God who calls you is also the One who will enable you to do His will. In the remainder of this unit we are going to be looking at the second and third points below:

Obedience Requires Adjustments

1. You cannot stay where you are and go with God at the same time.
2. Obedience is costly to you and those around you.
3. Obedience requires total dependence on God to work through you.

When you are willing to surrender everything in your life to the lordship of Christ, you, like Elisha, will find that the adjustments are well worth the reward of experiencing God. If you have not come to the place in your life where you have surrendered *all* to His lordship, decide today to deny yourself, take up your cross, and follow Him (Luke 9:23).

Review today's lesson. Pray and ask God to identify one or more statements or Scriptures that He wants you to understand, learn, or practice. Underline it (them). Then respond to the following:

What was the most meaningful statement or Scripture you read today?

_____

_____

Reword the statement or Scripture into a prayer of response to God.

_____

_____

What does God want you to do in response to today's study?

_____

_____

OBEDIENCE IS COSTLY, PART 1

DAY 3

You cannot stay where you are and go with God. You cannot continue doing things your way and accomplish God's purposes in His ways. Your thinking cannot come close to God's thoughts. For you to DO the will of God, you must adjust your life to Him, His purposes, and His ways.

Obedience is costly to you.

 In this unit we are looking at three statements about adjustments and obedience. Under each one, write the statement in your own words from your perspective. Use "I" and "me" instead of "you."

1. You cannot stay where you are and go with God at the same time.

_____

2. Obedience is costly to you and those around you.

_____

3. Obedience requires total dependence on God to work through you.

_____

Look at the second statement: Obedience is costly to you and those around you. You cannot know and do the will of God without paying the price of adjustment and obedience. Willingness to pay the price of following His will is one of the *major* adjustments. At this very point "many of his disciples turned back and no longer followed him" (John 6:66). This also is a point where churches will not know and experience the fulfilling of God's purposes and will through them, because they are not willing to pay the price of obedience.

Willingness to pay the price

The Cost: An Adjustment in Our Program

Some people in our Vancouver association sensed God might be calling them to a place of ministry. They asked me to share with them how they could know and follow God's call. For two days we spread the word that anyone sensing a call to ministry could come to an informal meeting. Seventy-five people came to hear me share. They all sensed God was calling them to some form of ministry. They said, "We need some training."

Lay leaders needed training

Within two weeks the number grew to 120. We began to identify needs and list training possibilities and so forth. In a small group of churches, a training program for 120 who sense God's call is a giant-size task. When we started to talk about providing training for this group, someone asked, "But, Henry, what about all of the program plans we have made for the fall?" This person knew that we probably could not do our fall program and the training for these 120 people.

 In light of what you have been studying, how would you respond to that question? What would you tell the 120 people?

_____

_____

I could have responded to this group of 120 people in several ways. I could have reported the large response in our newsletter and just asked people to praise God for what He was doing. Then I could have told these 120 that we already had our program set for the next year. They would have to wait a year so we could get these training plans into our program calendar. I could have stayed with our full program plans and done a token amount of training to pacify the 120. I didn't do that. I responded by explaining: "If God has called these folks to ministry and they need training, we must adjust our plans and program to what God is doing. We need to remember, we are servants of God." That's what we did. We adjusted our plans to join God in what He was doing.

We say that God is Lord and that He can interrupt us anytime He wants. We just don't expect Him to do it. We expect Him to affirm everything we are doing and never ask us to change anything we have planned. If we want God to go down the channels that we have already established and protect our own plans and programming, we are in trouble. When God invites us to join Him, we will have to make some major adjustments. Those adjustments and obedience to God's direction will be costly. Does God ever ask us to change personal plans or directions in order to follow Him?

Read Acts 9:1-25 and describe the adjustment Saul had to make. Describe the cost He had to pay to follow Christ.

_____

_____

_____

Does God ever ask a person to change his or her plans or directions in order to follow Him? Yes ❏   No ❏

Saul (Paul)

Saul (later named Paul) had to make a total about-face in directions. He went from persecuting Christians to proclaiming that Jesus was the Christ. God will ask you to follow Him in ways that will require adjustments in your plans and directions. For Paul the adjustment was costly. It even put his life at risk with the Jews. The adjustments you have to make will be costly as well.

The Cost: Enduring Opposition

Read the following paragraphs and underline some of the costs of obedience. I have underlined one for you.

Opposition to new churches

In Saskatoon our church sensed very clearly that God had called us to start new churches all across our province. Not everyone understood or agreed with what we were doing. Some actively opposed us at almost every mission church we started. Though we were totally convinced of the awesome spiritual darkness in Canada, some did not see it. In Regina, the capital of our province, a full page article appeared in the paper 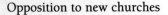condemning us for daring to start a new church in this city of 150,000. In our efforts to have a Bible study in Humboldt, a delegation of leaders from another church group came to my office and urged me to stop. They said our efforts were "of the devil" and that they would oppose the Bible study. In Deschambault, our pastor was met on the street and cursed by a witch doctor. From Prince Albert I received letters condemning our efforts. In Blaine Lake we were told of a prayer meeting dedicated to praying that we would fail and withdraw.

Some in our own conference felt we were foolish to attempt new mission churches when we were so small ourselves. We were told not to ask for help if we got into trouble with salary support for mission pastors or other staff workers. Those who had not been with us when God spoke to us saw our efforts as "presuming on God." I soon discovered that every step of faith could be interpreted as presumption by others. Only obedience and the affirmation of our obedience in the working out of God's activity would reveal that we were doing the will of God.

Later, as mission churches grew, flourished, and became self-supporting, our critics realized this work was indeed of God. Many of these former critics were encouraged to take these same steps of faith in starting new work for themselves. God helped us remain faithful to Him, with a heart full of love toward others; but that was costly.

List some of the "costs" described above that we had to pay in starting new churches.

_____

_____

_____

Read 2 Corinthians 11:23-33 and list some of the costs Paul had to pay for following and obeying Christ.

_____

_____

_____

_____

Sometimes obedience to God's will leads to opposition and misunderstanding. Because of his obedience, Paul suffered much for the cause of Christ. The list of beatings, imprisonments, and danger sound like more than one person could bear. He concluded one letter by saying, "I bear on my body the marks of Jesus" (Gal. 6:17). Paul had not had these experiences before he began to do the will of his Lord. Obedience was costly to him. Even so, Paul still could say:

> I want to know Christ and the power of his resurrection and the fellowship of sharing in his sufferings, becoming like him in his death, and so, somehow, to attain to the resurrection from the dead. Not that I have already obtained all this, or have already been made perfect, but I press on to take hold of that for which Christ Jesus took hold of me (Phil. 3:10-12).

The apostle Paul revealed the adjustments that he made to do the will of God when he said, "I have become all things to all men so that by all possible means I might save some" (1 Cor. 9:22). Your adjustments and obedience to Christ will be costly as well.

Have you ever had an experience where your adjustment or obedience to God was very costly? Yes ❑   No ❑ If so, briefly describe that experience and the cost you had to pay.

_____

_____

_____

David Livingstone was a famous Nineteenth Century missionary from Scotland. He gave his life making Christ known in Africa. Perhaps his words of commitment may inspire your own commitment to pay the cost of following Christ:

David Livingstone

> **Lord, send me anywhere, only go with me.**
>
> **Lay any burden on me, only sustain me.**
>
> **Sever any tie but the tie that binds me to Thyself.**
>
> —DAVID LIVINGSTONE

Review today's lesson. Pray and ask God to identify one or more statements or Scriptures that He wants you to understand, learn, or practice. Underline it (them). Then respond to the following:

What was the most meaningful statement or Scripture you read today?

_____

_____

Reword the statement or Scripture into a prayer of response to God.

_____

_____

_____

_____

What does God want you to do in response to today's study?

_____

_____

_____

Practice quoting or writing your Scripture memory verses.

DAY 4   OBEDIENCE IS COSTLY, PART 2

Obedience is costly to those around you.

One of the most demanding adjustments to doing the will of God will be deciding to obey even when obedience will be very costly to those around you. Obedience is costly to you *and* to those around you.

Answer the following questions. Read the Scripture passage if you do not know the answer already.

1. When Moses was obedient and told Pharaoh to let Israel go, what did it cost the Israelites? (Ex. 5:1-21)

_____

2. When Jesus obeyed and went to the cross, what was the cost to His mother as she stood there and watched Him die? (John 19:17-37)

_____

3. When Paul was obedient in preaching the gospel to the Gentiles at Thessalonica, what did it cost Jason? (Acts 17:1-9)

_____

Moses and the Israelites

When Moses obeyed God, the work load of the children of Israel was increased and the Israelite foremen were beaten. The Israelites paid a high cost for Moses to do the will of God.

Jesus and Mary

When the Lord Jesus did the will of the Father and died on the cross, his mother, Mary, had to suffer the agony of watching her Son be cruelly killed. Jesus' obedience put His mother through an experience where her heart was broken. His obedience put fear and pain in the lives of every one of His disciples. For *Jesus* to do the will of God, others had to pay a high cost.

Paul and Jason

When Paul followed God's will in preaching the gospel, others were led to respond to God's work in their own lives. Jason and some others were arrested by a rioting mob and accused of treason because of their association with Paul. Frequently Paul's obedience to God's will endangered the lives of those who were with Him.

You must not overlook this very real element in knowing and doing the will of God. God will reveal His plans and purposes to you, but your obedience will cost you and others around you. When, for instance, a pastor surrenders his life to missions, it may cost those around him (his family, his church) more than what it will cost him. If he leads his church to become directly involved in doing missions, it may cost some in the church more than it will cost the pastor.

Fill in the blanks in the following statements.

1. You cannot _____ where you are and

go with _____ at the same time.

2. Obedience is _____ to you and

those _____ you.

3. Obedience requires total dependence on God to work through you.

Check your answers on page 132.

Cost to My Family for Me to Do God's Will

When Marilynn and I committed ourselves to do mission work, one of the great costs we had to face was what it would cost our children for me to be gone so much. Our oldest was was eight when we went to Saskatoon. Our youngest was born a few months after the move. I was gone from home much of the time during those years the children were growing up. Marilynn also had to pay a high price by rearing all five children with me gone so much.

I have heard many people of God say, "I really think God is calling me; but, after all, my children need me. I can't put my family through that." Well, your children really do need your care. But, do you suppose that if you were to respond obediently to the activity of God, He would have a way to take care of your children? We did!

We believed God would honor our obedience to Him. We believed the God who called us would show us how to rear our children. We came to believe that the heavenly Father, who loves His servants, could take better care of our children than we ever could. We believed that God would show us how to relate to our children in a way that would make up for the lost time with them. Now, I could not let that become an excuse for neglecting my family. But, when I was obeying the Father, I could trust Him to care for my family.

I could trust Him to care for my family.

We baptized three persons the first year we were in Saskatoon. After two and a half years of hard, hard labor, we were running 30 in Sunday School. Marilynn said to me, "Henry, Richard came to me today and said he really feels sorry for you. He said, 'Dad preaches such good sermons. He gives an invitation week after week, and nobody comes.' "

I went to Richard and said, "Richard, don't ever be sorry for your father. Even if God lets me labor for ten years and see very little results, I will hardly be able to wait for the day when He brings the harvest." I had to help Richard understand what was taking place. I explained God's promise: "He who goes out weeping, carrying seed to sow, will return with songs of joy, carrying sheaves with him" (Ps. 126:6). God worked through me at that moment to teach my son a deeply meaningful spiritual truth.

I remember a time when Marilynn hit a low point. She had gotten discouraged. The next Sunday, after I preached, Richard came down the aisle to make a decision. He said, "I feel called to the ministry."

God took care of Marilynn.

Right behind him came our neighbor, also named Richard. Marilynn had spent hundreds of hours taking care of this young lad from a troubled home. He came saying, "I also feel that God has called me to the ministry." Then he turned and said, "And a lot of the credit goes to Mom Blackaby."

Another boy named Ron stood up in that same service and said, "I want you to know that God is calling me to the ministry also. And I want you to know that it is due largely to Mother Blackaby." At a crisis time in his life, our family had ministered to him and encouraged him to seek God's will for his life. Marilynn had done much to show love to Ron. At this very critical time for Marilynn, God took care of her.

Now, all five of our children sense God's call to vocational ministry or mission work. Only God could have done such a beautiful work with our children. I want you to know that you can trust God with your family! I would rather entrust my family to God's care than to anyone else in the whole world.

You can trust God with your family!

Can you recall an experience when your family had to pay a high price for you to do the will of God in a matter? Yes ☐ No ☐ If so, briefly describe the experience.

_____

_____

_____

Can you recall a time when you chose not to obey God because of the high cost to those around you? Yes ☐ No ☐ If so, briefly describe the situation.

_____

_____

_____

What are some things you know about God that could help you trust God to care for your family? List several.

_____

_____

_____

Let Christ Communicate with His People

If you ever ask God's people to seek the mind of the Lord, be prepared to accept what they tell you. You need to honor what they say. I have seen some who would ask a church, a committee, or group to pray and seek God's will in a matter. The people would express what they sensed God was saying. Then, the leader would say something like: "Now, let me tell you what God wants us to do." If the people of God are the body of Christ, only Christ can be the Head. The whole body needs to come to Christ for an understanding of God's will for that body. We all need to learn to trust Christ to communicate with His people.

Only Christ can be the Head.

☀ **Suppose your church began praying for a special financial need and a retired person sensed God wanted her to give half of her $4,000 life savings to meet that need. How do you think you would respond? Check your response.**
   ❏ 1. I would refuse her gift and ask the more financially secure people to give instead.
   ❏ 2. I would receive the gift, thank God for answering prayer, and weep about the high cost she had to pay for our church to do God's will.
   ❏ 3. I would receive the gift, but I would try to work out a way to replace the money as soon as possible.
   ❏ 4. I would ask her to wait for two more weeks and pray to make sure this is what God wants her to do.

Cost to an Individual for Our Church to Do God's Will

I had to face a situation similar to this. One of our new missions needed a building. The financial agency we were working with required that a certain percentage of the cost be paid as a down payment in order for us to get the loan.

The mission was very small, so I asked our church members if they would be willing to pray about the possibility of contributing toward the down payment. They agreed to pray and watch to see how God would provide. Ivah Bates, one of our real prayers, was a widow. In addition to a small pension, she had a total of $4,000 in the bank to last her the rest of her life. She gave a check for $2,000 to the building fund.

As her pastor, a whole lot of emotions went through my own heart. Here I was leading our church to do what we believed God wanted us to do. I had pain in my own heart to see what it was costing our people to respond. I talked with Ivah's daughter. She said, "Don't deny my mother the right to give. She has always trusted her Lord. She wants to do that now, too."

"Don't deny my mother the right to give."

Some pastors or finance committees say, "We can't ask our people to give too often, or it will hurt our ongoing budget giving." I learned to never deny God's people the opportunity to give. I never tried to pressure or manipulate people to give. That was not my job. I would create the opportunity and encourage them to give only what God led them to give. God's people will cheerfully do the will of God. Some of them will respond with generosity and count it an honor that God has allowed them to sacrifice for Him. Some will have life-changing experiences as a result of such an opportunity.

☀ **Do you know of a situation where a person or a family had to pay a high price because your church followed God's will? Yes ❏   No ❏ If so, briefly describe the situation.**

_____

_____

Complete the first two statements, then check your answers on page 132.

1. You cannot stay where you are and _____

_____

2. Obedience is costly to _____

3. Obedience requires total dependence on God to work through you.

The Cry of a Mother's Heart

Hudson Taylor, a great man of prayer and faith, responded to God's call to go to China as a missionary. His father had already died. He had to leave his widowed mother to go to China. By the end of his life in 1905, he had been used by God to found the China Inland Mission. There were 205 preaching stations, 849 missionaries, and 125,000 Chinese Christians—a testimony of a life absolutely surrendered to God. Hudson Taylor described something of the cost he and his mother experienced as he obeyed God's will to go to China as a missionary.

Hudson Taylor

 Imagine that you are Hudson Taylor. Your father is dead. You realize that you may never see your mother again here on earth. Slowly read Taylor's account of their parting and try to imagine the emotions they must have felt.

> *"My beloved, now sainted, mother had come to see me off from Liverpool. Never shall I forget that day, nor how she went with me into the little cabin that was to be my home for nearly six long months. With a mother's loving hand she smoothed the little bed. She sat by my side, and joined me in the last hymn that we should sing together before the long parting. We knelt down, and she prayed—the last mother's prayer I was to hear before starting for China. Then notice was given that we must separate, and we had to say good-bye, never expecting to meet on earth again.*
>
> *"For my sake she restrained her feelings as much as possible. We parted; and she went on shore, giving me her blessing! I stood alone on deck, and she followed the ship as we moved towards the dock gates. As we passed through the gates, and the separation really commenced, I shall never forget the cry of anguish wrung from that mother's heart. It went through me like a knife. I never knew so fully, until then, what 'God so loved the world' meant. And I am quite sure that my precious mother learned more of the love of God to the perishing in that hour than in all her life before.*
>
> *"Praise God, the number is increasing who are finding out the exceeding joys, the wondrous revelations of His mercies, vouchsafed to those who 'follow Him,' and emptying themselves, leave all in obedience to His great commission."[6]*

Based on this brief account, answer the following questions:

1. What did it cost Hudson Taylor to adjust his life to God and obediently go to China?

_____

_____

2. What did it cost Hudson's mother for him to obey God's will?

_____

_____

3. What did they learn about God's love through this experience?

_____

_____

Leaving home and family on a dangerous mission was a very costly step for Hudson Taylor to take. His mother so loved the Lord that she was willing to pay the cost of releasing her son to missions. Both of the Taylors had to pay a high cost for obedience. Yet, they both experienced the love of God in a way they had never known before. History reveals that God rewarded the faithfulness of His servant Hudson Taylor. God used him in miraculous ways to reach interior China with the gospel of Christ.

Do you think God might call you to a costly adventure of faith? Yes ❑   No ❑ How will you respond to God when He calls you to a costly commitment? Check one:
Yes, Lord! ❑   No, that costs too much. ❑

You may think that the last question is a little premature. Not really. That is what the lordship of Christ is all about. You should be able to answer the last question without knowing anything about what God may call you to. Your whole life should be lived with the attitude of "Lord, whatever you may ask of me today or in the future, my answer is YES!" Come to the place in your life where you are willing to surrender ALL to Him.

Review today's lesson. Pray and ask God to identify one or more statements or Scriptures that He wants you to understand, learn, or practice. Underline it (them). Then respond to the following:

What was the most meaningful statement or Scripture you read today?

_____

_____

Reword the statement or Scripture into a prayer of response to God.

_____

_____

_____

What does God want you to do in response to today's study?

_____

_____

SUMMARY STATEMENTS

- My obedience is costly to those around me.
- I can trust God to care for my family.
- Don't deny others the opportunity to sacrifice for their Lord.
- I need to trust Christ to communicate with His people.
- Lord, whatever you may ask of me today or in the future, my answer is yes!

DAY 5 TOTAL DEPENDENCE ON GOD

Obedience requires total dependence on God to work through you.

Another adjustment that is a part of knowing and doing the will of God is your coming to *a total dependence on God* to complete what He wants to do through you. Jesus said our relationship to Him would be like a vine and the branches. He said, "Apart from me you can do nothing" (John 15:5). When you are God's servant, you must remain in an intimate relationship with God in order for Him to complete His work through you. You must depend on God alone.

The adjustment requires moving from doing work *for* God according to *your* abilities, *your* gifts, *your* likes and dislikes, and *your* goals to being totally dependent on *God* and *His* working and *His* resources. This is a MAJOR adjustment! It is never easy to make.

Fill in the blanks to complete the statements we have been studying in this unit.

1. You cannot _____ where you are and _____ with God at the same time.

2. Obedience is _____ to _____ and those around you.

3. Obedience requires _____ _____ on God to work through you.

Check your answers on page 132.

Read the following Scriptures and notice why you must depend on God to carry out His purposes. Answer the question that follows.

John 15:5—"I am the vine; you are the branches. If a man remains in me and I in him, he will bear much fruit; apart from me you can do nothing."

1 Corinthians 15:10—"By the grace of God I am what I am, and his grace to me was not without effect. No, I worked harder than all of them—yet not I, but the grace of God that was with me."

Galatians. 2:20—"I have been crucified with Christ and I no longer live, but Christ lives in me. The life I live in the body, I live by faith in the Son of God, who loved me and gave himself for me."

Isaiah 14:24—"The Lord Almighty has sworn, 'Surely, as I have planned, so it will be, and as I have purposed, so it will stand.'"

Isaiah 41:10—"Do not fear, for I am with you; do not be dismayed, for I am your God. I will strengthen you and help you; I will uphold you with my righteous right hand."

Isaiah 46:9-11—"I am God, and there is none like me. . . . My purpose will stand, and I will do all that I please. . . . What I have said, that will I bring about; what I have planned, that will I do."

Why must you depend totally on God to work through you?

_____

_____

_____

Without God at work in you, you can do nothing to bear Kingdom fruit. As you are crucified with Christ, He lives through you to accomplish His purposes by His grace. When God purposes to do something, He guarantees that it will come to pass. He is the One who will accomplish what He purposes to do. If you depend on anything other than God, you will be asking for failure in Kingdom terms.

The Bus Ministry Parable

Once a church asked, "Oh God, how do you want to reach our community through us and build a great church?" God led them to start a bus ministry and provide transportation for children and adults to come to church. They did what God told them to do, and their church grew into a great church.

They were flattered when people from all over the country began to ask, "What are you doing to grow so rapidly?" They wrote a book on how to build great churches through a bus ministry. Thousands of churches began to buy buses to reach their communities, feeling that the method was the key to growth. Later many sold those same buses. They are saying, "It didn't work for us."

"IT" never works! HE works! The method is never the key to accomplishing God's purposes. The key is your relationship to a Person. When you want to know how God would have you reach your city, start a new church, or whatever, ask HIM. Then, when He tells you, don't be surprised if you can't find any church that is doing it just that way. Why? God wants you to know Him. If you follow someone else's plan, use a method, or emphasize a program, you will have a tendency to forget about your dependence on God. You leave the relationship with God and go after a method or a program. That is spiritual adultery.

"IT" never works!
HE works!

Answer the following questions by checking your responses.

1. Where do you usually go to find out how to accomplish God's purposes for your life or for your church? Check all that apply.
   ❑ a. I go to the bookstore or library to find a good book on the subject—one written by a person who has a reputation for success in the area.
   ❑ b. I talk to people or churches that are successful.
   ❑ c. I contact the denominational offices and ask them to tell me which program to use to get the job done.
   ❑ d. I spend time in prayer and the Word asking God to guide me (us) to do things in His way.

2. Which of the following is most important for you to know in seeking to do God's will? Check one.
   - ❑ a. What God wants to do where I am
   - ❑ b. A successful method
   - ❑ c. What program will work best in my situation
   - ❑ d. How other people or churches are succeeding in the Lord's work

Good books, successful methods, creative programs, and the success of others cannot take the place of your relationship with God. They never do the work. God does the work. Apart from Him, you can do nothing. By focusing on anything other than God as "the answer," you rob yourself and your church from seeing God at work. You keep yourself and your church from knowing God. That is a great tragedy for many in our day. May God deliver us from that.

Only God has the right to tell you what to do.

Does that mean that you will never be led by God to develop an organized program or follow a method? No. But only God has the right to tell you what to do. You do not take the initiative to decide for yourself what you will do. You must wait before God until He tells you what to do.

Wait on the Lord.

Read the following Scriptures and circle the word *wait* in each.

Psalm 5:3—"In the morning, O Lord, you hear my voice; in the morning I lay my requests before you and wait in expectation."

Psalm 33:20—"We wait in hope for the Lord; he is our help and our shield."

Psalm 37:34—"Wait for the Lord and keep his way. He will exalt you to inherit the land."

Psalm 38:15—"I wait for you, O Lord; you will answer, O Lord my God."

Isaiah 40:31, KJV—"They that wait upon the Lord shall renew their strength; they shall mount up with wings as eagles; they shall run, and not be weary; and they shall walk, and not faint."

Why do you think you should wait until you have heard a word of direction from the Lord?

_____

_____

"Ask and it will be given to you; seek and you will find; knock and the door will be opened to you. For everyone who asks receives; he who seeks finds; and to him who knocks, the door will be opened."
—Matthew 7:7-8

You may think of waiting as a passive, inactive time. Waiting on the Lord is anything but inactive. While you wait on Him, you will be praying with a passion to know Him, His purposes, and His ways. You will be watching circumstances and asking God to interpret them by revealing to you His perspective. You will be sharing with other believers to find out what God is saying to them. As you wait on the Lord, you will be very active in asking, seeking, and knocking (Matt. 7:7-8). While you wait, continue doing the last thing God told you to do. In waiting you are shifting the responsibility of the outcome to God—where it belongs.

Then, when God gives you specific guidance, He will do through you more in days and weeks than you could ever accomplish in years of labor. Waiting on Him is always worth the wait. His timing and His ways are always right. You must depend on Him to guide you in His way and in His timing to accomplish His purpose.

The Holy Spirit Helps You Accomplish the Father's Will

The Holy Spirit will never misunderstand the Father's will for your life. The Father has a purpose to work out through your life. In order that you not miss it, He places His Spirit in you. The Spirit's job is to guide you according to the will of the Father. Then He enables you to do God's will. You are completely dependent on God for the knowledge and ability to accomplish His purposes. That is why your relationship to Him is so important. That is why you need to wait until you have heard a word from Him about His purposes and ways.

Jesus is your example of One who never failed to know and do the will of His Father. Every solitary thing the Father purposed to do through His life, the Lord Jesus did it immediately. What was the key to His success? He was always rightly related to the Father! If you walk in a consistent relationship with God's provision for you—the provision of His Son, His

Holy Spirit, and His own presence in your life—then you should never come to a time that you do not know the will of God. There should never be a time when you are not enabled to carry out the will of God.

In Jesus you have a picture of a solitary life in a love relationship with God, consistently living out that relationship. He is the perfect example. You and I will come quickly to the conclusion that we are a long way from that. True! But the Christ who lived His life in complete obedience is fully present in you to enable you to know and do His will. We need to adjust our lives to God and consistently live out that relationship with absolute dependence on Him. He will never fail to pull your life into the middle of His purpose and enable you to do it.

How would you describe the quality and purity of your relationship with God?

_____

_____

What, if any, adjustments do you think God wants you to make to renew a consistent and right relationship with Him?

_____

_____

Adjustments in Prayer and the Cost

When our church encountered a directive from God, I often experienced a crisis in my prayer life. I learn more about prayer at those times than almost any other time. There were some things that only prayer could bring about. Often God waits until we ask. The crisis was this: Was I willing to pray until God brought it about? Mark 11:24 has been a prayer promise that has been challenging to me regarding the relationship of faith and prayer.

Read Mark 11:24 again and write the promise in your own words.

_____

_____

"Whatever you ask for in prayer, believe that you have received it, and it will be yours."

—Mark 11:24

This verse is sometimes used to teach a "name-it-and-claim-it" theology. *You* decide what *you* want. *You* name that in *your* request, claim it, and it's *yours*. That is a self-centered theology. Remember that only God takes the initiative. He gives you the desire to do His will (Phil. 2:13). His Holy Spirit guides you to pray according to God's will (Rom. 8:26-28). The God-centered approach would be to let God lead you to pray according to His will (in the name and character of Jesus). Believe that what He has led you to pray, He Himself will bring to pass. Then continue praying in faith and watching for it to come to pass.

Prayer will be costly

When God encounters you, you face a crisis of belief that may require major adjustments in your life. You need to learn how to pray. Prayer will be exceedingly costly to you. You may need to let God wake you up in the middle of the night to pray. You may need to spend much time in prayer. Times may come when you pray into the night or even all night. Becoming a person of prayer will require a major adjustment of your life to God.

Another cost will come as you try to guide the people around you to pray. Most of our churches have not learned how to pray. The greatest untapped resource that I know of is the prayer of God's people. Helping your church become a praying church will be a rewarding experience.

Is your church known in your community as a "house of prayer"? Is your church a praying church? Which of the following do you think is true? Check one.

❏ 1. Our church is widely known as a praying church.
❏ 2. Our church is becoming a praying church, but we have a long way to go.
❏ 3. Our church prays some, but not very effectively. We need to become a praying church.
❏ 4. If I were honest, I would say that our church doesn't really know how to pray. Our church needs to become a praying church.

What evidence can you give to support your answer in the last question?

_____

_____

What, if anything, do you think God wants to do through you with regard to prayer in your church?

_____

_____

Every church needs to be a praying church!

Review today's lesson. Pray and ask God to identify one or more statements or Scriptures that He wants you to understand, learn, or practice. Underline it (them). Then respond to the following:

What was the most meaningful statement or Scripture you read today?

_____

_____

Reword the statement or Scripture into a prayer of response to God.

_____

_____

_____

_____

What does God want you to do in response to today's study?

_____

_____

_____

Review your Scripture memory verses and be prepared to recite them to a partner in your small-group session this week.

SUMMARY STATEMENTS

- Obedience requires total dependence on God to work through me.
- "IT" never works! HE works!
- The key is my relationship to a Person.
- Through me He will do more in days and weeks than I could ever accomplish in years of labor. Waiting on Him is always worth the wait.
- Fervent prayer will be one of the most demanding things I ever do.
- My church needs to be a praying church!

[1]David & Naomi Shibley, _The Smoke of a Thousand Villages,_ (Nashville: Thomas Nelson Publishers, 1989), 11.

[2]Elisabeth Elliot, _Shadow of the Almighty. The Life and Testament of Jim Elliot_ (New York: Harper & Brothers Publishers, 1958), 247.

[3]Franklin Graham with Jeanette Lockerbie, _Bob Pierce, This One Thing I Do,_ (Waco, Texas: Word Books, 1983), 220.

[4]Shibley, Thousand Villages, 90.

[5]Shibley, Thousand Villages, 98.

[6]J. Hudson Taylor, A Retrospect, (Philadelphia: The China Inland Mission, n.d.), 39-40.

EXPERIENCING GOD THROUGH OBEDIENCE

Obedience Provided Future Blessing

When we were still a very small church with a Sunday School attendance of 45, we had three mission churches we were trying to staff and support. We were asked to sponsor another mission in Winnipeg, Manitoba. It was 510 miles from Saskatoon. Someone would have to drive this 1,020 mile round-trip in order to provide them a pastor. At first glance, this sounded like an impossible task for our little group.

I shared with our congregation how a faithful group of people had been meeting for more than two years. They wanted to start a Southern Baptist church. We were the closest possible sponsoring church. We had to determine whether this was God's work and whether He was revealing His work to us. Was this our invitation to join Him in what He was doing? The church agreed this was God's doing. We knew we had to obey Him. We agreed to sponsor the new mission. Then we asked God to show us how and to give us the strength and resources to do it.

I drove a number of times to Winnipeg to preach and minister to the people. Sooner than for any of our other mission churches, God provided a pastor and a salary! The story of our obedience did not end there, however. Friendship Baptist Church has become the mother church to nine other mission churches and started an entire association of churches.

When our oldest son Richard finished seminary, this church in Winnipeg called him to be their pastor. This was his first pastorate! Our second son Tom was called to be on the staff of this church to guide music, education, and youth. Little did I know that this one act of obedience—that at first appeared impossible—held such potential for future blessing for my family.

Jesus replied, "If anyone loves me, he will obey my teaching. My Father will love him, and we will come to him and make our home with him." —JOHN 14:23

Verse to Memorize This Week

You come to know God by experience as you obey Him and He accomplishes His work through you.

God has always been at work in our world. He is now at work where you are. God always will take the initiative to come to you and reveal what He is doing, or what He is about to do. When He does, this will be His invitation for you to join Him.

Joining Him will require major adjustments of your life to Him, so He can accomplish His will through you. When you know what God has said, what He is about to do, and have adjusted your life to Him, there is yet one remaining necessary response to God.

> To experience Him at work in and through you, you must obey Him. When you obey Him, He will accomplish His work through you; and you will come to know Him by experience.

This unit brings us to a focus on the last of our seven realities—You come to know God by experience as you obey Him and He accomplishes His work through you.

For review, see if you can write the seven realities in your own words using the "hints" below.

1. Work— _____

2. Love relationship— _____

_____

3. Invitation— _____

4. Speaks— _____

_____

_____

5. Crisis— _____

_____

6. Adjust— _____

_____

7. Obey— _____

_____

Check your answers on the inside back cover of the book.

Below, I have listed three actions from reality 7. Number them in the order that they occur as you follow God's will. 1=first, 2=second, 3=third.

_____a. You come to know God by experience.
_____b. You obey Him.
_____c. He accomplishes His work through you.

After God has taken the initiative to involve you in His work, you believe Him and adjust your life to Him. Only then do you get to the place of obedience. You must obey Him first. Then, He will accomplish His work through you. When God does a God-sized work through your life, you come to know Him intimately by experience. The answer to the last question is a-3, b-1, c-2. In this unit you will study each of these aspects of God's work more fully.

You Obey Him

In unit 4, day 3 (pp. 61-64) you studied the relationship between love and obedience. You found that obedience is the outward expression of your love of God (John 14:15, 24a). By way of review, here are some statements from that lesson:

- Obedience is the outward expression of your love of God.
- The reward for obedience and love is that He will reveal Himself to you.
- If you have an obedience problem, you have a love problem.

"If you love me, you will obey what I command. He who does not love me will not obey my teaching."

—John 14:15, 24

- God is love. His will is always best.
- God is all knowing. His directions are always right.
- God is all powerful. He can enable you to do His will.
- If you love Him, you will obey Him!

☼ **If, in the last few weeks, one of the above statements has influenced the way you love and obey God, briefly describe what God has been doing regarding your love and obedience.**

_____

_____

Your memory verse for this unit speaks of love and obedience. Begin memorizing it. Write it below.

_____

_____

_____

Jesus said that the one who is in intimate relationship with Him ("brother," "sister," "mother") is the one who does the will of the Heavenly Father (Matt. 12:50). Jesus clearly said that by obedience a person indicates his love relationship with God (John 14:15-21).

James in his letter to the believers went to great lengths to indicate that faith that does not obey in actions is dead, or has no life. When the disciples obeyed Jesus, they saw and experienced God's mighty power working in and around them. When they did not act in faith and do His will, they did not experience His mighty work.

In many ways, obedience is your moment of truth. What you DO will:
1. Reveal what you believe about Him.
2. Determine whether you will experience His mighty work in you and through you.
3. Determine whether you will come to know Him more intimately.

☼ **Read 1 John 2:3-6 below. Circle the word _know_ each time it occurs. Underline the words _obey_ and _obeys_. Draw a box enclosing the word _love_.**

> 1 John 2:3-6   "We know that we have come to know him if we obey his commands. The man who says, 'I know him,' but does not do what he commands is a liar, and the truth is not in him. But if anyone obeys his word, God's love is truly made complete in him. This is how we know we are in him: Whoever claims to live in him must walk as Jesus did."

1. How can you know that you have come to know God in Jesus Christ?

_____

2. What is one clear indication that a person does not know Him?

_____

3. What does God do in the life of anyone who obeys His Word?

_____

As a review from unit 4, fill in each blank in the following statements with the correct word from the following list.

force	enable	right	true	best

4. Because God is love, His will is always _____.

5. Because God is all-knowing, His directives are always _____.

6. Because God is all-powerful, He can _____.me to do His will.

When you come to a moment of truth when you must choose whether to obey God, you cannot obey Him unless you believe and trust Him. You cannot believe and trust Him, unless you love Him. You cannot love Him, unless you know Him.

Each "new" command of Jesus will require a new knowledge and understanding of Him. The Holy Spirit will teach you about Jesus, so you can trust Him and obey Him. Then you will experience Him in new ways. This is how you grow in Him. As 1 John 2:3-6 says when

---

"For whoever does the will of my Father in heaven is my brother and sister and mother."
—Matthew 12:50

"Faith without works is dead."
—James 2:20, KJV

Moment of truth

you come to know Him you will obey Him. If you do not obey Him, that indicates that you do not know Him.

Jesus stated it a different way when He said, "Not everyone who says to me, 'Lord, Lord,' will enter the kingdom of heaven, but only he who does the will of my Father who is in heaven. Many will say to me on that day, 'Lord, Lord, did we not prophesy in your name, and in your name drive out demons and perform many miracles?' Then I will tell them plainly, 'I never knew you. Away from me, you evildoers!' " (Matt. 7:21-23). Obedience is very important.

Answers to questions 4-6: 4-best, 5-right, 6-enable.

The Importance of Obedience

When He gives you a directive, you are to obey it.

If you know that God loves you, you should never question a directive from Him. It will always be right and best. When He gives you a directive, you are not just to observe it, discuss it, or debate it. You are to obey it.

> **Read the following Scriptures and circle the word *obey* in each. Answer the question that follows.**

Deuteronomy 28:1, 8 "If you fully obey the Lord your God and carefully follow all his commands I give you today, the Lord your God will set you high above all the nations on earth. . . . The Lord will send a blessing on your barns and on everything you put your hand to."

Deuteronomy 28:15, 20 "If you do not obey the Lord your God and do not carefully follow all his commands and decrees I am giving you today . . . The Lord will send on you curses, confusion and rebuke in everything you put your hand to, until you are destroyed and come to sudden ruin because of the evil you have done in forsaking him."

How important is obedience? _____

_____

_____

List some of the benefits of obedience found in the following Scriptures .

Jeremiah 7:23 "Obey me, and I will be your God and you will be my people. Walk in all the ways I command you, that it may go well with you."

Benefit of obedience: _____

Luke 6:46-49 "Why do you call me, 'Lord, Lord,' and do not do what I say? I will show you what he is like who comes to me and hears my words and puts them into practice. He is like a man building a house, who dug down deep and laid the foundation on rock. When a flood came, the torrent struck that house but could not shake it, because it was well built. But the one who hears my words and does not put them into practice is like a man who built a house on the ground without a foundation. The moment the torrent struck that house, it collapsed and its destruction was complete."

Benefit of obedience: _____

John 7:16-17 "Jesus answered, 'My teaching is not my own. It comes from him who sent me. If anyone chooses to do God's will, he will find out whether my teaching comes from God.' "

Benefit of obedience: _____

God blesses those who are obedient to Him (Deut. 28:1-14). The benefits of obedience are beyond our imagination; but they include being God's people (Jer. 7:23), having a solid foundation when the storms of life come against you (Luke 6:46-49), and knowing spiritual truth (John 7:16-17).

Disobedience is serious.

Rebellion against God is the opposite of obedience. Disobedience is a serious rejection of God's will. Deuteronomy 28:15-68 speaks of some of the costs of disobedience. (For further study on the results of obedience and disobedience see Deut. 30 and 32.)

※ **How do you think God would describe your level of obedience?**

_____

What (if anything) do you know God wants you to do that you are not doing?

_____

Consider this prayer for your own life:

> Teach me, O Lord, to follow your decrees;
> then I will keep them to the end.
> Give me understanding, and I will keep your law
> and obey it with all my heart.
> Direct me in the path of your commands,
> for there I find delight.
> —Psalm 119:33-35

※ **Review today's lesson. Pray and ask God to identify one or more statements or Scriptures that He wants you to understand, learn, or practice. Underline it (them). Then respond to the following:**

What was the most meaningful statement or Scripture you read today?

_____

_____

Reword the statement or Scripture into a prayer of response to God.

_____

_____

What does God want you to do in response to today's study?

_____

_____

SUMMARY STATEMENTS

- I come to know God by experience as I obey Him and He accomplishes His work through me.
- If I love God, I will obey Him.
- Obedience is the outward expression of my love of God.
- Faith that does not obey in actions is dead.
- Obedience is my moment of truth.
- God blesses those who are obedient to Him.

OBEDIENCE, PART 2

Obedience means joy and uninterrupted fellowship with God.

Servants of God do what He directs. They obey Him. The servant does not have the option to decide whether he wants to obey or not. Choosing not to obey is rebellion, and such disobedience will bring serious consequences.

What Is Obedience?

Many people today are so self-centered they want to do their own "thing." They do not stop to consider what obedience may mean in their lives. Jesus told a parable about obedience:

> What do you think? There was a man who had two sons. He went to the first and said, "Son, go and work today in the vineyard."
> "I will not," he answered, but later he changed his mind and went.

Then the father went to the other son and said the same thing. He answered, "I will, sir," but he did not go.

—Matthew 21:28-30

Which son did the will of his father? Circle one: First Son   Second Son

What is the meaning of obedience? Check one.
❏ 1. Saying you will do what is commanded.
❏ 2. Doing what is commanded.

At the end of each day's lesson, you have been asked this question: "What does God want you to do in response to today's study?" I want you to look back at your re-sponses to that question for each lesson. Keep in mind that some of the things you have listed may be long-term commitments. Pray before you begin this review and ask God to help you see your overall pattern of obedience or disobedience. Then review your responses to the last question at the end of each day. Mentally answer these two questions about each day's response:

1. Do I believe God clearly guided me to respond to the study that way?
2. Have I done all God has asked me to do up to this time?

Do not proceed until you have completed your review.

Now, respond to the following. If you do not have an answer or response, go on to the next item.

A. What is one command or instruction you have obeyed?

_____

B. What is one long-term instruction to which you have only just begun your obedience?

_____

C. What is one response that probably was YOUR idea and *not* God's directive?

_____

D. What is one command you have not obeyed?

_____

E. Below is a scale from 0—Complete Disobedience to 10—Perfect Obedience (Only Jesus would qualify for a 10!). Place an X to indicate how you think GOD would rate your life of obedience since you began studying this course.

Complete   0——1——2——3——4——5——6——7——8——9——10   Perfect
Disobedience   Obedience

F. Why do you think He would rate you at that level?

_____

_____

G. If there is a level of disobedience, what do you sense is the root cause?

_____

_____

If this has not been a positive experience, don't despair. Let God use this time of evaluation to draw you back to Himself—into a relationship of loving obedience. God is interested in moving you from where you are to where He wants you to be in this love relationship. From that point you can experience all the joys that He has to offer.

Obey What You Already Know to Be God's Will

Some people want God to give them an assignment to do for Him. They vow that they will do whatever He asks. But when God observes their lives, He notices they have not obeyed in the things He already has told them to do.

Do you think God would give new assignments to a servant who will not obey? Yes ❏   No ❏   I don't know ❏

When God gives you Ten Commandments, are you obeying them? When Jesus tells you to love your enemies, are you doing that? When Jesus tells your church to make disciples of all nations, are you doing all you know to obey Him? When God tells you through Scripture to live in unity with your Christian brothers and sisters, are you doing it?

God's commands are not given to you so you can pick and choose the ones you want to obey and forget about the rest. He wants you to obey *all* His commands out of your love relationship with Him. When He sees you are faithful and obedient in a little, He will be able to trust you with more. The Holy Spirit will guide you daily to the specific commands God wants you to obey.

God's commands

Second Chances

Frequently, people will ask me the question, "When a person disobeys God's will, does God give him or her a second chance?"

Read Jonah 1:1-17 and answer these questions:

Jonah

1. What did God ask Jonah to do? (v. 2) _____

2. How did Jonah respond? (v. 3) _____

3. Then how did God respond to Jonah? (vv. 4-17) _____

_____

Now read Jonah 2:9—3:10 and answer these questions:

4. When God gave Jonah a second chance, how did Jonah respond? (3:3)

_____

5. When Jonah obeyed God, what did God do through Jonah's ministry? (3:4-10)

_____

I am comforted to know that God often gives a second chance. When God had a plan to call Nineveh to repentance, He asked Jonah to join Him in His work. Jonah disobeyed because he was prejudiced against these "pagan enemies." Jonah would have rather seen God carry out the destruction of the city. Disobedience to God is very serious. Jonah went through the trauma of being thrown into a raging sea and spending three days in the belly of a big fish. Jonah confessed and repented of His disobedience. Then God gave him a second chance to obey.

God often gives a second chance.

The second time Jonah did obey (though reluctantly). On his first day Jonah preached a one-sentence message, and God used the message to call 120,000 people to repentance. Jonah said, "I knew that you are a gracious and compassionate God, slow to anger and abounding in love, a God who relents from sending calamity" (Jonah 4:2). God's response to Jonah and Nineveh taught Jonah much about how deeply God cares for all peoples and wants them to come to repentance.

Some of the great people of God were broken by sin and disobedience, yet God did not give up on them. If God allowed people only one mistake, Moses would never have come to be the person he was. He made several mistakes (for example, Ex. 2:11-15). Abraham started out with a great walk of faith, but He went into Egypt and blew it—more than once (for example, Gen. 12:10-20). David muffed it (for example, 2 Sam. 11), and so did Peter (for example, Matt. 26:69-75). Saul (Paul) even began his "service for God" by persecuting Christians (Acts 9:1-2).

God does not give up on you.

Disobedience Is Costly

Disobedience, however, is never taken lightly by God. You read how Jonah's disobedience almost cost him his life. Moses' murder of the Egyptian cost him 40 years in the wilderness. David's sin with Bathsheba cost the life of his son. Paul's early ministry was greatly hindered because of his disobedience. Many people were afraid to get near him because of his reputation as a persecutor of Christians.

God is interested in developing your character. At times He lets you proceed, but He will never let you go too far without discipline to bring you back. In your relationship with God, He may let you make a wrong decision. Then the Spirit of God causes you to recognize that it is not God's will. He guides you back to the right path. He will clarify what He wants. He

God is interested in developing your character.

will even take the circumstance of your disobedience and work that together for good (Rom. 8:28) as He corrects you and teaches you His ways.

Nadab and Abihu disobeyed

Even though God forgives and often gives second chances, you must not take disobedience lightly. Sometimes He does not give a second chance. Aaron's two sons, Nadab and Abihu, were disobedient in offering unholy incense to the Lord; and God struck them dead (Lev. 10).

Moses stole God's glory

Moses stole God's glory in front of all Israel and struck the rock saying, "Listen, you rebels, must we bring you water out of this rock?" (Num. 20:10). Notice the word "we." God was the One who would bring water from the rock. Moses took God's glory, and God refused to take away the consequences of that disobedience. He refused to allow Moses to go with Israel into the Promised Land.

Mark the following statements as T (true) or F (false).

_____1. God never gives second chances.

_____2. When God forgives the sin of disobedience, He also removes all the consequences of the sin.

_____3. God can take the circumstances of disobedience and work them together for good for those who love Him.

_____4. God is interested in developing your character.

_____5. Disobedience can be very costly.

_____6. God does not always remove the consequences of sin.

God loves you. He wants what is the very best for you. That is why He gives you the commands and instructions He does. His commands are not to limit or restrict you but to free you to experience the most meaningful life possible. Answers to the true and false questions: 1 and 2 are False. The others are true.

Obedience means joy and uninterrupted fellowship with God. A hymn by John H. Sammis reminds us of the relationship between obedience and fellowship with God:

Trust and obey

> When we walk with the Lord In the Light of His Word
>   What a glory He sheds on our way!
> While we do His good will, He abides with us still,
>   And with all who will trust and obey.
> But we never can prove The delights of His love
>   Until all on the altar we lay;
> For the favor He shows And the joy He bestows
>   Are for them who will trust and obey.
> Then in fellowship sweet We will sit at His feet
>   Or we'll walk by His side in the way;
> What He says we will do, Where He sends we will go;
>   Never fear, only trust and obey.
> *Trust and obey, for there's no other way*
>   *To be happy in Jesus, But to trust and obey.*

Affirmation

A sign for Moses

When we hear God invite us to join Him, we often want a sign: "Lord, prove to me this is you, and then I will obey." When Moses stood before the burning bush and received his invitation to join God, God told him that he would receive a sign that God sent him. God told Moses, "This will be the sign to you that it is I who have sent you: When you have brought the people out of Egypt, you will worship God on this mountain" (Ex. 3:12). In other words: "Moses, you obey me. I will deliver Israel through you. You will come to know me as your Deliverer, and you will stand on this Mountain and worship Me." God's affirmation that He had sent Moses was going to come after Moses obeyed, not before. This is most frequently the case in Scripture. The affirmation comes after the obedience.

God is love. Trust Him and believe Him. Because you love Him, obey Him. Then you will so fellowship with Him that you will come to know Him intimately. That affirmation will be a joyous time for you!

※ **Review today's lesson. Pray and ask God to identify one or more statements or Scriptures that He wants you to understand, learn, or practice. Underline it (them). Then respond to the following:**

What was the most meaningful statement or Scripture you read today?

_____

_____

Reword the statement or Scripture into a prayer of response to God.

_____

_____

What does God want you to do in response to today's study?

_____

_____

SUMMARY STATEMENTS

- Obedience is doing what is commanded.
- I should obey what I already know to be God's will.
- When God sees I am faithful and obedient in a little, He will be able to trust me with more.
- God often gives second chances.
- Sometimes He does not give a second chance.
- Disobedience is costly.
- God is interested in developing my character.
- Affirmation comes after the obedience.

GOD WORKS THROUGH YOU

DAY 3

You, too, will be blessed when God does a special, God-sized work through you.

When you obey God, He will accomplish through you what He has purposed to do. When God does something through your life that only He can do, you will come to know Him more intimately. If you do not obey, you will miss out on some of the most exciting experiences of your life.

When God purposes to do something through you, the assignment will have God-sized dimensions. This is because God wants to reveal Himself to you and those around you. If you can do the work in your own strength, people will not come to know God. However, if God works through you to do what only He can do, you and those around you will come to know Him.

Today's lesson is related to your study in unit 7. The God-sized dimensions of an assignment from God create the crisis of belief. You have to believe that God is who He says He is and that He can and will do what He says He will do. When you obey Him, you have to allow Him to do what He has said. He is the one who accomplishes the assignment, but He does it through you.

※ **Read the following statements from unit 7 and check the ones that have been especially meaningful to you.**
- ❑ When God invites you to join Him in His work, He has a God-sized assignment for you.
- ❑ When God calls you to join Him in a God-sized task, faith is always required.
- ❑ When you face a crisis of belief, what you do next reveals what you really believe about God.
- ❑ Faith is in a Person.
- ❑ Faith is confidence that what God has promised or said *will* come to pass.

❑ When God speaks, He always reveals what He is going to do—not what He wants you to do for Him.

❑ If you have faith in the God who called you, you will obey Him; and He will bring to pass what He has purposed to do.

❑ Obedience indicates your faith in God.

❑ With faith, you can proceed confidently to obey Him; because you know that He is going to bring to pass what He purposes.

Briefly describe one thing God has done to bring meaning to your life regarding God-sized tasks, faith, and/or obedience.

_____

_____

_____

Moses Obeyed and God Accomplished . . .

Moses obeyed

Only in the act of obedience did Moses begin to experience the full nature of God. What he began to know about God grew out of his obedience to God. In Moses' life we can see this pattern of God speaking, Moses obeying, and God accomplishing what He purposed to do.

 Read the following Scriptures and answer the questions for each.

Exodus 7:1-6

1. What was Moses commanded to do? (v. 2) _____

2. What did God say He was going to do? (v. 4) _____

3. What would be the result when Moses obeyed and God did what He said? (v. 5)

_____

Exodus 8:16-19

4. What did God command Moses and Aaron to do? (v. 16) _____

5. How did Moses and Aaron respond? (v. 17) _____

6. Who turned the dust into gnats? Moses and Aaron ❑ or God ❑ (v. 19) Check one.

A pattern of God's working

We see this pattern throughout Moses' life:

• God invited Moses to join Him in what He was doing to deliver Israel.
• God told Moses what he was to do.
• Moses obeyed.
• God accomplished what He purposed to do.
• Moses and those around him came to know God more clearly and intimately.

When the people stood between the Red Sea and the oncoming Egyptian army, God told Moses to hold his staff over the sea. Moses obeyed. God parted the sea and the people crossed on dry ground (Ex. 14:1-25). Then Miriam led the people in a hymn of praise describing their new understanding of God.

When the people were thirsty and had no water to drink they complained to Moses. God told Moses to strike a rock with the staff. Moses obeyed, and God caused water to flow from the rock (Ex. 17:1-7). We see this pattern in Moses' life again and again.

 The stages in this pattern of God's working through Moses are in the wrong order below. Number them in the correct order from 1 to 5.

_____a. Moses and those around him came to know God more clearly and intimately.

_____b. Moses obeyed.

_____c. God told Moses what he was to do.

_____d. God accomplished what He purposed to do.

_____e. God invited Moses to join Him in what He was doing to deliver Israel.

When Noah obeyed, God preserved his family and repopulated the earth. When Abraham obeyed, God gave him a son and built a nation. When David obeyed, God made him a king. When Elijah obeyed, God sent down fire and consumed a sacrifice. These people of faith came to know God by experience when they obeyed Him and He accomplished His work through them. Moses came to know God through experience as he obeyed God. The correct order of stages in the pattern of God's working with Moses is: e, c, b, d, a.

The Disciples Obeyed and God Accomplished . . .

Luke records a beautiful experience of Jesus's disciples that follows this same pattern. Jesus invited 70 (72, NIV) to join Him in the Father's work. They obeyed and experienced God doing through them something they knew only God could do.

70 disciples sent out

Read Luke 10:1-24 and answer the following questions.

1. What did Jesus command the 70 followers to do?

In verse 2? _____

In verses 5 and 7? _____

_____

In verse 8? _____

In verse 9? _____

_____

2. What does verse 16 indicate about the relationship between servants and the Master, between the 70 and Jesus?

_____

_____

3. How do you think the 70 felt about their experience? (v. 17)

_____

4. What do you think the 70 came to know about God through this experience?

_____

Jesus gave these followers some specific directions. They obeyed Him and experienced God working through them to heal and cast out demons. Jesus told them that their own salvation ought to bring more joy than the submission of the spirits (v. 20). Jesus praised God the Father for revealing Himself to these followers (vv. 21-22). Then Jesus turned to His disciples and said, "Blessed are the eyes that see what you see. For I tell you that many prophets and kings wanted to see what you see but did not see it, and to hear what you hear but did not hear it" (Luke 10:23-24).

These disciples were blessed. They had been chosen especially by God to be involved in His work. What they saw, heard, and came to know about God was something even prophets and kings wanted to experience and did not. These disciples were blessed!

The disciples were blessed.

You, too, will be blessed when God does a special, God-sized work through you. You will come to know Him in a way that will bring rejoicing to your life. When other people see you experiencing God that way, they are going to want to know how they too can experience God that way. Be prepared to point them to God.

God-sized work through you.

Has God done something recently through you that has caused you to rejoice? Yes ❏   No ❏ If so, briefly describe it.

_____

_____

If you are obedient, God will work some wonderful things through you. You will need to be very careful that any testimony about what God has done only gives glory to Him. Pride may cause you to want to tell your experience because it makes you feel special. That will be a continuing tension. You will want to declare the wonderful deeds of the Lord, but you must avoid any sense of pride. Therefore:

"Let him who boasts boast in the Lord" (1 Cor. 1:31).

Review today's lesson. Pray and ask God to identify one or more statements or Scriptures that He wants you to understand, learn, or practice. Underline it (them). Then respond to the following:

What was the most meaningful statement or Scripture you read today?

_____

_____

Reword the statement or Scripture into a prayer of response to God.

_____

_____

What does God want you to do in response to today's study?

_____

_____

Practice quoting or writing your Scripture memory verses.

SUMMARY STATEMENTS

- When I obey God, He will accomplish through me what He has purposed to do.
- God wants to reveal Himself to me and those around me.
- I will be blessed when God does a special, God-sized work through me.
- I need to be very careful that any testimony about what God has done only gives glory to Him.
- "Let him who boasts boast in the Lord" (1 Cor. 1:31).

God reveals Himself to His people by what He does.

YOU COME TO KNOW GOD

God reveals Himself to His people by what He does. When God works through you to accomplish His purposes, you come to know God by experience. You also come to know God when He meets a need in your life. In unit 4 you learned that in Scripture God's names indicate how He has revealed Himself to humanity.

As a review, turn to page 57 and read "Knowing God by Experience" and "Names of God."
How does God reveal Himself to us? How do we come to know God?

_____

_____

In Scripture when God did something through an obedient person or people, they came to know Him in new and more intimate ways. (For more examples see Judg. 6:24; Ps. 23:1; Jer. 23:6; Ex. 31:13.) God revealed His personal name to Moses, "I AM WHO I AM" (Ex. 3:14). When God "became flesh and made his dwelling among us" (John 1:14), Jesus expressed Himself to His disciples by saying:

The I am's of Jesus

"I am the bread of life" (John 6:35).
"I am the light of the world" (John 8:12).
"I am the gate" (John 10:9).
"I am the good shepherd" (John 10:11).
"I am the resurrection and the life" (John 11:25).
"I am the way and the truth and the life" (John 14:6).
"I am the true vine" (John 15:1).

Jesus identified Himself with the I AM (name of God given to Moses at the burning bush) of the Old Testament. Knowing and experiencing Jesus in these ways requires that you "believe in Him" (have faith in Him). For instance, when He says to you, "I am the way," what you do next in your relationship with Him will determine if you come to experience Him as "the way" in your own life. When you believe Him, adjust your life to Him, and obey what

He says next, you come to know and experience Him as "the Way." This is true about everything God reveals to you day by day.

☀ **Using the names, titles, and descriptions of God in Appendix A (p. 220), list below some names by which you have come to know God by experience.**

_____

_____

_____

_____

_____

_____

Which name of God is most precious or meaningful to you at this point in your life?

_____

Use the remainder of this day in a time of prayer and thanksgiving to God for what He has revealed to you about Himself. You may want to use the helps on pages 60-61 to guide this into a time of worship and adoration of the Lord.

After your time of prayer and worship, write a description of how you have come to know God by experience during this course of study.

_____

_____

_____

_____

QUESTIONS AND ANSWERS

DAY 5

For a little change of pace, let's look at some questions related to this unit that I am commonly asked. Perhaps these are questions you, too, have been asking.

Q: Why does God seem to be working so slowly in my life?

Jesus had been with His disciples about three years when He said, "I have much more to say to you, more than you can now bear. But when he, the Spirit of truth, comes, he will guide you into all truth. He will not speak on his own; he will speak only what he hears, and he will tell you what is yet to come" (John 16:12-13). He had more He needed to teach them, but they were not ready to receive it. Jesus knew, however, that the Holy Spirit would continue to guide these disciples into truth on God's time table.

You may be saying, "God, hurry up and make me mature."

And God is saying, "I'm moving just as fast in your life as you will allow me. When you are ready for your next lesson, I will bring a new truth into your life."

☀ **Ask yourself these questions:**

- Am I responding to all God already is leading me to do?
- Have I obeyed all I already know to be His will?
- Do I really believe that He loves me and will always do what is best and right?
- Am I willing to patiently wait on His timing, and obey everything I know to do in the meantime?

Why do you think God sometimes works slowly in a person's life as He matures him or her?

_____

God will never give me an assignment that He will not enable me to complete.

*Allow God to take all
the time He needs.*

Grass that is here today and gone tomorrow does not require much time to mature. A big oak tree that lasts for generations requires much more time to grow and mature. God is concerned about your life through eternity. Allow Him to take all the time He needs to shape you for His purposes. Larger assignments will require longer periods of preparation.

Would you be willing for God to take all the time He needs to prepare you for the assignments He may have purposed for your life? If so, write out a prayer to Him.

_____

_____

_____

Q: Why doesn't God give me a big assignment?

God might say to you, "You are asking Me to involve you in my great movements, but I am trying to get you simply to understand how to believe Me. I can't give you that assignment yet." God has to lay some basic foundations in your life before He can prepare you for the larger tasks.

Have you ever said something like, "Lord, if You just give me a great assignment, I will serve You for all I am worth"?

God might respond, "I really want to, but I can't. If I were to put you into that kind of assignment, you would never be able to handle it. You are just not ready."

Are you able?

Then you may argue, "Lord, I am able. I can handle it, just try me." Do you remember any of the disciples who thought they were able to handle a bigger assignment?

Trust Him.

On the night before Jesus' crucifixion Peter said, "Lord, I am ready to go with you to prison and to death." Jesus answered, "I tell you, Peter, before the rooster crows today, you will deny three times that you know me." (Luke 22:33-34). Is it possible that He also knows exactly what you would do? Trust Him. Do not insist that God give you something that you think you are ready for. That could lead to your ruin.

God is far more interested in accomplishing His kingdom purposes than you are. He will move you into every assignment that He knows you are ready for.

How do you think you should respond when God has not given you the kind of assignment you want?

_____

_____

Let God orient you to Himself. The servant does not tell the Master what kind of assignment he needs. The servant waits on his Master for the assignment. So be patient and wait. Waiting on the Lord should not be an idle time for you. Let God use times of waiting to mold and shape your character. Let God use those times to purify your life and make you into a clean vessel for His service.

*Any assignment from God is
an important assignment.*

As you obey Him, God will prepare you for the assignment that is just right for you. Any assignment, however, that comes from the Maker of the universe is an important assignment. Don't use human standards to measure the importance or value of an assignment.

Q: What is happening when I obey and the "doors" close?

Suppose you sense the call of God to a task, or to a place, or to an assignment. You set about to do it and everything goes wrong. Often people will say, "Well, I guess that just was not God's will."

God calls you into a relationship with himself. Be very careful how you interpret circumstances. Many times we jump to a conclusion too quickly. God is moving us in one direction to tell us what He is about to do. We immediately jump to our own conclusion about what He is doing because our conclusion sounds so logical. We start following the logic of our own reasoning and then nothing seems to work out. We have a tendency to leave the relationship and take things into our own hands. Don't do that.

Most of the time when God calls you or gives a direction, His call is not what He wants you to do for Him. He is telling you what He is about to do where you are. For instance, God told Paul that He was going to reach the Gentiles through him. God, not Paul, was going to reach the Gentiles. Paul started to go in one direction and the Spirit stopped him (Acts 16:6-10). He started to go another direction. Again, the Spirit stopped him. What was the original plan of God? To reach the Gentiles. What was Paul's problem? He was trying to figure out what he ought to do, and the "door" of opportunity closed. Did the door close? No. God was trying to say, "Listen to me, Paul. Go and sit in Troas until I tell you where you are supposed to go."

In Troas Paul had the vision to go over to Macedonia and help them. What was happening? God's plan was to turn the gospel to the west toward Greece and Rome. God was at work in Philippi and wanted Paul to join Him.

When you begin to follow and circumstances *seem* to close doors of opportunity, go back to the Lord and clarify what God said. Better yet, always try to make sure on the front end of a sense of call exactly what God is saying. He most often is not calling you to a task, but a relationship. Through that relationship He is going to do something through your life. If you start off in a direction and everything is stopped, go back and clarify what God has said. Do not deny what God has said, clarify what God has said.

☀ **Read the following illustration about a couple that sensed God's call to student work. Watch for instructions on what to do when you begin to move in the direction you sense God is leading and circumstances "close the door." Underline or circle the instructions. I have circled one for you.**

I talked with a wonderful couple who said they were invited to go to Saskatoon to do student work. They started the process for assignment as missionaries and the Missions Board said, "No."

Their conclusion was: "Then, we made a mistake." I advised them not to jump to that conclusion, but to go back and recall what God said when they sensed His call. They were canceling the whole plan of God, because one detail did not work out as they thought it would.

I asked them to go back and clarify what God had called them to do. Was He calling them to missions? Was He calling them to student work? Was He calling them to Canada? They did sense God was calling them to Canada and student work.

Then, I said, "Keep that sense of call in place. Because one door closed don't assume that the assignment is over. Watch to see how the God who called you is going to implement what He said. When God speaks a word of direction, He will bring it to pass. Be very careful that you do not let circumstances cancel what God said."

God may have a different city in mind for them. He may want them to have a different means of financial support. Or He may need more time to prepare them for the assignment. Let Him work out the details in His timing. In the meantime, do all you know to do, then wait for the next word of instruction.

☀ **What are some of the things you would do when faced with a circumstance that seemed to close the door on God's will.**

_____

_____

_____

_____

When things seem to go wrong after you take a step of obedience:
• Clarify what God said and identify what may have been your "additions" to what He said.
• Keep in place what God has said.
• Let Him work out the details in His timing.
• Do all you know to do.
• Then wait on the Lord until He tells you what to do next.

"Paul and his companions traveled throughout the region of Phrygia and Galatia, having been kept by the Holy Spirit from preaching the word in the province of Asia. When they came to the border of Mysia, they tried to enter Bithynia, but the Spirit of Jesus would not allow them to. So they passed by Mysia and went down to Troas. During the night Paul had a vision of a man of Macedonia standing and begging him, 'Come over to Macedonia and help us.' After Paul had seen the vision, we got ready at once to leave for Macedonia, concluding that God had called us to preach the gospel to them."
—Acts 16:6-10

Clarify what God said.

When things seem to go wrong . . .

The God who initiates His work in a relationship with you is the One Himself who guarantees to complete it.

God's greatest single task is to get His people adjusted to Himself. He needs time to shape us until we are exactly what He wants us to be. Suppose you sense that God is going to do something great because of what He has said in His Word and prayer. You sense He is going to do it because of the way circumstances are working out and other believers (church) agree. Then six months pass and you still haven't seen anything great. Don't get negative and depressed and discouraged. Watch to see what God is doing in you and in the people around you to prepare you for what He is going to do. The key is your relationship with God.

Q: How can I know whether the word I receive is from God, my own selfish desires, or Satan?

Some people go to much trouble studying Satan's ways so they can identify when something appears to be a deception of Satan. I don't do that. I have determined not to focus on Satan. He is defeated. The One who is guiding me, the One who is presently implementing His will through me is the Victor. The only way Satan can effect God's work through me is when I believe Satan and disbelieve God. Satan always will try to deceive you. Satan cannot ultimately thwart what God purposes to do.

Read the following illustration and see if you can make an application to your spiritual life.

The Mounties and counterfeit money

Royal Canadian Mounted Police, the Mounties, train men in anti-counterfeiting work. They never let a trainee see a counterfeit bill. They know only one genuine type of ten-dollar bill exists. They so thoroughly study the genuine bill that anything that does not measure up to that is counterfeit.

You can't imagine all the ways people can counterfeit money. But Mounties don't study how people counterfeit money. They just study the real thing. Anything that doesn't measure up to that is fake.

When you are faced with a sense of direction, you may ask yourself, "Is this God, me, or Satan." How can you prepare yourself to know clearly a Word from God?

_____

_____

_____

Jesus quoted the last word He had from the Father.

How should you approach spiritual warfare with Satan? Know the ways of God so thoroughly that if something doesn't measure up to God's ways, turn away from it. That's what Jesus did in the temptations. In essence Jesus just quietly said, "I understand what you are saying, Satan; but that is not the last word I had from God. The Scriptures say . . . " (See Matt. 4:1-11.) Jesus never discussed it with Satan. He never analyzed it. He just kept doing the last thing God told Him to do until God Himself told Him what to do next.

Q: Does God Have One Plan for My Life For Eternity?

God's plan is for a relationship.

Does God plan your life for eternity and then turn you loose to work out His plan? God's plan is for a relationship. We get in trouble when we try to get God to tell us if He wants us to be a Christian business person, a music director, an education director, a preacher, or a missionary. We want to know if He wants us to serve in our home country or go to Japan or Canada. God doesn't usually give you a one-time assignment and leave you there forever. Yes, you may be placed in one job at one place for a long time; but God's assignments come to you on a daily basis.

He calls you to a relationship where He is Lord—where you are willing to do and be anything He chooses. If you will respond to Him as Lord, He may lead you to do and be things you would have never dreamed of. If you don't follow Him as Lord, you may lock yourself into a job or an assignment and miss something God wants to do through you. I've heard people say things like: "God called me to be a . . . , so this other thing couldn't possibly be

His will." Or "My spiritual gift is. . . so this ministry couldn't be God's will for me."

God will never give you an assignment that He will not, at the same time, enable you to complete it. That is what a spiritual gift is—a supernatural empowering to accomplish the assignment God gives you. Don't focus on your talents, abilities, and interests in determining God's will. I have heard so many people say, "I would really like to do that; therefore, it must be God's will." That kind of response is self-centered. You need to become God-centered. When He is Lord, your response should be something like this:

> *Lord, I will do anything that your kingdom requires of me. Wherever you want me to be, I'll go. Whatever the circumstances, I'm willing to follow. If you want to meet a need through my life, I am your servant; and I will do whatever is required.*

Suppose a teenager in your church were to come to you for counsel. He says, "I think God may be calling me to the ministry. Can you tell me how to know whether I should be a pastor, missionary, or minister of education? I want to be very careful. I don't want to miss God's plan for my life!"

How would you respond? List or outline what you would say.

_____

_____

_____

_____

Did you point him to God's plan as a relationship, not just a job description? Did you help him see his need to submit to Christ's lordship on a daily basis? I trust you would have been able to help him to a God-centered approach to knowing and doing God's will.

Review today's lesson. Pray and ask God to identify one or more statements or Scriptures that He wants you to understand, learn, or practice. Underline it (them). Then respond to the following:

What was the most meaningful statement or Scripture you read today?

_____

_____

Reword the statement or Scripture into a prayer of response to God.

_____

_____

What does God want you to do in response to today's study?

_____

_____

Review your Scripture memory verses and be prepared to recite them to a partner in your small-group session this week.

SUMMARY STATEMENTS

- I will allow Him to take all the time He needs to shape me for His purposes.
- Any assignment that comes from the Maker of the universe is an important assignment.
- God calls me to a relationship.
- I won't leave the relationship and take things into my own hands.
- Let Him work out the details in His timing.
- Know the ways of God so thoroughly that if something doesn't measure up to God's ways, I will know it is not from Him and turn away from it.
- God will never give me an assignment that He will not enable me to complete.

GOD'S WILL AND THE CHURCH

IVAH BATES WAS A KNEE

I've mentioned Ivah Bates before. She was a widow who had lived on a farm and was retired. She was one of the greatest prayers I have ever known. Our church was the body of Christ, and we called Ivah a knee. God put her in the body as a powerful prayer.

When we had new believers, I would send them over to Ivah and let her talk to them about how to pray. She equipped many prayers. When we began our ministry to the university campus, Ivah didn't know how to function in the body concerning the campus. Who was to equip her to function in the body in this new ministry? Well, our campus minister was. He shared with Ivah how she could pray regarding the campus. She did not change her role in the body. She just learned how to be the "knee" (prayer) for the campus. The students were told, "Whenever you are going to witness to somebody or you have a particular assignment in our ministry, go to Ivah and tell her about it. She will pray."

So a student named Wayne said to Ivah, "Next Tuesday I will be witnessing to Doug, would you pray for me?" Ivah agreed. She dropped everything and began to pray over the noon hour while Wayne was witnessing. She did that every time the students told her what they were doing. Only the "hand" was touching the campus, but the whole body was fitly joined together. Each part functioned where God put it, so that the hand could be effective.

About three months later, a young man came down the aisle during the invitation. He was trusting the Lord. I said to the congregation, "This is Doug. He has just become a Christian." I looked over at Ivah and she was deeply moved and weeping. She had never met Doug, but she had prayed for him for three months.

Who won Doug to the Lord? The body did!

Verse to Memorize
This Week

In Christ we who are many form one body, and each member belongs to all the others.   —ROMANS 12:5

Church members need to be taught how to walk with God. They need to know how to hear Him speaking. They need to be able to identify things that only God can do. As pastor, I was responsible for that. During the first year of my ministry as a pastor, I took time to find out what God had been doing before I got there. Then it took me time to lead the people into the kind of relationship with God so that they understood what a church was and how it was to function.

In the Bible, God gave vision and enabled the spiritual leaders He called. These leaders then led the people. Their walk with God and sensitivity to what God was doing among the people was crucial. A picture of this pattern is seen in Acts 6.

Perhaps one of the greatest challenges for Christianity in our day is for churches to so walk with God that the world comes to know Him through their witness. When a church allows God's presence and activity to be expressed, a watching world will be drawn to Him. How can your church be that kind of church? First you must come to understand who you are in relation to God and each other.

1. A church is a creation of Christ. He builds His church (Matt. 16:18) using Spirit-directed pastors and leaders (Eph. 4:11-13), and arranges the members in it according to His will (1 Cor. 12:18). Therefore, spiritual leaders and members should have respect for the pastor and every member God has placed in their church.
2. A church is a living body of Christ with many members (1 Cor. 12:27). The church is not a building or an organization. It is a group of people built up into a living body.
3. A church is uniquely related to Christ as Head of the body (Eph. 1:22; 4:15-16). All matters in a church are to come under His lordship.
4. Members of a church are uniquely related to every other member of the church (Eph. 4:11-16; 1 Cor. 12). All members are interdependent on one another. All members need each other.
5. A church is on mission with Christ in our world carrying out the Father's redemptive purpose (Matt. 28:18-20; 2 Cor. 5:17-20). "We are God's fellow workers" (1 Cor. 3:9).

In each of the following pairs of statements, one is human-centered and one is God-centered. Check the God-centered statements.

❑ 1a. An effective church is built by strong leadership, active participation of the laity, and good organization.
❑ b. Christ builds His church through the Holy-Spirit-empowered service of the pastor, other spiritual leaders, and members of His body.
❑ 2a. Jesus Christ gives life to the church, which is His living body.
❑ b. A church is a group of people who have been effectively organized into an institution in a local community.
❑ 3a. Every church needs a CEO and Board of Directors.
❑ b. Christ is Head of the church.
❑ 4a. When the church gathers together, members experience God at work in the body through the lives of other members.
❑ b. Church attendance is important to show our support for the organization.
❑ 5a. A church watches to see where God is at work and joins Him in His redemptive mission.
❑ b. A church sets worthy and reachable goals and members give their best to achieve them.

The God-centered statements are 1-b, 2-a, 3-b, 4-a, 5-a. God does work through the pastor, other spiritual leaders, and people in the church to accomplish His purposes. Many statements that are commonly used around churches indicate, however, that often we are very human-centered in our religious work. We give our human intelligence and abilities far more credit than they are due. God is the One who gets the glory rightfully due Him for Kingdom work.

Being More Important than *Doing*

Just like individuals, churches are often more interested in what God wants them to do than what He wants them to be. Being the kind of people that please God is far more important than doing something for Him. Yes, God does want a church to obey Him by doing what He asks. Yet, He is not interested in a church violating His commands in order to get a task done. Can you imagine how God must feel when a church splits out of hatred for each other, because one group wanted to do something for God and the other group refused?

What do you think? Circle your opinion below.

1. God wants a church to complete an assigned task even if it brings about a major division.   Yes   or   No?

2. God wants His people to demonstrate love above all else.   Yes   or   No?

3. As long as a church is doing God's work, they can do it in ways that are unethical or illegal.   Yes   or   No?

For some people these are tough questions. Individuals often think that a work for God can be done with whatever means are necessary. They don't hesitate to violate God's written will in order to accomplish something they think is His will. God is interested in His people being holy, clean, and pure. He is interested in the unity of the church—"there should be no division in the body" (1 Cor. 12:25). He is interested in members loving one another, because the world will know we are His disciples by our love (John 13:35). God is able to accomplish His work through His people in a way that is consistent with all His commands and His nature.

Throughout the New Testament, God expresses some of His desires for the church. I want you to keep some of these in mind as we study this unit together:

1. **God wants His people to be holy and pure.**
2. **God wants His people to display unity.**
3. **God wants His people to love each other.**

Read the following Scriptures. For each Scripture match it with one of the three statements above. Write the appropriate statement on the line below each Scripture.

A. "I pray . . . that all of them may be one, Father, just as you are in me and I am in you. May they also be in us so that the world may believe that you have sent me. . . . May they be brought to complete unity to let the world know that you sent me" (John 17:20, 21, 23).

_____

B. "This is the message you heard from the beginning: We should love one another. . . . Let us not love with words or tongue but with actions and in truth. . . . This is his command: to believe in the name of his Son, Jesus Christ, and to love one another as he commanded us" (1 John 3:11, 18, 23).

_____

C. "Do not conform to the evil desires you had when you lived in ignorance. But just as he who called you is holy, so be holy in all you do; for it is written: 'Be holy, because I am holy' " (1 Pet. 1:14-16).

_____

D. "Do everything without complaining or arguing, so that you may become blameless and pure, children of God without fault in a crooked and depraved generation, in which you shine like stars in the universe as you hold out the word of life" (Phil. 2:14-16).

_____

E. "Make every effort to keep the unity of the Spirit through the bond of peace" (Eph. 4:3).

_____

How would you evaluate your church's faithfulness to these commands? Is your church holy, pure, united, and loving?

_____

_____

Answers are: A-2; B-3; C-1; D-1; E-2.

Knowing and Doing God's Will as a Church

Much of what you have studied applies to churches as well as individuals. For instance:

- God is always at work in and around a church.
- God pursues a continuing love relationship with His church that is real and personal.
- God invites a church to become involved in His work.
- When a church sees where God is at work, that is their invitation to join Him in what He is doing.
- God speaks by the Holy Spirit through the Bible, prayer, circumstances, and the church.
- A church will face a crisis of belief when God invites them to become involved in a work only He can accomplish. Faith and action will be required.
- A church will have to make major adjustments in order to join God in His work.
- A church is totally dependent on God for accomplishing tasks of Kingdom value.
- Apart from God a church can do nothing of Kingdom value.
- As a church obeys God, they will come to know Him by experience as He does wonderful things through them.

The list could go on. Something is different about the way a church comes to know God's will and the way an individual knows God's will. A church is the body of Christ. A body functions as one unit with spiritual leaders and members. All are interdependent—they need each other. Each leader and member of the body needs the others to fully know God's will. Each member has a role in the body (Gal. 6:1-5) and each leader has a responsibility to the body to equip the members (Eph. 4:11-13). The pastor is responsibile for the body as well as to the body.

The church functions as a body—one unit with many participating spiritual leaders and members.

The Parable of the Train Tracks

Suppose your eye could say to your body, "Let us walk down these train tracks. The way is all clear. Not a train is in sight." So you begin to walk down the tracks.

Then suppose your ear says to the body, "I hear a whistle coming from the other direction."

Your eye argues, "But nothing is on the track as far as *I* can see. Let's keep on walking." So your body listens only to your eye and keeps on walking.

Soon your ear says, "That whistle is getting louder and closer!"

Then your feet say, "I can feel the rumbling motion of a train coming. We better get our body off these tracks!"

If this were your physical body, what would you do? Check your response.

- ❏ 1. I would get off the train tracks as soon as possible!
- ❏ 2. I would take a vote of all my body members and let the majority rule.
- ❏ 3. I would try to ignore the conflict and hope it passed away.
- ❏ 4. I would trust my eye and keep on walking. My eye has never let me down, yet.

That may have seemed like a silly question. God gave our bodies many different senses and parts. When each part does its job, the whole body works the way it should. In our physical bodies we do not take votes based on majority rule, ignore conflicting senses, or choose to listen only to one sense and ignore the others. To live that way would be very dangerous.

Because a church is the body of Christ, it functions best when spiritual leaders and members share what they sense God wants the church to be and do. A church needs to hear the whole counsel of God through its spiritual leaders and members. Then it can proceed in confidence and in unity to do God's will.

Write a brief summary about the difference between the way a church comes to know God's will and the way an individual comes to know God's will.

_____

_____

_____

What questions do you have about how a church comes to know God's will?

_____

_____

Your memory verse for this unit focuses on the church as a body. Write it on the following lines and begin memorizing it. Then review your other memory verses.

When God wants to reveal His will to a church, He will begin by speaking to one or more individuals. Because of the nature of his call and assignment from God, this is often the pastor, although it may be another member of the body. The pastor's job is to bear witness to the church about what he senses God is saying. Other members may also express what they sense God is saying. The whole body looks to Christ—the Head of the church—for guidance. He guides all the members of the body to understand His will fully.

You may have questions about how to practice that in your church. A church of 50 members would do this somewhat differently than one with 5,000 members. The most important factor is not a method but a relationship with a Person. Christ is Head of His church and He knows how each one can work uniquely with Him to understand His will. The Jerusalem church had over 3,000 members and Christ was able to do His work through them, with the guidance of the apostles as spiritual leaders.

In Saskatoon, as God moved and expressed His will to church members, I guided them as their pastor to share with the other members of the body. All were given an opportunity and encouraged to share. Each was encouraged to respond as God guided him or her. This happened, not only in worship (usually at the close of a service), but also in prayer meetings, committee meetings, business meetings, Sunday School classes, home Bible studies, and in personal conversations. Many called the church office and shared what God was saying to them in their quiet times. Still others shared what they experienced at work or at school. The entire church became experientially and practically aware of Christ's presence in our midst.

When are some times that members of a church body could share with others what they sense God wants the church to be and do? Include ideas from the previous paragraph with any other ideas you may have.

_____

_____

_____

_____

_____

Does your church take time for members in the body to share with the church what they sense God wants the church to be and do? Yes ❑   No ❑

Sharing what God is doing in your life may help someone else encounter God in a meaningful way. For instance, when someone was led to make a significant commitment to the Lord in one of our services, I gave that person an opportunity to share with the body. Sometimes that testimony prompted others to respond in a similar way.

Review today's lesson. Pray and ask God to identify one or more statements or Scriptures that He wants you to understand, learn, or practice. Underline it (them). Then respond to the following:

What was the most meaningful statement or Scripture you read today?

_____

_____

Reword the statement or Scripture into a prayer of response to God.

_____

_____

What does God want you to do in response to today's study?

_____

_____

DISCERNING GOD'S WILL AS A BODY

The church does not come to know the will of God in just the same way an individual does. A church comes to know the will of God when the whole body understands what Christ—the Head—is telling them.

Individuals come to know God's will through an intimate love relationship with God. The Holy Spirit speaks through the Bible, prayer, circumstances, and the church to reveal Himself, His purposes, and His ways.

A church comes to know the will of God when the whole body understands what Christ—the Head—is telling them.

☀ **Review the lesson in unit 6, "God Speaks through the Church" (pp. 105-107). Write below the most meaningful statement or Scripture you identified in that lesson.**

_____

_____

How does an individual come to know God's will?

_____

_____

How does your church currently make decisions about what to be and do?

_____

_____

Before Pentecost (in the New Testament), the Holy Spirit did not dwell in the lives of all of God's people. He only came upon chosen individuals for God's purposes. In the Old Testament God spoke to His people through a leader—a prophet, a priest, a king, and so forth. For instance, God would tell Moses His will for Israel; and Moses would tell the people what they were to do. Israel then (most of the time) did what Moses said. (For an example see Num. 9:1-5.)

Israel

☀ **In the Old Testament how did Israel come to know God's will?**

_____

_____

"The Lord spoke to Moses . . . 'Have the Israelites celebrate the Passover . . .' So Moses told the Israelites to celebrate the Passover, and they did so. . . . The Israelites did everything just as the Lord commanded Moses." —Numbers 9:1-5

With the coming of the Holy Spirit on the church at Pentecost, God came to dwell in every believer. He created the body—a local church—so that every member needed every other member. In the body of Christ every believer has direct access to God. God can speak to any and every member of the body. He can work through the whole body in revealing His will.

The church

In the New Testament, the Holy Spirit also led the apostles as they guided the church. God led the members and leaders in a mutual interdependence of serving and decision-making. New Testament examples illustrate joint decision making under Christ's lordship:
- The Choosing of Judas' Replacement—Acts 1:12-26
- The Choosing of the Seven—Acts 6:1-7

- Peter's Witness to the Gentile Conversions—Acts 11:1-18
- Barnabas and Saul Sent Out—Acts 13:1-3
- The Jerusalem Council—Acts 15:1-35

Notice in these examples that there are different methods of arriving at a decision. For instance, the Jerusalem Council settled an important doctrinal and practical issue. After Peter and James had spoken, the "whole assembly . . . listened to Barnabus and Paul" (Acts 15:12) also. "Then the apostles and elders, with the whole church, decided . . ." (Acts 15:22). "It seemed good to the Holy Spirit and to us" (Acts 15:28).

When God speaks to a person about the church, the person should share with the body what he or she senses God is saying. As each member shares what he senses God is saying, the whole body goes to God in prayer to discern His will for the body. In His timing God confirms to the body what He is saying. *Individual* opinions are not that important. The will of God is very important. No single method can be given for discerning God's will as a body. Pastors, other church leaders, and members are to have such a relationship with God and the church body that spiritual guidance is the outcome. When Christ is able to guide each spiritual leader and member of the body to function properly, the whole body will know and be enabled to do God's will.

The church is a body, and every leader and member has direct access to God. Which of the following is the way a church should relate to God to understand His will? Check your response.

❏ 1. The church should set the pastor up as the mediator between God and the church. God tells only the pastor His will, and the pastor tells the people.
❏ 2. Members of the church should present their own opinions about what the church should be and do. Then they debate with each other about whose opinion is right. They take a vote and let the majority rule.
❏ 3. The pastor, leaders, and members should pray and ask God for guidance. Then each person shares what he or she senses God is saying to the church. All the leaders and members then look to the Head of the body—Christ—and continue praying until Christ has convinced them of His will.
❏ 4. Other: _____

The Head does the convincing on His timetable.

A church comes to know God's will when the whole body comes to understand what Christ wants them to do. For a church, knowing God's will may involve many members, not just one. Yes, God often will speak to the leader about what He wants to do. That leader then bears witness to the body about what he senses God's will is. The leader does not have to try to convince the church that this is God's will. The leader does not have to ask the congregation to follow him without question. The leader encourages the body to go to Christ and get confirmation from the Head (Christ). The Head does the convincing on His timetable. Then the whole body follows Christ—the Head. This is why a church must learn to function as a body with Christ as the Head of His church.

Problems arise when a church does not function as a body.

A new mission church entered into an agreement to buy land for their first building. The pastor led the church to buy the land based on some promises made by the realtor. Problems arose for the church because the realtor did not keep his promises after closing on the property. The group ran into financial problems and grew very discouraged about the whole project. Finally, the pastor brought the church together and told them about all the negotiations and the current problems. Two members spoke up and said, "Pastor, we knew that realtor was dishonest. He has deceived us in business dealings before. We were just afraid to disagree with your plans, because it would have appeared that we were opposing God." Fortunately, God was gracious, and soon the problems were resolved. This points out, however, that the church needs to function like a body with every member free to share what he or she knows or senses as God's will.

How does a church come to know God's will? Write a brief summary.

_____

_____

Church Decision Making

When God gave directions to our church in Saskatoon, He often gave them through persons other than me. Many of them came from the members of the body who

sensed a clear direction of God and shared it with the body. We created the opportunity for people to share what they sensed God was leading us to be or do. Our desire was not to find out who was for it and who was against it. In our business meetings we never took a vote asking, "How many of you are for this and how many of you are against it?" That is the wrong question. Every time you ask that question you have a potential church split.

The right question is: "With all of the information and all of the praying that we have been doing, how many of you sense that God clearly is directing us to proceed in this direction?" This is a very different question. It does not ask members for their opinions. It asks them to vote based on what they sense God is saying to His church. On critical issues we never voted at the time we discussed the issue. This relieved the pressure of trying to get their point across that some would sense. After discussion, we would take time to pray and seek the mind of Christ.

Suppose 55 percent of the members voted saying, "Yes, we sense God clearly is leading us to proceed in this direction." Forty-five percent voted saying, "We do not sense God is clearly leading us in this direction." What did we do? We never proceeded. That expression told me as pastor two things: (1) God seemed to be leading us in that direction; and (2) the timing wasn't right, because the head had not yet brought all the rest of the body to the same sense of direction. We definitely felt God was leading in this direction because 55 percent of us sensed that. But we knew the timing wasn't right because 45 percent had not yet come to that understanding. We prayed, worked, and watched. We let the Head bring the body to understand what He wanted to do through us. God was in charge and was present to bring us to one mind and heart (Rom. 15:5-6; 1 Cor. 1:10). We trusted Him to do that.

People often ask, "Did you always wait until you got a 100 percent vote?" No, I knew that we might have one or more that were so out of fellowship with the Lord that they could not hear His voice. Another might be purposefully disobedient. However, we usually did wait until the votes were almost unanimous.

"I appeal to you, brothers, in the name of our Lord Jesus Christ, that all of you agree with one another so that there may be no divisions among you and that you may be perfectly united in mind and thought."
—1 Corinthians 1:10

I did not get angry or disappointed with those who did not agree with the rest of the body. Their disagreement indicated that they might have a fellowship problem with the Lord. As the pastor, I would then set my life alongside theirs to see how God might need to work through me to help them back to proper fellowship with the Lord. I always had to pray this through and only respond as the Lord led me.

1.

2.

3.

4.

☀ **Reflect on the following questions. In the margin write a brief answer to each one.**

   1. Do you believe God wants the body to come to one heart and one mind on His will for the body?
   2. Do you believe God is able to bring His people to understand His will?
   3. Do you believe God is able to bring YOUR church to this kind of unity?
   4. Would you be willing to wait on God until He has had time to adjust the members of the body to His will?

This may be another one of those places where you have reached a crisis of belief. Ask God for help through this one. Can God bring a whole church to a sense of unity about His will? Yes:

> "May the God who gives endurance and encouragement give you a spirit of unity among yourselves as you follow Christ Jesus, so that with one heart and mouth you may glorify the God and Father of our Lord Jesus Christ."
>
> —Romans 15:5-6

☀ **What does God have to say to you through the two verses above?**

God's Timing

Good directions from God may be lost by missing God's timing. Not only does a church need to know *what* God wants them to do, but they need to know *when* He wants them to do it. We must wait until God's time. We need to wait on Him as a body until He has adjusted us to Himself. This develops a confident patience in the Lord and a loving trust in each other.

We must wait until God's time.

Real Motivation

I never tried to get the people just to support an organization, a program, or a person (human). I challenged them to ask God what He wanted. When they knew what God wanted, the only option was faithful obedience. That obedience could and often was expressed through an organization, a program, or corporate ministry of the church.

Which one of the following will best motivate God's people to faithful obedience to the will of God? Check your response.

   ❏ 1. Ask them to find out what God wants as they walk in an intimate love relationship with Him. When He clearly speaks, they should obey Him.
   ❏ 2. Ask them to support a program promoted by the denomination.
   ❏ 3. Ask them to support an influential leader in the church.
   ❏ 4. Ask them to go along with a committee recommendation.
   ❏ 5. Tell them, "I have a word from God" and expect them to just agree.

The churches I have served have had many traditions. I kept teaching and teaching and teaching until the Spirit of God, who is our common Teacher, brought us to one heart and one mind. We began to release ourselves and let God take all the time He needed. I felt that my responsibility as a pastor was to lead God's people into such a relationship with Jesus Christ that they would know clearly when He was speaking. Then I asked them to obey God—not follow a program, an influential lay leader, a committee, or me. God the Holy Spirit is the Christian's real Motivator.

The Holy Spirit is the Christian's real Motivator.

Our business meetings became some of the most exciting times in the life of our church. People knew that at the business meeting we would clearly see the directions and activity of God. They wanted to come to the business meeting because it became such a thrilling moment when our church saw God reveal His purposes and His ways to us.

The church is a body with Christ as the Head. The Spirit of God guides every believer. His indwelling presence can teach us and help us. I always allowed my understanding of the will of God to be tested in the life of the congregation—not because of what I thought the people were, but because of what I knew the church was.

I can trust God to guide the members of the body.

When I sensed that God wanted our church to do something, as pastor I always asked the church family to work through it with me. If the people walk with God, then I can trust God to guide them. This can be true for pastors and for other church members as well. If the people do not walk in right fellowship with God, then I depend on God to guide me in helping them become what He wants them to be. God doesn't give up on His people, so neither should I.

I can trust God to guide a group of churches.

As a director of missions, I led the churches in our association (a group of churches) to function this way also. It took me awhile to help the pastors understand how to walk that way. The work we were doing was not my program, it was God's work. Can a whole association of churches function this way? Yes, if you will help them understand how to walk with God that way.

What is God saying to you about your church and how it currently makes decisions?

_____

_____

_____

Review today's lesson. Pray and ask God to identify one or more statements or Scriptures that He wants you to understand, learn, or practice. Underline it (them). Then respond to the following:

What was the most meaningful statement or Scripture you read today?

_____

_____

_____

Reword the statement or Scripture into a prayer of response to God.

_____

_____

_____

What does God want you to do in response to today's study?

_____

_____

THE BODY OF CHRIST, PART 1

The Body of Christ in Romans 12

Paul wrote to the church at Rome and gave the members some instructions about how the body of Christ should live in relation to each other. A church needs to learn to function as the body of Christ. These instructions from Paul will help you in relation to your church.

Turn in your Bible to Romans 12. Read the verses listed below and answer the questions.

1. **Verses 1-2.** What two things did Paul recommend to members of the body, so that the whole body would be able to discern God's will? Complete the sentence.

   Offer your bodies as . . . _____

   Do not conform . . . but be transformed by . . . _____

   _____

2. **Verses 3, 10, and 16.** What are some specific things you can do to prevent problems caused by pride?

   _____

   _____

   _____

3. **Verses 4-6:** "Members do not all have the same function, so in Christ we who are many form one body, and each member belongs to all the others. We have different gifts."

   Why are other members of the body important to you?

   _____

   _____

   Verse 5 is your Scripture memory verse this week. Write it below and begin memorizing it.

   _____

   _____

   _____

DAY 3

A church needs to learn to function as the body of Christ.

4. Verses 9-21. Which of the many instructions given in these verses do you think members of your church need to practice more than they do? (For example, you might respond: "We need to do more to share with God's people who have needs.") Check all that apply.

❏ Love others sincerely.   ❏ Bless those who persecute you.

❏ Hate evil.   ❏ Rejoice with those who rejoice.

❏ Cling to what is good.   ❏ Mourn with those who mourn.

❏ Be devoted to one another.   ❏ Live in harmony with one another.

❏ Honor one another.   ❏ Don't be proud or conceited.

❏ Serve the Lord with zeal.   ❏ Associate with people of low position.

❏ Be joyful in hope.   ❏ Don't repay evil for evil.

❏ Be patient in affliction.   ❏ Do what is right.

❏ Be faithful in prayer.   ❏ Don't take revenge.

❏ Share with God's people in need.   ❏ Overcome evil with good.

❏ Practice hospitality.

Living sacrifices and renewed minds are necessary to "test and approve what God's will is" (v. 2). Pride can cause problems in the body. You should think of yourself with sober judgment, honor others above yourself, live in harmony, and associate with people of low position. Church members need to practice all the instructions given in verses 9-21. Warning: following these instructions may be very costly!

☀ **Pause to pray for specific ways God may want your church to act more like the body of Christ.**

The Holy Spirit Equipping Each Member to Function in the Body

The first part of 1 Corinthians 12 talks about the Holy Spirit enabling each member. Verse 7 says, "To each one the manifestation of the Spirit is given for the common good" (1 Cor. 12:7). The Holy Spirit is the Gift (Acts 2:38). The Holy Spirit manifests (makes visible, clear, known; reveals) Himself to each member of the body for the common good of the body.

The Holy Spirit is the Gift.

☀ **Check the correct answer for each of the following questions. Base your answers on 1 Corinthians 12:7 above.**

1. To whom does the Spirit manifest Himself?

  ❏ a. Only to a few very spiritual individuals.

  ❏ b. Only to church leaders.

  ❏ c. To every believer.

2. Why does the Holy Spirit manifest Himself to believers?

  ❏ a. So the individual can be blessed.

  ❏ b. So the individual can call attention to himself.

  ❏ c. So the whole body can benefit from His work.

Did you check the last item in both questions? Good job! ALL members of the church—Christ's body—are gifted by the Holy Spirit's presence. Each person's experience of the Holy Spirit is for the good of the body not for himself or herself. That is why we need each other. Without a healthy and functioning body, a church will miss much of the good God provides for a church.

In the Old Testament the Holy Spirit gifted a person for an assignment.

The Old Testament is the kindergarten for understanding the Holy Spirit's work. In the Old Testament the Spirit came upon individuals to help them achieve an assignment God had given them. Moses had an assignment as an administrator, so God equipped him with His Holy Spirit to administrate.

God gave each of the judges an assignment. Then the Spirit of God came upon each one and equipped him or her to complete the assignment given. David was called to be king when he was a shepherd. How could he possibly be king when he had never been king? The Spirit of God came upon him and equipped him to be king. Ezekiel was called to be a prophet. How could he possibly be a prophet? The Scripture says the Spirit of God came upon him and caused him to do everything God asked of him (Ezek. 2-3).

Here is the pattern we see in the Old Testament:
1. God gave an assignment to a person.
2. The Holy Spirit was given to that person to equip him or her for the assignment.
3. The proof of the Spirit's presence was that the person was able to complete the assignment effectively through the supernatural enabling of the Holy Spirit.

An Old Testament pattern

The workmen of the tabernacle are a clear example. God gave Moses specific details about how to build the Tabernacle (Ex. 25—31). He wanted it done exactly as He had instructed Moses. Then God said, "I have chosen Bezalel son of Uri, the son of Hur, of the tribe of Judah, and I have filled him with the Spirit of God, with skill, ability and knowledge in all kinds of crafts. . . . Moreover, I have appointed Oholiab . . . to help him. Also I have given skill to all the craftsmen to make everything I have commanded you" (Ex. 31:2-3, 6). How would Moses have known if the Spirit of God was upon those men? He would have watched them at work. If they were enabled to carry out the assignment God had given, Moses would have known the Spirit of God was upon them.

Bezalel and Oholiab

Throughout the Old Testament, the Spirit of God always was present to equip an individual to carry out a divine assignment. God didn't give a person some thing. He Himself was the Gift. The Spirit manifested His presence by equipping each individual to function where God had assigned him.

 What is the pattern for the Holy Spirit's work in the Old Testament? Use the hints below and describe the pattern. Peek back if you need help.

Assignment— _____

_____

The Gift— _____

_____

The proof— _____

_____

When members of a church begin considering spiritual gifts, they sometimes run into difficulty by thinking that God gives them some *thing*—like an ingredient called administration. No, He doesn't give some thing; He gives Himself. The Gift is a Person. The Holy Spirit equips you with *His* administrative ability. So His administration begins to become your administration. What you observe when you see a spiritual gift exercised is a manifestation of the Holy Spirit—you see the Holy Spirit equipping and enabling an individual with His abilities and capabilities to accomplish God's work.

spiritual gifts

 Read John 14:10 and 1 Corinthians 12:7 in the left margin. Which of the following is the better definition of a spiritual gift? Check your response.
- ❏ 1. A spiritual gift is a manifestation of the Holy Spirit at work in and through a person's life for the common good of the body of Christ.
- ❏ 2. A spiritual gift is a special ability God gives a person so he or she can accomplish the work God has assigned to the church.

"It is the Father, living in me, who is doing his work."
—*John 14:10*

"To each one the manifestation of the Spirit is given for the common good."
—*1 Corinthians 12:7*

Jesus said: "It is the Father, living in me, who is doing his work" (John 14:10). Even in Jesus's miraculous works, the Father was manifesting Himself. The Father was in Jesus, and He worked through Jesus to accomplish His purposes. The first definition above focuses on God and what He does through us. The second definition focuses more on what I get so I can do something for God or for His church. Remember, Jesus said, "Apart from me you can do nothing" (John 15:5). A spiritual gift is a manifestation of God at work through you.

The Body of Christ in 1 Corinthians 12

The first part of 1 Corinthians 12 talks about the Holy Spirit manifesting Himself in different ways. He manifests Himself to every believer. The second part of that chapter talks about the body.

 Read the following list of summary statements. Then read 1 Corinthians 12:11-31 and see if you can locate at least one verse that supports each of the statements below. Write the numbers of the verses beside the statements.

Verse(s) _____ 1. The Holy Spirit decides who to give assignments to and enables each spiritual leader and member to accomplish God's work.

Verse(s) _____ 2. The body is a single unit made up of many parts.

Verse(s) _____ 3. Members of the body do *not* decide their own role in the body.

Verse(s) _____ 4. God puts spiritual leaders and members in the body where He wants them to be.

Verse(s) _____ 5. The body is not complete without all the spiritual leaders and members God has given the body.

Verse(s) _____ 6. Members of the body need every other member of the body.

Verse(s) _____ 7. The body should be united as one, not divided.

Verse(s) _____ 8. Members of the body should have equal concern for each other.

Verse(s) _____ 9. Spiritual leaders and members of the body have different assignments from God for the good of the whole body.

For the statements above you may have identified fewer verses or different verses, but here are some possible answers: 1—verse 11; 2—verses 12-14; 3—verses 15-17; 4—verse 18; 5—verses 17-20; 6—verses 21-24; 7—verse 25; 8—verses 25-26; 9—verses 28-30.

Review today's lesson. Pray and ask God to identify one or more statements or Scriptures that He wants you to understand, learn, or practice. Underline it (them). Then respond to the following:

What was the most meaningful statement or Scripture you read today?

_____

_____

Reword the statement or Scripture into a prayer of response to God.

_____

_____

_____

What does God want you to do in response to today's study?

_____

_____

_____

SUMMARY STATEMENTS

- The Holy Spirit is the Gift.
- The Spirit of God always is present to equip me to carry out a divine assignment.
- A spiritual gift is a manifestation of the Holy Spirit at work in and through a person's life for the common good of the body of Christ.
- The Spirit decides who to give assignments to, and enables spiritual leaders and members to accomplish His work.
- God puts spiritual leaders and members in the body where He wants them to be.
- The body is not complete without all the spiritual leaders and members God has given the body.
- Members of the body should have equal concern for each other.
- Spiritual leaders and members of the body have different assignments from God for the good of the whole body.

THE BODY OF CHRIST, PART 2

Paul wrote the Corinthian church, a local body of believers, and said: "You are the body of Christ, and each one of you is a part of it" (1 Cor. 12:27). Just as your physical body needs every part in order to live a normal and healthy life, so the church needs every member in order to live a normal and healthy church life. No member can say of any other member, I don't need you. Apart from the other members of the church (the body) you will not be able to experience the fullness of life God has intended for you. When one member is missing or not functioning as God intended, the rest of the body will miss out on the fullness of life God has intended for the church.

God places members in the body as it pleases Him. If He makes a person an "eye," the Holy Spirit will equip him to see. If God makes a person an "ear," the Holy Spirit will equip her to hear. If He makes a person a "hand," the Holy Spirit will equip him to function as a hand. In New Testament Scriptures relating to the body of Christ, the Holy Spirit's work is to enable a person to function in the assignment where God puts him in the body. Not every member is an apostle, prophet, teacher, and so forth; but each one does have a God-given function. Each one functions where God puts him or her in the body so the whole body functions together as it should.

> **Below are some statements that might be heard from a church member. They may reflect an incorrect view of the church as the body of Christ. If you heard a member of your church make the statement on the left, which of the biblical principles on the right could you use to help the person understand how God intends for the church to function? You may list more than one principle that may apply. Write the number of the principle before each statement on the left. If you agree with a statement, write "agree" beside it. If you have serious questions about any of the statements, write your questions in the margin for discussion in the small-group session.**

I understand the will of God for my church when I listen to the whole body express what they are experiencing in the life of that body.

Statements

_____ A. "I think we should clean up our church rolls and get rid of all those names of people who don't attend any more."

_____ B. "Bill got himself into trouble by breaking the law. It doesn't bother me that he has to serve time in jail."

_____ C. "I think I should be elected chairman of the deacons. After all, I have been a faithful member of this church for 42 years."

_____ D. "If I can't be a Sunday School teacher, I'll just quit coming to this church."

_____ E. "I don't care that the rest of the body thinks God is leading them to ask me to serve in that role. I have never been a . . . and I know I couldn't do it. I don't have the talents necessary."

_____ F. "If those 10 families can't agree with the majority, that's tough. In this church the majority rules. If they don't like what we are doing, they can go somewhere else."

_____ G. "Since God has told me what His will is for this church, all you have to do is listen to me. Anybody who doesn't agree with me is unspiritual and out of God's will."

Principles

1. The Spirit decides who to give assignments to, and enables members to accomplish His work.

2. The body is a single unit made up of many parts.

3. Members of the body do not decide their own role in the body.

4. God puts members in the body where He wants them to be.

5. The body is not complete without all the members God has given the body.

6. Members of the body need every other member of the body.

7. The body should be united as one, not divided.

8. Members of the body should have equal concern for each other.

9. Members of the body have different assignments from God for the good of the whole body.

I believe each of these statements may reflect an incorrect understanding of the church as the body of Christ. Some of the principles I would use are A—5 and 6; B—8; C—3 and 4; D—1 and 3; E—1; F—7; G—2, 5, and 6. Anytime you evaluate the way a church body functions, you should keep at least three concerns in mind:

> **God's Concerns for the Body of Christ**
>
> 1. Jesus is Head of the body. The body ought to be Christ-centered.
> 2. God is very concerned about the body maintaining unity and oneness of heart.
> 3. Love like that described in 1 Corinthians 13 should prevail. Members of the body ought to love each other as they love themselves.

In the list of three concerns above, circle one or two key words in each that might help you remember the three concerns. As you read the following responses, underline statements that will help you function correctly in the body of Christ. If you have questions or concerns, write them in the margin for discussion in your small-group session.

A church needs all the members God has given the body.

A. "I think we should clean up our church membership rolls and get rid of all those names of people who don't attend any more." The first question this church needs to ask is, Are these people members of the body of Christ—are they Christians? If God added them to your body because that is where He wanted them (1 Cor. 12:18), do you have a right to delete them? A church needs all of the members God has given their body (principles 5 and 6). This church should pray and ask God to show them how to reclaim these wayward members for active fellowship.

If one suffers, all suffer.

B. "Bill got himself into trouble by breaking the law. It doesn't bother me that he has to serve time in jail." When one member suffers, all suffer (1 Cor. 12:26), even if the suffering is the consequence of sin. Members of Christ's body are commanded to love one another. Read 1 Corinthians 13 if you want to see how love would respond in the body. Show concern for all members of the body (Principle 8).

Are you remembering to underline statements that will help you function rightly in the body of Christ? Be sure to do so. I will be asking you to review these later today.

We do not choose our own function.

C. "I think I should be elected Chairman of the Deacons. After all, I have been a faithful member of this church for 42 years." This could be a self-centered desire. We serve in the church by God's assignment (Principles 3 and 4). We do not choose our own function. If God intends for you to serve in a particular capacity, the Head (Jesus Christ) can bring the rest of the body to recognize that. Will you trust Him to do that through the body?

God decides where one should function in the body.

D. "If I can't be a Sunday School teacher, I'll just quit coming to this church." The church needs to be sensitive to what others sense God may be leading them to do. Principles 1 and 3 focus attention on the fact that God is the one who should decide where one functions in the body. Trust Him to let the body know. A nominating committee for church leadership positions must be very prayerful in discerning God's will. Both the individual and the church must carefully seek God's will and trust Him to make His will clear.

You can't do it. The Holy Spirit enables you to complete any assignment He gives.

E. "I don't care that the rest of the body thinks God is leading them to ask me to serve in that role. I have never been a . . . and I know I couldn't do it. I don't have the talents necessary." One problem we face in the body is that we seldom see God at work. We just see people. I try to see God at work *in* His people. Principle 1 points out that the Holy Spirit will enable a person to carry out any assignment that God gives the person. Just because you have never done something before, or because you don't think you have the skills does not necessarily mean that God is not giving you that assignment. Moses gave some objections like this one when God was calling him at the burning bush. Take very seriously what the body senses to be God's will. Take what the body senses to the Lord and trust God to guide you correctly.

Respond and serve as unto the Lord.

Be willing to respond as unto the Lord. Serve with all your heart as unto the Lord. That place in the church life could become one of the most exciting places of the activity of God. Don't do it just to fill a job. Do it as unto the Lord.

The Untouchables

Can teaching unruly teenage boys become a special assignment from God? Shortly after I began teaching teenage boys at a church in California, 23 leather-jacketed teenagers walked into the back of that church. None of them were Christians. God put me in the midst of a group of hurting young people. Within three months, 22 of the 23 teenagers had come to know the Lord. Their changed lives broke up a gang called The Untouchables. The low-rent housing area were they lived had a high concentration of crime. The crime rate dropped dramatically when God brought 22 teenage boys to saving faith in Christ.

God can display Himself anywhere in the life of the church that you are willing to let Him put your life. Ask God to fill that position and that place in the life of the church with His presence. You could become the catalyst to turn that church completely upside down.

 In statements A-E, what are some things you underlined that might help you function more effectively in the body of Christ?

_____

_____

_____

_____

_____

F. "If those 10 families can't agree with the majority, that's tough. In this church the majority rules. If they don't like what we are doing, they can go somewhere else." The church functions by the rule of the Head—Jesus Christ. We often settle for majority rule, because we don't want to wait until the Head has time to convince the body of His will. If we are willing to sacrifice the unity of the body so the majority can have their way, we are not taking 1 Corinthians 12:25 (Principle 7) very seriously. Didn't Jesus pray for the unity of the church in John 17 so the world could believe in Him? We ought to have a similar burden for unity. Give Jesus—the Head—time to do the convincing. When He has brought the body to an understanding of His will, the timing will be just right to proceed! Each member is precious to God.

Unity of the body is very important to God

G. "Since God has told me what His will is for this church, all you have to do is listen to me. Anybody who doesn't agree with me is unspiritual and out of God's will." Principles 2, 5, and 6 apply here. When the eye begins to see, the eye has a tendency to say, "Hand, why don't you see what I see? You're not spiritual."

"My prayer is . . . that all of them may be one, Father, just as you are in me and I am in you. May they also be in us so that the world may believe that you have sent me."
—John 17:20-21

Then the poor hand says, "I can't see, because I am a hand."

The eye has forgotten that the body is not one part but many (1 Cor. 12:14). The Spirit of God manifests Himself to every person. Why? For the common good. When the eye sees, it is not for the eye. His sight is for the body. Sight is not for the eye's sake so he can say, "I thank God that I have the gift of seeing. I wish all the rest of you did, too." Sight is for the body's sake. All the other members depend on the eye to tell them what he sees.

As I illustrated with the parable of the train tracks in day 1, the eye will seldom get the whole picture of what God has for a church. The body needs everyone to express what he or she senses. When the church puts together what each member senses, then the body comes to know the will of God perfectly. No one individual can know all the will of God for a church. Leaders understand the will of God for the church when they listen to the members of the body express what they are experiencing in the life of that body.

You understand the will of God for the church when you listen to the whole body express what they are experiencing in the life of that body.

I may come with a sincere heart and share what I sense God is saying through me as pastor, but I never assume that I know all that God has for the church. I share and then listen to what all the rest of the body says. Often I find that the blending of what God is saying through me and what He is saying through someone else is God's will. Neither one of us knew the whole will of God. At other times, I share and realize: the Lord wants us to begin making some adjustments, but the timing is not right to start the work now. When God brings the body to unity, then we know the timing is right. What I sense God wants us to do may not be wrong, it is just not complete. I need to hear what the other members are saying in order to understand fully what God is saying to me.

 Review your underlining in the preceding material. As the questions apply to you, respond to the following:

1. What questions do you have that you would like to discuss in your small-group session?

_____

2. What is one thing you think God would like to change in the way your church functions as a body?

_____

_____

3. What is one thing you think God wants you to do differently as you relate to other members of the body of Christ—your church?

_____

_____

Review today's lesson. Pray and ask God to identify one or more statements or Scriptures that He wants you to understand, learn, or practice. Underline it (them). Then respond to the following:

What was the most meaningful statement or Scripture you read today?

_____

_____

Reword the statement or Scripture into a prayer of response to God.

_____

_____

_____

What does God want you to do in response to today's study?

_____

_____

Practice quoting or writing your Scripture memory verses.

SUMMARY STATEMENTS

- Jesus is Head of the body.
- God is very concerned about the body maintaining unity.
- God-like love ought to prevail in the body.
- God decides where I ought to function in the body.
- I understand the will of God for my church when I listen to the whole body express what they are experiencing in the life of that body.
- Each member is precious to God.

DAY 5   LIFE IN THE BODY

Right relationships with God are far more important than buildings, budgets, programs, methods, church personnel, size, or anything else.

As you and your church allow God to teach you how to effectively live as a body, you will see a love and unity spring forth that you may not have experienced before. Effective body life begins with each individual being rightly related to God in an intimate love relationship. It continues as all the members are rightly related to Jesus Christ as the Head of your church. Right relationships with God are far more important than buildings, budgets, programs, methods, church personnel, size, or anything else.

The Scriptures give many helps for a church body to be rightly related to each other.

Read each of the following Scriptures. Under each one, write a brief statement or summary of God's will for relationships in the church body. You may want to look these up in your Bible, so you can read the context for the verses.

Romans 14:1, 12-13—"Accept him whose faith is weak, without passing judgment on disputable matters. . . . each of us will give an account of himself to God. Therefore let us stop passing judgment on one another. Instead, make up your mind not to put any stumbling block or obstacle in your brother's way."

God's will: _____

1 Corinthians 10:24—"Nobody should seek his own good, but the good of others."

God's will: _____

Ephesians 4:25—"Each of you must put off falsehood and speak truthfully to his neighbor, for we are all members of one body."

God's will: _____

Ephesians 4:29—"Do not let any unwholesome talk come out of your mouths, but only what is helpful for building others up according to their needs, that it may benefit those who listen."

God's will: _____

Ephesians 4:31-32—"Get rid of all bitterness, rage and anger, brawling and slander, along with every form of malice. Be kind and compassionate to one another, forgiving each other, just as in Christ God forgave you."

God's will: _____

Ephesians 5:19-20—"Speak to one another with psalms, hymns and spiritual songs. Sing and make music in your heart to the Lord, always giving thanks to God the Father for everything."

God's will: _____

Ephesians 5:21—"Submit to one another out of reverence for Christ."

God's will: _____

Colossians 3:13-14—"Bear with each other and forgive whatever grievances you may have against one another. Forgive as the Lord forgave you. And over all these virtues put on love, which binds them all together in perfect unity."

God's will: _____

As you read the New Testament, you will find many instructions that speak specifically to how God's people ought to live in relation to others. These instructions are not in the Bible just for you to study, memorize, discuss, or debate. They are written so you may know how to experience abundant life in Christ. When you have doubts about how to apply a Scripture, take your concern to the Lord. His Spirit can help you come to understand spiritual truth.

You should have found these instructions in your study.
- Be patient and accepting of those whose faith is weak or those who are immature.
- Don't be quick to judge others in matters that are disputable.
- Don't be selfish. Seek the good of others even at your own expense.
- Be absolutely truthful in all you say.
- Don't be critical and tear people down with your speech. Don't focus your conversation on unwholesome subjects. Be an encourager. Build people up. Keep their needs in mind as you speak.
- Forgive each other like Christ forgave you. Don't let any root of bitterness remain between you and another. Get rid of anger, inside fighting, and slander. Don't intentionally try to hurt another person (physically, emotionally, or spiritually).
- Encourage one another in your joint worship of God. Make music together.
- Die to self daily and submit to one another. Do this in reverence for Christ who submitted Himself to death on the cross for you.
- Be patient with each other, even when you have been mistreated or offended. Forgive even the worst offenses like God does. Love one another.

This unit is not long enough for me to share all I want to share. You may finish today's lesson and say, "I wish Henry had told me what to do in this circumstance." I have some good news for you! You don't need me to do that. The God who led Faith Baptist Church to function like the body of Christ is the very same one who is present in your church. Christ is present and He alone is the Head of your church. You don't need a method from me; you need instructions that are especially customized for your church from the Head. Those kind of instructions are the very best.

Let me take the remaining space to share about a few subjects that the Lord may want to use in your life or your church.

A Covenant Relationship in the Body

First Corinthians 12:7 and 18 tell us that God is the one who adds members to the body as it pleases Him. He adds them to the body for the common good of the whole body. When God added a member to our body, we had a cause for rejoicing. When a person came for membership in our church, we immediately began talking about what being the body of Christ meant. As pastor, I led the congregation to establish a covenant relationship with the person. (A covenant is a sacred pledge or agreement.) Though I varied the process depending on the individual's experience, the covenant making usually went something like this:

I would ask persons desiring membership to briefly share their personal testimonies. Then I would ask the person to respond to the following:
- Do you affirm before this congregation that Jesus Christ is your Saviour and Lord?
- Have you obediently followed the Lord in believer's baptism? (Or: Do you desire to follow the Lord in believer's baptism?)
- Do you clearly believe God is adding you to this body of Christ? (Or: Tell us how you have come to sense that God is adding you to this body.)

Then I would say, "God is not adding you to our church accidently. If God is adding you to our body, He wants to do something through your life to help us become more complete."
- Will you allow God to work through you to make this body more complete?
- Will you open your life to allow this body to minister to you to help you become more complete?

After the person testified to these questions, I would turn to the congregation and ask:
- From the testimony you have heard, Do you believe that God is adding this person to our body?
- Would you open your life to this person to let God work in your life through him (her)?
- Would you let God work through each of you to help this one become all God has purposed for him (her)?

Then, I would remind the church: "None of us know what this person may go through in the days to come. God may have added him to our body because He knew he was going to need our ministry. Will you covenant with this person to let God flow through you to help him become all God wants him to be? If you will so pledge yourself, stand and let's thank God for what He has just done by adding this person to our body. Because God added this person to our church, God will do something that will make us more of what He wants us to be."

We took this covenant relationship very seriously. Once a young girl asked me to remove her name from our membership roll. She had joined a cult. I told her, "We cannot do that. We have entered into a sacred covenant agreement with you. We believe you are making a mistake in the decision you have made. Though you have broken your part of the covenant, we are obligated to keep our part. Our church family will continue to love and pray for you. Whenever you need us, we will be here for you."

About six to nine months later she came back. She came to realize how she had been deceived. She said, "Thank you for continuing to love me. Thank you for not giving up on me." That's what the body of Christ is all about. The body cares for each member of the body, so that together all the members become more complete in love and in Christ.

Turn in your Bible and read 1 Corinthians 12 once more. This time ask God to speak to you about your church and how it can better function as the body of Christ. Ask Him to speak to you about your relationship to the body of Christ. Record anything you sense God is saying to you through His Word.

For my church: _____

_____

_____

For me: _____

_____

_____

Optional: **If you want to continue letting God speak through His Word, read Romans 12 again and ask God to speak to you about how you and your church can function like the body of Christ should. On a separate sheet of paper record what you sense God is saying to you.**

God Builds the Body to Match the Assignment

If I were going to be a weight lifter, I would train my body so that it could lift weights effectively. If I were going to be a sprinter, I would train my body differently. When I want to do a job well, I train my body to match the assignment.

When God builds a local church as the body of Christ, He adds members to the body and trains them to match the assignment He has for that body. He builds a local church body in a way that enables that body to respond to Him. Then God can accomplish an assignment through that body.

Let me illustrate. In the early days in Saskatoon, our church had about 15 or 20 people. We sensed that God wanted to use us to start churches in towns and villages all across Canada. As we prayed about this, we sensed God wanted to work through us to reach students on the university campus. We came to believe that if we would be faithful to witness on that campus, God would save many of those students. If we would then be faithful in involving them in the life of the body, we believed God would call many of them to be pastors, church staff members, and missionaries all across Canada.

Student ministry

We had two major problems: we didn't have a single college student and we didn't know how to reach students on a university campus. But we had an assignment. We began to pray and watch to see what God would do to help this body become the kind of body that could fulfill that assignment to that campus. The first persons I baptized were a professor at the university and his daughter. Then God began to bring other students into the church, and the body began to grow.

God led us to Robert Cannon, the Baptist Student Union Director at a university in Texas. He sensed God was calling him to Canada to work with students, but we had no money to move him or pay him. Robert came and God provided. When Robert came, I said, "Robert, you are here to equip the body so that the body can fulfill its ministry of reaching students for Christ on the campus. The assignment for campus ministry has been given to our church." Read Ephesians 4:11-13.

Robert Cannon

☀ **Do you follow what we were doing? Who had the assignment to reach the campus for Christ? Circle one: Robert Cannon   Our Church**

Where did the assignment come from?

What was Robert's primary job? Check one.
❏ 1. Start a Christian student organization on campus.
❏ 2. Go door-to-door in the dorm witnessing.
❏ 3. Equip the body to carry out its ministry to the campus.

The assignment came from God to the church. God added Robert to our body to equip the body to carry out its ministry to the campus. Robert helped prayers know how to pray concerning the campus. He helped those given to hospitality to linkup with students who needed a home away from home. He equipped others to witness. He helped the church know how to minister to the needs of the campus.

God added Robert to our body to equip the body to carry out its ministry to the campus.

At least 50 students have gone on to the seminaries to train for ministry. Many are returning to pastor churches. God built the body, gave it an assignment, and equipped it so He could accomplish the assignment through the members. The church was faithful, and God did what He told us He wanted to do.

Because I know God builds the body to match the assignment, I pay close attention to the people God adds to the body. Sometimes that is an indication of an assignment God is getting us ready for. Over a short period of time, several people related to the medical profession joined our church. We began praying to see why God had added them to our church. When the assignment to reach the native Indians on the reservations came to us, this group felt led to be a part of that work. They went to the reservations and provided a wide variety of free medical help. While people waited in line to receive help, other members of the church were there to talk and witness. The medical clinic opened doors for us to start Bible studies, lead people to the Lord, and start churches with the native Indians.

Pay attention to the people God adds to your church.

Think about the people in your church. Pray right now and ask God to guide you and others in your church to identify the assignments He already has prepared you for.

Have any ideas come to your mind as you have prayed? Write them below.

_____

_____

Continue praying for God's guidance. If the ideas grow into a burden, share what you are thinking and feeling with other members of the body. Their response may help you understand what God is wanting to do.

Review today's lesson. Pray and ask God to identify one or more statements or Scriptures that He wants you to understand, learn, or practice. Underline it (them). Then respond to the following:

What was the most meaningful statement or Scripture you read today?

_____

_____

Reword the statement or Scripture into a prayer of response to God.

_____

_____

What does God want you to do in response to today's study?

_____

_____

Review your Scripture memory verses.

SUMMARY STATEMENTS

- Right relationships with God are far more important than buildings, budgets, programs, methods, church personnel, size, or anything else.
- God doesn't add members to the body accidently.
- God builds the body to match the assignment.
- God builds the body, gives it an assignment, and equips the body to carry out the assignment.
- I will pay close attention to the people God adds to my church.

KINGDOM PEOPLE

Vincent Paul and East Indians

Our Vancouver association had decided we would do everything God led us to do to reach every person with the gospel. I was driving through Vancouver and saw some East Indians (persons from the nation of India). We had an East Indian community of about 60,000 people. I realized that we didn't have a single East Indian congregation. At that time no evangelical group in Vancouver had a congregation reaching East Indians.

God gave me a burden for reaching East Indians. I began to share with our churches about the need for a congregation among the East Indians. In our area one of the strong prejudices is toward East Indians. Which church would be willing to sponsor a mission with a group that the community has a prejudice against? That would require a major adjustment in the thinking of one of our churches.

I shared the need and asked people to pray that God would show us how He was going to reach East Indians through us. We prayed. Then we watched expectantly for how God would unfold His plan. We made an adjustment in our lives to receive what God was going to do. We wanted to ready ourselves; so when God began to move, we could join Him immediately.

At the end of the summer a pastor called me and said, "Henry, we have had an unusual thing happen in our Vacation Bible School. We had a large group, and two-thirds of them were East Indian."

I shared with him what we had been praying. I asked, "Would you go back and ask your church if they would sponsor an East Indian mission church?" He did, and they agreed to sponsor that mission. Then I said, "Let's pray that God will give us a trained East Indian pastor." I had no idea where to find such a man. But, God knew!

Two months later, I received a phone call. A man with an accent said, "My name is Vincent Paul. My wife and I were born in India. We started five Baptist churches in India. I am just now graduating from Southern Baptist Seminary in Louisville, Kentucky. God has laid on my heart that I am to come and start an East Indian congregation in Vancouver. Do you have a need?" Vincent Paul came, and the Lord put together all of his financial support. God is good!

UNIT

11

If we walk in the light, as he is in the light, we have fellowship with one another, and the blood of Jesus, his Son, purifies us from all sin. —1 JOHN 1:7

Verse to Memorize
This Week

You cannot be in relationship with Jesus and not be on mission.

When you respond to God's invitation to an intimate love relationship with Him, He brings you into a partnership with Himself. God has added you to a local body of believers. Together you are the body of Christ in your community. As Head of your church, Christ Himself is guiding and working through your church to accomplish the will of the Father.

The Spirit that bonds you to other believers in a local church also bonds you to ALL believers. God's people from every local body of Christ are part of God's kingdom. Christians are kingdom people, and Christ Himself is the eternal King over His kingdom. He "has made us to be a kingdom and priests to serve his God and Father" (Rev. 1:6). In this partnership with Christ as King, you become involved in His mission to reconcile a lost world to God. To be related to Christ is to be on mission with Him. You cannot be in relationship with Jesus and not be on mission. Jesus said, "As the Father has sent me, I am sending you" (John 20:21).

God Has a World on His Heart!

"God so loved the world that he gave his one and only Son, that whoever believes in him shall not perish but have eternal life" (John 3:16). God fashioned Christ's first body by the Holy Spirit and placed Him in Mary. He became flesh and dwelt among us (John 1:14). Jesus provided for our salvation through His death and resurrection. Once Jesus returned to heaven, God fashioned a new body of Christ through the Holy Spirit. This body was and is the believers whom God has added to the church.

Jesus now functions as Head of His body (local church) to guide it in carrying out the will of the Father. God established each church as a body of Christ, so that He could continue His redemptive work in the world. When Christ is allowed to function as Head of His church, God can use that body to carry out His will in every part of the earth.

☀ **Pause to reflect on the following questions. Check yes or no.**

- Did Christ know the will of the Father while He was on earth? Yes ❏   No ❏
- Did Christ ever misunderstand the purposes of the Father? Yes ❏   No ❏
- Did Christ ever fail to do the will of the Father? Yes ❏   No ❏
- If Christ is allowed to be the Head of a local congregation, will He ever misunderstand what the Father wants to achieve through that body of believers? Yes ❏   No ❏
- Can Christ reveal to the members of His body how they are to be involved in the purposes of the Father? Yes ❏   No ❏

Every congregation is a world missions strategy center.

A church is a living organism. It is a living body with Christ present as the Head. Each part of that body is related to Christ and to each other. Anytime God has access to His people, He can touch a world through that congregation. Every congregation is a world missions strategy center. God can touch a world through you. You just need to adjust your life to God's activity where you are.

A Laotian refugee

In Vancouver I served as interim pastor of a little church. A Laotian refugee family had joined the church the week before I came. I knew that God never adds to the body by accident. Those added to the church *are* my ministry. My responsibility as pastor was to see what God was doing when He added them to our church. I needed to see what God wanted to do in their lives through our church. I needed to see what God wanted to do through them in the life of our church.

Thomas

Thomas, the father, had been saved in a refugee camp in Thailand. His life was so gloriously transformed that he wanted all of his Laotian people to know Jesus. He went all over the community trying to find his Laotian brothers and lead them to Christ. The first week Thomas led 15 adults to the Lord. The next week he led 11 to the Lord, and he wept because he felt he was so unfaithful to the Lord.

In our next church business meeting I said, "We need to start a Laotian mission church." I shared all I knew of what God was doing. "I believe God is leading those people to the Lord so we can start a Laotian mission," I explained. Then I asked the church to decide how they sensed God wanted us to respond. They voted to start a Laotion mission church.

Then I said, "We ought to call Thomas as the pastor." I told them what God was doing in

Thomas' life. God had given him a pastor's heart. He had a burden for evangelism. He had just enrolled in a local Baptist theological college to get training to do anything God wanted to do through him. They voted to call Thomas as pastor of the new mission.

Two months later Thomas was invited to a meeting for ethnic pastors in Saint Louis. Thomas asked if he could go. I said, "Sure."

Then he asked, "Can I take some friends with me?" I didn't know what that meant until he said he wanted to take 18 friends with him. Then he said, "Henry, would you mind if I came back through all the major cities of Canada? My brothers are in all these cities. God wants me to go and lead some of them to the Lord. If God will help me, I'll find a pastor for them. Then they can have a church in every major city of Canada." Then I knew that God was doing something.

I knew that God was doing something special.

I said, "Oh, Thomas, please go!" He did. Later that year at Christmas, Laotian people from all across Canada came to celebrate the new life in Christ they had found.

Some time later I went back to Vancouver to visit. I asked about Thomas. The Laotian government had granted permission to start churches. Thomas returned to Laos and preached the gospel, and 133 members of his family came to know the Lord. He started four mission churches. He linked the church in Vancouver with the Laotian churches with the heart's desire of seeing all the Laotian people come to know the Lord.

All we saw was one Laotian refugee. What did God see? He saw a people and a whole nation being drawn to Himself. When God honors your church by placing a new member in the body, ask God to show you what He is up to. He wants to touch your community and maybe even the world through your church.

Impacting the World

Read the story of Philip and the Ethiopian in Acts 8:26-39. Then answer the following questions.

1. Who guided Philip to involve him in what God was going to do for the Ethiopian? (vv. 26, 29)

   _____

2. How much information about what he was to do did Philip have at the beginning? (v. 26)

   _____

3. When Philip saw the Ethiopian, he was watching to see what the Father was doing. What do you think he saw of God's activity? (vv. 27-28)

   _____

   _____

4. What did the Spirit tell Philip to do next? (v. 29)

   _____

5. What did Philip do to find out what God was doing in this man's life? (v. 30)

   _____

6. What did God do in this Ethiopian's life through Philip? (vv. 35-39)

   _____

   _____

7. Based on what we know of the Ethiopian (v. 27), what impact do you think this encounter could have had on the spread of the gospel?

   _____

   _____

Answers: (1) An angel of the Lord—the Spirit—guided Philip. (2) He only knew that he was to travel south on the road from Jerusalem to Gaza. (3) He saw a God-fearing man who had been to Jerusalem to worship. Since the Ethiopian was reading from Isaiah, Philip saw a

man who was seeking after God, a man interested in spiritual matters. Philip knew only God could draw a person to Himself like that. (4) The Spirit told Philip to get near the chariot. From that point Philip could then find out what he needed to do to join God in what He was doing. (5) Philip asked a probing question. (6) God used Philip to tell the good news about Jesus Christ. The Ethiopian believed the gospel message, was saved, and baptized. (7) God evidently had a plan of getting the gospel message to Ethiopia. He chose a key leader in the government and used Philip to lead him to Christ. Philip's obedience on one single day was used of God to carry the gospel to a strategic kingdom in Africa.

Think about your community. Where in your community could a person be used of God in ways that could impact world missions? Check those below that might apply and list others you can think of.
❏ International students at the local college or university
❏ International business personnel at local companies
❏ Tourists from foreign countries
❏ International seamen on ships in port
❏ Ethnic persons who have contact with their native country
❏ Local individuals who do business in foreign countries
❏ Christian youth and college students who might be called of God to be missionaries
❏ Laypersons who would be willing to serve as volunteers in short-term foreign mission projects (evangelism, medical and health care, disaster relief, agriculture, teaching English, and so forth).

Others: _____

_____

Pray and ask God if He wants you to become involved in some way with one of these groups.

When you adjust your life to God and become a Kingdom person, He can involve you in His work anywhere in the world. He is at work all over the world building His kingdom.

I was speaking to a conference in Minneapolis/St. Paul about participating with God to touch a world. A pastor from an inner-city church, said, "That's how God told me to function as a pastor! We began to look for what God was doing. Someone from Jamaica joined our church and asked, 'Would you come and preach in our country. We need the Lord so much.' I took some people with me. We started three churches while we were there. The next month God added to our church someone from another Caribbean nation. We went there and started churches. Now we are sponsoring mission churches in three Caribbean nations."

Then he smiled and said, "Last Sunday we had a man join our church from Ghana, West Africa. I don't know what God's up to, but we're ready to see!"

They discovered they were Kingdom citizens. To experience God and to know and do the will of God is to put your life alongside the activity of God and let the Spirit of God show you why that happened in your church. Adjust your life to Him, and let Him work through you to draw a world to Himself.

Isn't it sad when we become so self-centered that we come into the presence of God and say, "Oh God, bless me. Bless my family. Bless my church."

Then God says something like: "I've been trying to do that all along, but in a completely different way than you have anticipated. I want you to deny self. Pick up a cross and follow me. I will lead you to places where I am working, and I'll include you. You will be an instrument in My hand so I can touch a world. When I do that through you, you will really experience My blessings."

Review today's lesson. Pray and ask God to identify one or more statements or Scriptures that He wants you to understand, learn, or practice. Underline it (them). Then respond to the following:

What was the most meaningful statement or Scripture you read today?

_____

_____

Touching the Caribbean and Africa from Minneapolis

Reword the statement or Scripture into a prayer of response to God.

_____

_____

_____

What does God want you to do in response to today's study?

_____

_____

KINGDOM WAYS, PART 1

When God speaks to you through the Holy Spirit, He is going to reveal Himself, His purposes, and *His ways*. Citizens in God's kingdom are to function to accomplish God's purposes in *kingdom ways* not in human ways. " 'My thoughts are not your thoughts, neither are your ways my ways' declares the Lord. 'As the heavens are higher than the earth, so are my ways higher than your ways and my thoughts than your thoughts' " (Isa. 55:8-9).

The principles of God's kingdom and the principles of the world are vastly different. Jesus said, "My kingdom is not of this world. If it were, my servants would fight to prevent my arrest by the Jews. But now my kingdom is from another place" (John 18:36). Servants in God's kingdom do not function the way the world would expect. Paul cautioned the Christians at Colosse, "See to it that no one takes you captive through hollow and deceptive philosophy, which depends on human tradition and the basic principles of this world rather than on Christ" (Col. 2:8).

 Once God invites you to join Him in His work, how will you be able to accomplish *His* kingdom purposes? Check one.
- ❏ 1. In any way I choose.
- ❏ 2. By following human reason, human principles, and human traditions.
- ❏ 3. By using my best thinking and working in my own way.
- ❏ 4. By following God's way.

Your human ways will not bring forth lasting spiritual fruit. God's purposes are accomplished only by God's ways. In the next two lessons I want you to go to the Scriptures under the Holy Spirit's guidance and let Him reveal some of the basic truths about the Kingdom and Kingdom ways. Remember that spiritual truth is not just a concept to be thought about, debated, or discussed. Truth is a Person. As God reveals Himself, His purposes, and *His ways* you need to be prepared to respond to Him in obedience.

Parables of the Kingdom

Jesus told many parables about the Kingdom. (A parable is a true-to-life story that illustrates a spiritual truth.) Jesus tried to help His disciples understand some of the characteristics of His kingdom and of Kingdom ways. Although some of Jesus' parables have much symbolic meaning (like the wheat and weeds below), most of the parables have one primary idea to teach.

Read the following parables of the Kingdom and respond to the questions that follow. Ask the Holy Spirit to give you spiritual understanding and guide you in application of these Kingdom truths. If the meaning for you and your church is not clear, just write "not clear."

The principles of God's kingdom and the principles of the world are vastly different.

The Wheat and the Weeds

Read Matthew 13:24-30, 36-43—The Parable of the Wheat and the Weeds (Tares)

1. According to Jesus' interpretation (vv. 37-43), match the items on the left with the interpretation on the right. Draw a line between the ones that go together.

Parable	Kingdom
One who sowed good seed	the devil
The good seed	sons of the evil one
The field	angels
One who sowed weeds	the Son of Man
The weeds	the end of the age
The harvest	the world
The harvesters	sons of the kingdom

2. According to this parable, what two kinds of people will appear to be members of Christ's kingdom?

_____

3. The two kinds of people will be separated. When and by whom?

_____

4. What meaning do you think this parable has for you or your church?

_____

_____

Membership rolls of churches are not the true test of whether a person belongs to the Kingdom. Just because a person has some resemblance to other Christians does not mean he is a Christian. Using this parable, Jesus teaches that some lost and evil people are mixed with true believers in churches. Notice, however, that God is the one who will make the final judgment about each person's relationship to Him. We should give ourselves to helping true believers grow and bear fruit. God will do the weeding out of unbelievers. That is His job. When a person is not bearing fruit, we should let God work through us to help the person with his deepest spiritual need. He knows what that need is, and what needs to be done about it. Sometimes, however, Christian discipline is required as an expression of God-like love (Matt. 18:15-17; Heb. 12:6).

The Mustard Seed

Read Matthew 13:31-32—The Parable of the Mustard Seed

1. Based on size, how does the Kingdom start and how does it end?

_____

2. What meaning do you think this parable has for you or your church?

_____

_____

Even though you may feel small and insignificant, you can find hope in the story of the mustard seed. God can take something small and seemingly insignificant and use it to produce something large and helpful. Are there changes you think God wants to make in your family or church? Do you feel like you are just not strong enough or influential enough? Be encouraged! God can do anything He wants with one person who believes Him and will obey Him. Does your church feel like it is too small to do much? What seems impossible with man is possible with God (Matt. 19:26). A church committed to the lordship of Christ can touch the world!

The Yeast

Read Matthew 13:33—The Parable of the Yeast (Leaven)

1. Which of the following best describes the way the Kingdom grows or spreads? Check one.
   - ❏ a. The kingdom grows rapidly like an explosion.
   - ❏ b. The kingdom grows steadily, but thoroughly.
   - ❏ c. The kingdom grows very little.

2. What meaning do you think this parable has for you or your church?

_____

_____

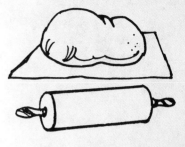

Do you ever want to see things change quickly at church or in your community? They can. But in the Kingdom, growth is more often like the yeast in a lump of bread dough. Yeast affects the dough nearby. Then that dough affects the dough nearest it. Before long a little yeast can bring about change in the whole lump. Be patient and faithful to the Lord. God will cause your small influence to have far reaching effects in His timing. Don't try to force change with your own strength. Trust God to do His work of bringing change through you.

Read Matthew 13:44-46—The Parables of the Hidden Treasure and the Pearl

1. How valuable is entrance into the Kingdom? _____

The Hidden Treasure and the Pearl

2. What would a wise person be willing to do to enter the Kingdom?

_____

3. What meaning do you think this parable has for you or your church?

_____

_____

The Talents

Participation in the Kingdom is more valuable than anything you can imagine. Jesus said it would be worth giving up everything you have in order to gain entrance to the Kingdom. In fact that is exactly what He demands (Luke 14:33). You must deny yourself and yield every-thing to His Lordship in order to be a disciple—the benefits are well worth the cost.

Read Matthew 25:14-30—The Parable of the Talents (Money)

1. What reward was given to the faithful servants who were good stewards of what the master had given them? (vv. 21, 23)

_____

2. How did the wicked, lazy servant misuse the money the master entrusted to him? (vv. 24-27)

_____

3. What meaning do you think this parable has for you or your church?

_____

_____

A very important Kingdom principle is found in the parable of the talents. (Talents were *units of money* in the time of Jesus.) When God gives you or your church resources, people, or assignments to develop and use for the Kingdom, He expects faithful stewardship. To those who are faithful, He will entrust even more and greater things. Jesus sums this princi-ple up this way:

If you are faithful in a little, Godwill make you ruler over much.

If you (or your church) are not faithful with what God entrusts to your care, don't be sur-prised if He refuses to give you more. Don't be surprised if He even takes away what He gave you. For instance, suppose God gives a church several new people who join on profession of their faith. If the church just leaves them to grow and mature on their own, these new believers may get discouraged and drop out. Have you ever heard a church say something like, "We are bringing people in the front door, and they are leaving out the back door"? If God is giving them, and a church is loosing them, the church would do well to take a seri-ous look at the stewardship of those lives God is giving.

Suppose God seems to stop or decrease the people, resources, or assignments He is entrust-ing to you or your church. That ought to cause you to stand before the Master and find out what He wants you or your church to do and be. There may be a serious flaw that He wants to correct (Luke 19:26).

Match the Kingdom principle on the left with the parable on the right that teaches the principle. Write the correct letters in the blanks.

___ 1. Belonging to God's kingdom is worth giving up everything.

___ 2. He that is faithful with a little will be made ruler over much.

___ 3. Although non-Christians have joined our churches, God knows the ones who belong to Him. He will separate Christians from non-Christians in judgment.

___ 4. A small godly influence steadily grows and eventually affects those around it.

___ 5. Small beginnings can grow into great ministries for the Kingdom's sake.

A. Wheat and Weeds

B. Mustard Seed

C. Yeast

D. Hidden Treasure/Pearl

E. Talents

Answers are: 1-D; 2-E; 3-A; 4-C; 5-B.

Review today's lesson. Pray and ask God to identify one or more statements or Scriptures that He wants you to understand, learn, or practice. Underline it (them). Then respond to the following:

What was the most meaningful statement or Scripture you read today?

_____

_____

Reword the statement or Scripture into a prayer of response to God.

_____

_____

What does God want you to do in response to today's study?

_____

_____

SUMMARY STATEMENTS

- God can do anything He wants with one person who believes Him and will obey Him.
- God can cause my small influence to have far-reaching effects in His timing.
- The Kingdom is worth everything.
- If I am faithful in a little, God will make me ruler over much.

DAY 3 KINGDOM WAYS, PART 2

The teachings of Jesus are filled with principles for living in His kingdom.

Here are some other parables of the Kingdom. I have listed at least one Kingdom truth that comes from each. You may want to read and study them as an optional activity.

 Select two of the following parables for further study. Circle the Scripture reference for the two parables you will study.

- **Matthew 13:47-50—The Parable of the Net—**God and His angels are the ones who distinguish between the wicked and the righteous in judgment.
- **Matthew 18:23-35—The Parable of the Wicked Servant—**Forgive and show mercy to others the way God does to you.
- **Matthew 20:1-16—The Parable of the Laborers in the Vineyard—**God is sovereign and generous. God is being fair when He treats new converts just as generously as He does people who have served Him for many years.

- **Matthew 25:1-13—The Parable of the Ten Virgins—**Keep watch and be prepared for the Lord Jesus to return. When He comes you must be ready.
- **Matthew 25:31-46—The Parable of the Sheep and Goats—**Those who really belong to the Kingdom will demonstrate their love for God by loving their fellowman. This love will be demonstrated in acts of kindness to meet real needs of others.
- **Mark 4:26-29—The Parable of the Seed Growing Secretly—**Human effort alone cannot produce fruit. Apart from Him, we can do nothing. Yet, we are privileged to work together with God in His kingdom work. But only He is able to bring forth the fruit.
- **Other parables** relate to the Kingdom but do not specifically mention "the kingdom." Here are some passages you also may want to study: Matthew 7:1-6; Matthew 7:24-27; Matthew 9:16-17; Matthew 11:16-17; Matthew 12:43-45; Matthew 13:3-8, 18-23; Matthew 21:28-30; Matthew 21:33-43; Matthew 24:32-35; Mark 4:21-22; Luke 7:41-42; Luke 10:30-37; Luke 11:5-8; Luke 12:16-21; Luke 13:6-9; Luke 14:16-24; Luke 14:28-30; Luke 14:31; Luke 15:4-7; Luke 15:8-9; Luke 15:11-32; Luke 16:1-9; Luke 16:19-31; Luke 17:7-10; Luke 18:2-5.

Answer the following questions for the parables you selected.

Parable 1:

1. What is the name of the parable and what is the Scripture reference?

_____

2. What do you sense Jesus was trying to teach by telling this parable?

_____

_____

3. What application of this principle do you think God wants you to make in your life? in your church?

_____

_____

Parable 2:

1. What is the name of the parable and what is the Scripture reference?

_____

2. What do you sense Jesus was trying to teach by telling this parable?

_____

_____

3. What application of this principle do you think God wants you to make in your life? in your church?

_____

_____

Kingdom Principles

The teachings of Jesus are filled with principles for living in His kingdom. The Sermon on the Mount (Matt. 5—7), for instance, is a valuable guide for right living in an evil world.

Turn in your Bible to Matthew 5—7. You do not have to read the entire sermon right now, but look for at least one principle for right living that God might want to apply to your life today. Answer the following questions:

The Sermon on the Mount

1. What is the Scripture reference? _____

2. What is the principle? State it in your own words.

_____

_____

3. How do you think God wants you to apply this principle to your life today?

_____

At sometime you may want to read through Matthew 5—7 and make a list of principles for right living. Your Experiencing God group may want to do this and then get together for a time of sharing. Through the help of the body of Christ, let God guide you to pure and faithful ways of living.

I want to list for you a few other Kingdom principles that may help you and your church more fully experience Koinonia.

As you read the following list, ask God to identify one of the principles that He wants you to pay more attention to. Circle the number of the principle. If God calls your attention to more than one, circle all the ones He identifies for you to apply more faithfully.

1. Don't worry about your life. Seek first the purposes of the Kingdom, and God will take care of your physical needs (Matt. 6:25-33).
2. To achieve greatness in the kingdom of heaven, humble yourself as a little child (Matt. 18:1-4).
3. Leadership and greatness in the Kingdom are NOT based on power, influence, or position. A leader who wants to be great will serve the needs of others. The one who wants to be first must become like a slave to others (Matt. 20:25-27).
4. The purpose of a believer or a church is to serve others, not to be served (Matt. 20:28).
5. "Whoever exalts himself will be humbled, and whoever humbles himself will be exalted" (Matt. 23:12).
6. If an individual (or a church) tries to save his spiritual life and vitality by keeping things to himself, he will lose it. If he (or a church) is willing to give himself away for the sake of others, he will find the fullness and abundance of life as God intended it to be (Luke 9:24)
7. "Stop passing judgment on one another" over disputable matters. "Make every effort to do what leads to peace and to mutual edification. . . . It is better not to . . . do anything else that will cause your brother to fall" (Rom. 14:13-21).
8. In the body of Christ, submit yourselves to one another out of reverence to Christ, the Head of the body (Eph. 5:21).
9. "Whoever is not against us is for us." Don't require everyone of God's children to 'join you.' Treat each one as a brother. (See Mark 9:38-41.)

In your own words, write the principle that God has called to your attention.

_____
_____
_____

For this principle to be correctly applied in your life, what would God want you to do differently in the way you live?

_____
_____

Write your Scripture memory verse for this week below:

_____
_____
_____

Review today's lesson. Pray and ask God to identify one or more statements or Scriptures that He wants you to understand, learn, or practice. Underline it (them). Then respond to the following:

What was the most meaningful statement or Scripture you read today?

_____
_____

Reword the statement or Scripture into a prayer of response to God.

_____
_____

What does God want you to do in response to today's study?

_____

_____

Write your own summary for today's lesson.

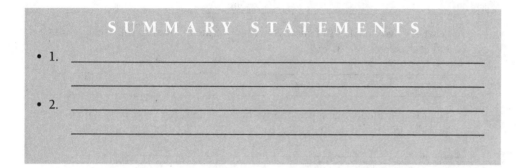

SUMMARY STATEMENTS

• 1. _____

_____

• 2. _____

_____

KOINONIA

In the mind and teaching of Jesus a church was a vital, living, dynamic fellowship of believers. The Greek word *koinonia*, most frequently translated "fellowship," is the best way to describe what a church ought to be. In these last two units I will use the word *Koinonia* to mean the fullest possible partnership and fellowship with God and with other believers.

Underline in the following paragraph words and phrases that help you understand the meaning of *Koinonia*.

Koinonia, or intimate fellowship, in the church is based on a personal *Koinonia* with God in Christ by individual believers. *Koinonia* with God only comes from a real, personal encounter with the living Christ and surrender to Him as absolute Lord of life. This is the intimate love relationship we have talked about. God pursues that kind of a relationship with you.

How would you define *koinonia*? _____

_____

Which of the following words can you use to describe your relationship to God? Check all that apply.

❏ alive   ❏ close   ❏ cold   ❏ distant

❏ growing   ❏ intimate   ❏ personal   ❏ real

❏ removed   ❏ stagnant   ❏ uneasy   ❏ vibrant

Read 1 John 1:1-7 below and circle the word *fellowship (koinonia)* each time it occurs. Then answer the questions that follow.

> [1]That which was from the beginning, which we have heard, which we have seen with our eyes, which we have looked at and our hands have touched—this we proclaim concerning the Word of life. [2]The life appeared; we have seen it and testify to it, and we proclaim to you the eternal life, which was with the Father and has appeared to us. [3]We proclaim to you what we have seen and heard, so that you also may have fellowship with us. And our fellowship is with the Father and with his Son, Jesus Christ. [4]We write this to make our joy complete.
> [5]This is the message we have heard from him and declare to you: God is light; in him there is no darkness at all. [6]If we claim to have fellowship with him yet walk in the darkness, we lie and do not live by the truth. [7]But if we walk in the light, as he is in the light, we have fellowship with one another, and the blood of Jesus, his Son, purifies us from all sin" (1 John 1:1-7).

DAY 4

You cannot be in true fellowship with God and be out of fellowship with your fellow Christians.

Koinonia: the fullest possible partnership and fellowship with God and with others.

A real, personal encounter with the living Christ!

1. What are some words in verses 1-3 that indicate John had a personal and real relationship with the living Lord Jesus Christ?

_____

2. Why did John write about what he had seen and heard of Jesus? (v. 3)

_____

_____

3. What are two benefits to believers because of the fellowship they share with God and each other? (vv. 4, 7)

_____

_____

4. What is indicated when a person says he has fellowship (*koinonia*) with God, but he walks in sin and darkness? (v. 6)

_____

_____

5. What will be true of a person who walks in the light as God is in the light? (v. 7)

_____

_____

Answers for questions 1-5: (1) John said he had seen, heard, and touched Jesus. John had an experiential knowledge of Jesus. He had come to know Him as the "eternal life" (v. 2). John is also the one who recorded Jesus' words: "This is eternal life: that they may know you, the only true God, and Jesus Christ, whom you have sent" (John 17:3). Eternal life means knowing God by experience in a real and personal way. This is *Koinonia*—fellowship with God. (2) John proclaimed Jesus so others would believe in Him and thus have fellowship with John and the other believers. (3) When we fellowship with God and when others come into fellowship with Him and with us, our joy is made complete and we experience the cleansing work of Jesus' blood. (4) Such a person is a liar. His or her life is a lie. (5) If a person walks in the light as God is in the light, he or she will have fellowship with other believers and experience forgiveness and cleansing of sin.

Fellowship Among Believers

Our *Koinonia* as believers is with God and His Son Jesus Christ. This fellowship is an intimate partnership. It is the sharing of all God is with us and all we are with God. To me, *Koinonia* is the most complete expression of a love (*agape*) relationship with God. When you live in this kind of love relationship with God, you will have the same quality of loving fellowship with other believers.

> You cannot be in fellowship with God and His Son and not walk in godly fellowship with one another!

First John clearly states that your relationships with your Christian brothers and sisters are an expression of your relationship with God. You cannot be in true fellowship with God and be out of fellowship with your fellow Christians (brothers).

☀ **Read each of the following Scriptures. Circle the words *brother* and *brothers*. Underline the words *love* and *loves*.**

1 John 2:9-11 "Anyone who claims to be in the light but hates his brother is still in the darkness. Whoever loves his brother lives in the light, and there is nothing in him to make him stumble. But whoever hates his brother is in the darkness and walks around in the darkness."

1 John 3:10 "This is how we know who the children of God are and who the children of the devil are: Anyone who does not do what is right is not a child of God; nor is anyone who does not love his brother."

1 John 3:14-15 "We know that we have passed from death to life, because we love our brothers. Anyone who does not love remains in death. Anyone who hates his brother is a murderer, and you know that no murderer has eternal life in him."

1 John 3:16-17 "This is how we know what love is: Jesus Christ laid down his life for us. And we ought to lay down our lives for our brothers. If anyone has material possessions and sees his brother in need but has no pity on him, how can the love of God be in him?"

1 John 4:7-8 "Let us love one another, for love comes from God. Everyone who loves has been born of God and knows God. Whoever does not love does not know God, because God is love."

1 John 4:11-12 "Since God so loved us, we also ought to love one another. No one has ever seen God; but if we love one another, God lives in us and his love is made complete in us."

1 John 4:20-21 "If anyone says, 'I love God,' yet hates his brother, he is a liar. For anyone who does not love his brother, whom he has seen, cannot love God, whom he has not seen. And he has given us this command: Whoever loves God must also love his brother."

1 John 5:1-2 "Everyone who loves the father loves his child as well. This is how we know that we love the children of God: by loving God and carrying out his commands."

How is your relationship with God reflected in your relationship with your "brother"? How does your relationship with your brother indicate the kind of relationship you have with God?

_____

_____

_____

Do you believe these Scriptures from 1 John are true? _____
If you are in a right relationship with God, how will you treat your Christian brothers and sisters?

_____

Suppose a person claimed to be a Christian. Suppose he claimed to love Jesus, yet he treated his Christian brothers and sisters harshly. He was unkind and hateful toward them. He was consistently in arguments with them. He publicly ridiculed them or slandered their name or reputation. He was unwilling to help them when they were in need. In the light of 1 John, what would you say about this person's relationship with God? Check one or more responses that you agree with, or write your own response on the line for "other."

❏ 1. I would take this person's word that he is a Christian who really loves Jesus.
❏ 2. I would question whether this person really knew and loved God at all.
❏ 3. I would think that this person had a very serious problem in his relationship with God.
❏ 4. Other:

Turn in your Bible to 1 Corinthians 13. Slowly read verses 4-8 and write on the lines below words and phrases that describe what Christian love is and is not. I have written one for you.

Love is …	Love is not…
patient	

If you love God, your love for your fellow Christians will show. You will be patient and kind. You will not be envious, boastful, proud, rude, self-seeking, or easily angered. You will not hold grudges. You will rejoice in truth and right, not in evil. You will protect and trust your Christian brothers and sisters. You will hope the best for others, and you will persevere in your love. This God-like love grows out of an intimate love relationship with God. In John 13:35 Jesus said:

"By this all men will know that you are my disciples, if you love one another."

Take some time to pray. **Ask God to reveal the truth to you about your fellowship (love relationship) with Him and with your Christian brothers and sisters. Remember that anyone who is in Christ is a brother or sister in the Lord.**

What do you sense God is saying about your fellowship with other Christians?

_____

_____

What do you sense God is saying about your fellowship with Him?

_____

_____

These two evaluations of your fellowship ought to be similar. If you say your fellowship with the Lord is good, but your fellowship with other Christians is poor, something is wrong. If you walk in intimate fellowship with God, you also will walk in intimate fellowship with your brothers and sisters in Christ.

Review today's lesson. Pray and ask God to identify one or more statements or Scriptures that He wants you to understand, learn, or practice. Underline it (them). Then respond to the following:

What was the most meaningful statement or Scripture you read today?

_____

_____

_____

Reword the statement or Scripture into a prayer of response to God.

_____

_____

_____

_____

What does God want you to do in response to today's study?

_____

_____

_____

SUMMARY STATEMENTS

- A church is a vital, living, dynamic fellowship of believers.
- *Koinonia* is the fullest possible partnership and fellowship with God and with others.
- I cannot be in fellowship with God and His Son and not walk in godly fellowship with other believers.

Kingdom people are interrelated with the other members and believers of the Kingdom worldwide. After 12 years at Faith Baptist Church in Saskatoon, I became Director of Missions for an association of 11 churches and mission churches in the greater Vancouver area of British Columbia, Canada. Guiding a church to walk with Christ as Head of His body is one matter. Guiding an association of 11 congregations to walk together with God with one heart and one mind is a different matter. I had to face some serious questions:

- Would God speak to the churches individually, and then bring them to one mind as they came together as an association?
- Would the churches respond to God when He spoke?
- Would the churches have the same kind of *Koinonia* (fellowship) with other churches as believers have with other believers in a local church?
- Would churches be willing to give freely of themselves in order to experience the fullest life God has to offer (Luke 9:23-24) ?
- Would godly fellowship be expressed by the free sharing of resources with churches that had needs?

I came to this new assignment with the conviction that "the God we serve is able . . . and he will" (Dan. 3:17). Biblical principles of God's working with His people do not change. Yes, helping a group of churches to learn to walk with God in intimate *Koinonia* with Him and with each other took some time. But God is the One who does that kind of miraculous work. I was only a vessel through which He chose to work.

Though we were a small band with few resources, God manifested His presence in the life of the churches and the association. At the beginning of unit 1 (p. 7), you read about how God led our churches to walk by faith as we witnessed to the people attending Expo '86. At the beginning of this unit (p. 183) you read about how God worked through our association to begin ministry to East Indians. In four years the number of churches and missions in our association doubled. Student work grew from one part-time student director to five full-time directors. Almost one hundred persons expressed a sense of call into ministry or missions work. Once-strained relationships with other church groups flourished into dynamic cooperative efforts of fellowship and outreach. God did so much more than we could ever ask or think, according to the Holy Spirit's enabling power at work in His churches (Eph. 3:20-21).

☀ **As you read the following paragraphs about the relationships between churches in our association, underline some things that indicate we had a functioning *Koinonia* between the churches.**

Our association in Saskatchewan had a unique *Koinonia* created by the Holy Spirit. Together our churches drew grids over the province. We developed a network to reach the entire province for Christ. Much like the New Testament churches, we considered everything each of us possessed as belonging by love to each other. A church's resources don't belong to the people themselves. The church is merely a steward of the resources. Everything a church has belongs to the Kingdom. Anything that our church in Saskatoon had was available to all the others. When one church called a student minister, he became a resource for every other church to call on for help in developing student ministry. When our church had a summer youth program, we invited other churches that were too small to have their own to participate with us. We even shared copy machines and other physical resources. If one needed financial help, we didn't hesitate to let God's people know. Then we would take an offering. Once we even mortgaged our building to help a mission church get a building of their own.

This kind of sharing developed a deep sense of *Koinonia* among our churches. We belonged to each other. We needed each other. We went out of our way to help each other and meet the needs that each church had. We learned to love each other. We planned times to get together for fellowship and mutual encouragement. That is what Christ's kingdom ought to be like. The watching world ought to be able to say, "Look how they love one another." That unique kind of love can only come from God. When people see that kind of God-like love, they will be drawn to Christ and His church.

Koinonia **takes on new dimensions, new possibilities, and new richness as churches relate in the wider circles of the Kingdom.**

"The God we serve is able . . . and he will" (Dan. 3:17).

We considered everything each church possessed as belonging by love to each other.

Sharing developed a deep sense of Koinonia among our churches.

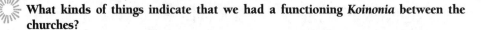 **What kinds of things indicate that we had a functioning *Koinonia* between the churches?**

_____

_____

_____

_____

_____

When *Koinonia* exists between churches, it will show in their relationships. We cooperated in our commission to reach our world for Christ. We were able to do things together that no one of the churches alone could have done effectively. We shared anything we had if it would meet the need of a sister church. We spent time together and loved each other.

Can that kind of *Koinonia* exist between churches not only on an associational level but also on a state, provincial, national, or international level? Yes! Can God-like *Koinonia* exist between churches of different denominations as they cooperate to achieve greater Kingdom purposes? Yes! However, humans left to their own ways cannot achieve those kinds of relationships. Only God through His Holy Spirit can create and sustain *Koinonia* between His people. He wants to be the King, Ruler, and Sovereign over all His kingdom. When He is allowed to rule, man-made barriers will fall.

When we have *Koinonia* with God the same quality and nature of that *Koinonia* will be reflected when we relate to:
* brothers and sisters in our local church
* other churches in a local area
* other churches in a state or province
* other churches in a nation
* other churches in the world
* other churches of different Christian denominations

When Christ is allowed to rule, man-made barriers will fall.

Based on the relationships your church has with other churches and denominations in your local area and worldwide, what kind of *Koinonia* would a watching world see?

_____

_____

What does your church do, or fail to do, that indicates it is not a functioning *Koinonia* in relationship to other churches or Christian groups? (For instance, some church league sports teams develop a poor reputation in the community because of their displays of anger, jealousy, rudeness, violence, and even hatred. That reflects a deep fellowship problem.)

_____

_____

If your church has a *Koinonia* problem with other Christian churches or groups, that is an indicator of a deeper *Koinonia* problem with the Lord. I am not suggesting that doctrinal differences ought to be compromised, but we can act like brothers and sisters who love each other. *Koinonia* takes on new dimensions, new possibilities, and new fullness as we relate in the wider circles of the Kingdom. This is the same way love works.

Love on a Scale of 1 to 10

Suppose, on a scale of one to ten, you are loving at level two—you love your parents and family who love you; and you love your friends who love you. Now, suppose God enables you to love your arch enemy like Jesus commanded in Matthew 5:43-48. If you can love your enemy at level ten, your capacity to love other persons will increase. If you can love on a level of ten, every other person that you have been loving will receive a greater dimension of love than you have ever been able to give them.

Evaluate your Christian love life. Check all of the following statements that are true of your Christian love.

❑ 1. I don't love anybody.
❑ 2. I love my family.
❑ 3. I love those who love me first.
❑ 4. I love those whom I know will love me, too.
❑ 5. God has helped me love those around me who are irritable and unfriendly.
❑ 6. God has taught me to love those in my community who are unlovely, people who are very different from me.
❑ 7. God has taught me to show love for people who are openly living in sin.
❑ 8. God has given me the grace to love my enemies.

You and I usually do not try to improve our capacity to love by loving the hard to love. We try to love our "enemy" and frustration and anger confront us, instead of a new kind of love. Then we say, "Lord, I didn't want you to bring anger into my life. I wanted you to bring love into my life." But God can deepen our capacity to love as He enables us to love the unlovely. When we learn to love at these deeper levels, our capacity to love others grows.

While I was in Vancouver, our association of churches made a commitment to love everyone and to help every person in Vancouver know the Lord. Isn't that what Jesus commanded us in the Great Commission (Matt. 28:18-20) ? God put me in a relationship with a person who had a deep love for anarchists. They were young adults who were mad at everybody and wanted to destroy established order and authority. This man said, "Henry, go with me to the anarchists' restaurant. I want you to listen to this group of people with all of their anger and bitterness. I want you to see how God can bring the gospel to them."

That was a very powerful experience for me. I sat in that restaurant for three hours listening to an outpouring of hate and bitterness. By the aid of the Spirit of God, with my heart, mind, and life I came to love those people. I tell you, the next Christian I met got love poured out on him. He didn't know what had come over me. God brought me to a deeper capacity to love when He taught me to love anarchists.

Is God impressing you to demonstrate your love to a specific individual, a specific group of people, or perhaps people who are different from you? Ask Him. If God is impressing you to demonstrate your love at a deeper level, write below the name of the one or ones He wants you to love.

_____

_____

Cooperative Relationships between Churches

The churches of the New Testament were INTERdependent. Each was independent before the Lord, yet they needed each other. They helped and encouraged each other. They had cooperative relationships that enhanced their experience of God.

As you read about each of the following relationships, underline or write in the right margin a few examples that clearly indicate that the New Testament churches had _Koinonia_ with each other. I've given you one example.

The Young Church of Jerusalem. On the day of Pentecost 3,000 people came to trust in Christ. We do not know how many of these lived or remained in Jerusalem after the Jewish feast was over. We do know, however, that the Jerusalem church had many members. Early on, they met in the temple courts and in many smaller groups in individual homes. They met daily for teaching, fellowship, eating, and prayer. They shared their material resources with any believer who had a need (Acts 2:42-47). These many small congregations were interdependent. Because of _Koinonia_ they were "one in heart and mind" (Acts 4:32).

Jerusalem Shares with Antioch. When the gospel began to bear fruit among the Greeks at Antioch, the Jerusalem church sent Barnabas to investigate and help the young church. When Barnabas saw God's activity there, he got Saul (Paul) to come and help. Together they stayed in Antioch teaching the new converts (Acts 11:19-26).

Antioch Shares with the Needs in Jerusalem. Word came to the church at Antioch that their Christian brothers and sisters in Judea were suffering from a famine. Because of _Koinonia_,

Loving anarchists

Interdependent churches

"The disciples, each according to his ability, decided to provide help for the brothers living in Judea. This they did, sending their gift to the elders by Barnabas and Saul" (Acts 11:29-30). These churches were not totally independent. They were bound together by their common *Koinonia* with Christ. They had to care for each other's needs out of love.

Antioch Sends Out Barnabas and Saul. The church at Antioch was missions minded. They shared Christ's heart for a lost world. One day "While they were worshiping the Lord and fasting, the Holy Spirit said, 'Set apart for me Barnabas and Saul for the work to which I have called them.' So after they had fasted and prayed, they placed their hands on them and sent them off" (Acts 13:2-3). The church at Antioch freely had received leaders, and they freely gave them for the spread of the Kingdom.

God spoke through the church to Barnabas and Saul.

Notice that Barnabas and Saul (Paul) already had been called to take the gospel to the Gentiles. Saul's conversion and call had occurred several years before (Acts 9:1-19; Gal. 1:16-24). Only in the midst of the body of Christ did they come to know the right timing for their missionary work. God spoke to them by the Holy Spirit and through the church. Don't be afraid to trust God and your church to help you know God's will and His timing for your Kingdom assignments.

Jerusalem Helps Maintain Sound Doctrine. When a dispute arose about the nature of salvation, Paul and Barnabas went to Jerusalem for consultation. The apostles, elders, and church at Jerusalem helped settle the dispute. Then they sent two of their own members to the church at Antioch to instruct, encourage, and strengthen the Gentile Christians.

Other Churches Cooperate for Kingdom Purposes. Throughout Paul's letters, we read of ways the churches cooperated with other Christians for the Kingdom's sake.
- The faith of the **Roman Christians** encouraged others all over the Christian world (Rom. 1:8-12). Paul planned on receiving assistance from this church for a journey to Spain he was planning (Rom. 15:24).
- **Churches in Macedonia and Achaia** sent contributions to the poor Christians in Jerusalem (Rom. 15:26-27).
- **The church at Philippi** frequently provided financial support for Paul so that he could preach the gospel and start churches in other cities (Phil. 4:14-16).
- **The churches at Colosse and Laodicea** shared workers (Epaphras) and letters from Paul (Col. 4:12-16).
- The believers in **the church at Thessalonica** inspired and became models to all the believers in Macedonia and Achaia (1 Thess. 1:6-10).

Which of the following best describes the relationship of churches in the New Testament? Check your response.
- ❏ 1. The churches were isolated and independent. They did not care about or need relationships with the others.
- ❏ 2. The churches were interdependent. They cared about each other, and they encouraged and helped each other.

What example can you give of how your church has experienced *Koinonia* because of a cooperative relationship with another church or Christian group?

_____

_____

_____

Experiencing More of God

A believer cannot experience God in all the dimensions God has for him or her apart from the body of Christ—a local church. In the body and together on mission to the ends of the earth, Christians begin to experience the fuller dimensions of life in God's kingdom. As we experience *Koinonia* with other groups of God's people, we experience greater dimensions of God's presence at work in our world. God already has in place channels through which you and your church can touch a world for Him. You need to allow Him to break down any barriers that may prevent you from experiencing all there is of God through *Koinonia* with others. Go to Him and watch for His initiative. He can show you how, with whom, and when.

Fill in the blank in the following statement.

The churches of the New Testament were not independent.

They were _____. They needed fellowship with each other to experience the greater dimensions of God and the *Koinonia* He provides.

Review today's lesson. Pray and ask God to identify one or more statements or Scriptures that He wants you to understand, learn, or practice. Underline it (them). Then respond to the following:

What was the most meaningful statement or Scripture you read today?

_____

_____

_____

Reword the statement or Scripture into a prayer of response to God.

_____

_____

_____

What does God want you to do in response to today's study?

_____

_____

_____

Write your Scripture memory verse (1 John 1:7) on the following lines.

_____

_____

Review your Scripture memory verses and be prepared to recite them to a partner in your small-group session this week.

SUMMARY STATEMENTS

- Everything each church possessed belonged by love to each other.
- Everything a church has belongs to the Kingdom.
- When *Koinonia* exists between churches, it will show in their relationships.
- When Christ is allowed to rule, man-made barriers will fall.
- The churches of the New Testament were interdependent.
- As my church experiences *Koinonia* with other groups of God's people, we experience greater dimensions of God's presence at work in our world.

CONTINUING FELLOWSHIP WITH GOD

UNIT

12

The Saskatoon Awakening

I went to Saskatoon to talk with Faith Baptist Church about coming as their pastor. I went to see if God wanted me to serve there. In Saskatoon God spoke to me through a local pastor who told me that Duncan Campbell had been in Saskatoon the previous year. [Duncan Campbell was used of God in a great and powerful way in a spiritual awakening in the Hebrides islands off the coast of Scotland.] Duncan said that the night before he had been assured by God that revival fires would break out here and spread all across Canada. That turned me inside out. Much of my life I have had a yearning to see spiritual awakening come to Canada. I saw how the spiritual markers God had placed in my life pointed me to this work in Saskatoon, so I accepted the call to come as to pastor of Faith Baptist Church.

I wanted to pray for awakening with fellow pastors from many denominations in the city. On Tuesdays I met with one group to pray for awakening, and on Thursdays I met with the other. For a year and a half we pastors prayed together. One day Bill McCleod called and said, "Henry that for which we have been praying is happening!" He explained that they had just finished a week of revival meetings. Two brothers in his church had not spoken to each other for six years. Both were deacons. They ran across that auditorium, hugged, wept, and renewed their relationship. A deep moving of God swept the congregation.

The services continued and many in the Christian community began to participate. The crowd outgrew Bill's church. We moved to the Anglican church that seats 700. In one night the church was filled. We moved to the Alliance church that seated 900 and overflowed in two days. Then we moved to the United church that seated 1,500. We held services every night for eleven weeks. The services would last until ten or eleven o'clock every night. Each night we held an after-meeting where people stayed in great numbers getting right with God. Sometimes the after-meetings lasted until four and five o'clock in the morning. From that awakening revivals broke out across Canada.

Verse to Memorize this Week

Let us consider how we may spur one another on toward love and good deeds. Let us not give up meeting together, as some are in the habit of doing, but let us encourage one another—and all the more as you see the Day approaching. —HEBREWS 10:24-25

God's Remedy for Broken Fellowship

Koinonia is not an option for a believer. Koinonia is not optional for a church. To be "in Christ" and to be a member of His body requires a fellowship with the living Christ. The love relationship, the Koinonia, the fellowship you have with God, is the most important aspect of your knowing Him, knowing His will, and being enabled to do His will.

Koinonia is not an option for me or my church.

Koinonia is essential for individuals and churches if they are to experience the vitality we see in New Testament Christians. Intimate fellowship with God and His Son, Jesus Christ, produces fellowship with Christian brothers and sisters. Only God can produce this genuine Koinonia (fellowship). The supreme expression of this divine fellowship is manifested when people with major differences are brought into a living spiritual fellowship.

Only God can produce genuine Koinonia.

🔆 **Which of the following is the greater demonstration of God's ability to create and maintain fellowship between people? Check one.**
- ❏ 1. Godly fellowship between people with similar ethnic background, language, education, and economic conditions or
- ❏ 2. Godly fellowship between people who are very different in background and social standing

When human barriers fall and people with significant differences can live together in peace, the world sees something only God can do. In God's kingdom "there is neither Jew nor Greek, slave nor free, male nor female, for you are all one in Christ Jesus" (Gal. 3:28). This Koinonia created by the Holy Spirit also is maintained by the Spirit. Koinonia with God and with others can, however, be threatened and even broken.

Sometimes broken fellowship with a brother or sister in Christ may be due to the other person's sin and broken fellowship with God. In that case you would want to pray for him or her and do everything you can to help the person return to the Lord.

Broken fellowship with a brother or sister in Christ indicates a broken fellowship with God.

Broken fellowship with a brother or sister in Christ indicates a broken fellowship with God. You always ought to begin by looking at your own relationship to the Lord. The break begins in your relationship with God. It does not start with your relationship to another person. If your fellowship with God is broken, you cannot *continue* in fellowship with Him or with your Christian brothers and sisters. You must first allow God to bring you back into right relationship with Himself.

Sin Breaks Koinonia with God

Sin separates you from intimate fellowship with God. Several words in the Bible (such as *sin, transgression, iniquity,* and *evil*) relate to what is commonly called "sin." You sin against God when you:
- Miss the mark of His purposes for you
- Rebel against Him, refuse to follow Him
- Commit acts of evil, wickedness, or immorality

When you sin against God, your fellowship with Him is broken. In the Old Testament this broken relationship is symbolized by God's hidden face. A person's face includes the major organs for communication. The *eyes* see. The *ears* hear. The *mouth* speaks. Though God does not have a physical body, God's "face" represented to the Hebrew God's presence, acceptance, and approval. For God to turn away His face was a sign of rejection, disapproval, and the absence of His presence.

God's face

🔆 **Circle the word *face* in each of the following verses.**

- "In a surge of anger I hid my face from you" (Isa. 54:8).
- "I was enraged by his sinful greed; I punished him, and hid my face in anger" (Isa. 57:17).
- "You have hidden your face from us and made us waste away because of our sins" (Isa. 64:7).
- "I will hide my face from this city because of all its wickedness" (Jer. 33:5).

Match the Scriptures with the part of God's "face" involved. Write *eyes, ears,* or *mouth* on the line beside each of the following passages of Scripture.

_____ 1. "If I had cherished sin in my heart, the Lord would not have listened" (Ps. 66:18).

_____ 2. "Your iniquities have separated you from your God; your sins have hidden his face from you, so that he will not hear" (Isa. 59:2).

_____ 3. "I will send a famine through the land—not a famine of food or a thirst for water, but a famine of hearing the words of the Lord. Men will stagger from sea to sea and wander from north to east, searching for the word of the Lord, but they will not find it" (Amos 8:11-12).

_____ 4. "Your eyes are too pure to look on evil; you cannot tolerate wrong" (Hab. 1:13).

When the Bible says God hid His face, what does it mean? Check ALL correct responses:
❏ a. God was scared.
❏ b. God withdrew the experience of His presence.
❏ c. God rejected a person or people because of sin.
❏ d. God refused to look, hear, or speak because of wickedness.

Why does God hide His face? _____

_____

_____

God does not hide His face because He is scared. He hides His face out of anger for sin. It shows His withdrawal of the experience of His presence, His rejection of sin, and His refusal to see, hear, or speak. When that happens, our fellowship with God is broken. (Other answers are: eyes—4, ears—1 and 2, and mouth—3.) No wonder the Psalmist cried out in anguish, "How long, O Lord? Will you forget me forever? How long will you hide your face from me?" (Ps. 13:1). Fellowship with God is the most cherished privilege of the child of God. God's hidden face is one of the most terrible disciplines.

Even God's discipline comes as an expression of love designed to draw us back into fellowship with Him (Heb. 12:1-11). This experience of an individual's broken fellowship with God also can happen to a group—a family, a church, a denomination, or a nation.

God's Remedies for Sin

Thank God He has given us a remedy for sin and broken fellowship:

> If we confess our sins, he is faithful and just and will forgive us our sins and purify us from all unrighteousness (1 John 1:9).

Confess

Repent

You *confess* your sin when you *agree* with God about the awful nature of your wrong. Confession and repentance go together. When you *repent* of sin you *turn away from* the sin and *return to God*. When your fellowship with God is broken because of sin, agree with Him about your sin and turn from it. Return to God and He will forgive you and reestablish your relationship to Him.

☀ **When Koinonia with God is broken because of sin, what must you do to be forgiven of your sin?**

_____

No one could number the ways a person can sin against God, and all sin breaks Koinonia with God. God's remedy for your sin is that you agree with Him, turn away from your sin, and return to Him. You must confess and repent.

When you sin, the Holy Spirit convicts you of the sin. God wants you to remain in right relationship with Him always. When you do not respond to the Holy Spirit's conviction, God will discipline you. God's discipline always is intended to draw you back into Koinonia with Him. If you do not immediately respond to God's discipline, He will bring on you more severe judgments to get your attention. (See Lev. 26.) These judgments may come on a family, a church, a denomination, or even a nation. When God brings judgment on His people, He also offers to forgive and bring healing to the land:

"How long, O Lord? Will you forget me forever? How long will you hide your face from me?"

—Psalm 13:1

"When I shut up the heavens so that there is no rain, or command locusts to devour the land or send a plague among my people, if my people, who are called by my name, will humble themselves and pray and seek my face and turn from their wicked ways, then will I hear from heaven and will forgive their sin and will heal their land" (2 Chron. 7:13-14).

Based on the promise of 2 Chronicles 7:14, answer the following questions:

1. When God brings judgment on His people, what four things should they do to find restored Koinonia?

_____

_____

2. What three things does God promise to do when His people return to Him?

_____

_____

God's remedy for restored fellowship with Him involves humility, prayer, seeking His face (seeking the experience of His presence), and repentance (turning from sin). He promises to hear, forgive sin, and heal the land! In Numbers 6:24-26 God told the priests to pray this beautiful blessing for the people:

> The Lord bless you and keep you;
> the Lord make his face shine upon you
>   and be gracious to you;
> the Lord turn his face toward you
>   and give you peace.

In the following box I have summarized what you have studied about God's remedy for sin, and I have included some other statements and Scriptures that may be helpful.

GOD'S REMEDY FOR SIN

- Humble yourself. Do not try to justify yourself. Do not hold on to pride.
- Pray. God hears the prayer of repentance.
- Confess your sin to God. Agree with Him that it is wrong. Confess to all who have been directly affected by your sin and ask for their forgiveness (Matt. 5:23-24).
- Repent. Turn away from your sinful ways and return to God and His ways.
- Seek God's face. Seek to renew fellowship with God. Talk to Him. Listen for His voice.
- If your sin has been an ongoing problem, confess the sin to one or more Christian friends and ask them to pray for you to be set free from sin's bondage (Jas. 5:16).
- Grieve. Ask God to help you understand how He feels about your sin. His desire is that you feel grief. When your heart is broken over your sin, you will be less likely to ever repeat the offense (Ps. 51:17).
- Submit yourself to God. Resist the devil. Purify your heart (Jas. 4:7-10).
- Claim the promises of forgiveness, cleansing, and healing (2 Chron. 7:14; 1 John 1:9).
- Then live in the victory Jesus gives through His resurrection power!

Review today's lesson. Pray and ask God to identify one or more statements or Scriptures that He wants you to understand, learn, or practice. Underline it (them). Then respond to the following:

What was the most meaningful statement or Scripture you read today?

_____

_____

Reword the statement or Scripture into a prayer of response to God.

_____

_____

What does God want you to do in response to today's study?

_____

_____

Write your Scripture memory verse for this unit on the following lines and review your verses from other units.

_____

_____

_____

_____

_____

_____

SUMMARY STATEMENTS

- Koinonia is created and maintained by the Holy Spirit.
- Broken fellowship with a brother or sister in Christ indicates a broken fellowship with God.
- Sin breaks Koinonia with God.
- Discipline and judgment of God are expressions of His love.

DAY 2   ESSENTIALS OF KOINONIA, PART 1

Koinonia with God is an experience of His presence.

Koinonia (a love relationship, intimate fellowship) with God is the basic element of salvation and eternal life (John 17:3). God takes the initiative to invite you into a love relationship. He places His Holy Spirit in you to enable you to live in a right relationship with Him. No human method or list of steps to follow can maintain fellowship with God. Koinonia with God is an experience of His presence. Although God does take the initiative, you must respond to God in order to fully experience His presence.

The seven realities of experiencing God identify the way you come to know God by experience. I have personalized the statements for you below. Check your memory and fill in the blanks. Then check your work on the inside back cover.

1. _____ is always at work around you.

2. God pursues a continuing love _____ with you that is real and
   _____.

3. God invites you to become _____ with Him in His _____.

4. God speaks by the _____ _____ through the Bible, _____,
   circumstances, and the _____ to reveal Himself, His _____, and
   His ways.

5. God's invitation for you to work with Him always leads you to a crisis of
   _____ that requires _____ and action.

6. You must make major _____ in your life to join God in
   what He is doing.

7. You come to know God by _____ as you
   _____ Him and He accomplishes His work through you.

Notice that the last three realities identify your response to God's initiative:
- You must act on faith in Him.
- You must make major adjustments to Him.
- You must obey Him.

When you respond to God's initiative, you come to know Him intimately by experience. Living in faithful obedience to Him allows you to experience His presence. This is Koinonia with God.

Continuing in fellowship with God does not happen by accident. This fellowship can be broken. Sometimes what seems to be a good intention can turn out to be a threat to fellowship with God and with our Christian brothers and sisters. To see how fellowship can be threatened or broken, we need to identify some essentials of genuine Koinonia with God.

ESSENTIALS OF KOINONIA

1. We must love God with our total beings.
2. We must submit to God's sovereign rule.
3. We must experience God in a real and personal way.
4. We must trust completely in God.

Essentials of Koinonia

1. We must love God with our total beings. "This is the first and greatest commandment" (Matt. 22:37-38). If you love God, you will obey Him (John 14:21-24). If you love Him, you also will love your brother (1 John 4:21; 5:3). If your fellowship with God is right—if you love Him with your total being—you will even be able to love your enemies.

The threat to fellowship is anything that causes you to lose your "first love" for God. This was the problem with the church at Ephesus (Rev. 2:1-7).

Read 1 John 2:15-16 at the left and list below some things that can threaten or compete with your love for God.

_____

_____

_____

Loving money or things more than God will break your fellowship with Him. Your sinful cravings and lust can capture your first love. You can even fall in love with what you have or what you are able to do. When your love is not pure toward God, fellowship with God is broken. Your fellowship with others will then reflect your broken fellowship with God.

For example: Suppose a person begins to love things more than God. When fellowship with God is broken, love for others will suffer. A person who loves things more than God will become stingy and greedy. When he sees a brother in need, he will keep *his* "things" to use for himself. He will not give to help others. He probably will even start using God's tithe (tenth) for himself. Greed is very dangerous (Eph. 5:5; 1 John 3:17).

Materialism is a terrible trap that robs many people of their love for God. Churches also can be selfish and greedy. This will cause them to use God's resources primarily on themselves rather than to help a lost and needy world.

What is one essential of Koinonia?

1. _____

Name at least two things that can threaten Koinonia by interfering with your love for God.

_____

2. We must submit to God's sovereign rule. God is your Master. Because of His perfect love for you, He demands absolute obedience. As Head of the church, Christ demands submission to Him and obedience to His will. Absolute surrender to His lordship is necessary for right fellowship with God.

Love God

"Jesus replied: ' "Love the Lord your God with all your heart and with all your soul and with all your mind." This is the first and greatest commandment.' "
—Matthew 22:37-38

"Do not love the world or anything in the world. If anyone loves the world, the love of the Father is not in him. For everything in the world—the cravings of sinful man, the lust of his eyes and the boasting of what he has and does—comes not from the Father but from the world."
—1 John 2:15-16

Submit to God

When a person becomes "a law unto himself," and does "what is right in his own eyes," the experience of Koinonia becomes impossible in his life, and often in the life of a church. Yielding your loyalty or allegiance to anyone other than Christ is spiritual adultery. If a pastor, the deacons, influential business persons, or a committee tries to "run" or rule the church, Koinonia is threatened.

The problem always starts with an individual's (or church's) relationship to God. When a person refuses to deny self and follow Christ, fellowship with God is broken. When self is in control, all other authority relationships will be out of control. Asserting self in the body of Christ robs Christ of His rightful authority as Head of the body.

Every member of the church must submit to the lordship of Christ over his own life and Christ's headship over the church.

Not only is fellowship broken when an individual tries to be head of the church, but it also is broken when the church expects their pastor, other individual, or group to rule the church. No individual or group can function as head of the body and that church be a healthy body. It may look healthy on the outside, but God sees the rebellion against His Son's rule and hates it. Every member of the church must submit to the lordship of Christ over his own life and Christ's headship over the church.

In your opinion, who does your church look to as the head of your church?

_____

In 1 Corinthians 1—3, divisions (broken fellowship) existed in the church because some were following Paul, some were following Apollos, and some were following Peter (Cephas). Paul condemned this kind of rebellion. He rebuked any attempt to follow anyone other than Christ. To follow him or Apollos would be childish, worldly, and ungodly (1 Cor. 3:1-4). The church must have the "mind of Christ" (1 Cor. 2:16) and follow Christ alone.

Koinonia is impossible if a church is made up of individuals who are unwilling to submit to the Lordship of Christ in the body of Christ. The same impossibility exists in a larger body of fellowship (association or denomination) where pastors and other participants refuse to submit to the lordship of Christ and function in that body under Christ's rule. Anything or anyone who hinders or usurps God's rule in your life, in the church, or in the larger bodies of the Kingdom causes broken fellowship with God. When fellowship with God breaks down, it is reflected in broken fellowship with others.

In your opinion, who is looked to as the head of your denomination?

_____

What is a second essential of Koinonia?

1. We must love God with our total beings.

2. _____

Describe how interference with Christ's rule threatens Koinonia in a church.

_____

_____

_____

In all honesty before God, who is Lord and Master of your life? Check one.
❏ Jesus Christ is.
❏ I am.
❏ My spouse is.
❏ My job is.
❏ Money and things are.
Other? _____

Today's lesson is shorter than most so you will have time to pray. Take time to pray. Pray through this lesson and . . .
- **Ask God if anything in your life is causing you to lose your first love for Him. Do you love anything more than Him? If He reveals anything, confess it and return to your first love.**
- **Ask God if you are absolutely given to His lordship in your life.**
- **Ask God if you are allowing Jesus to function as Head of your church.**

- Pray for your spouse, your family, your church, and your denomination that God will be allowed to rule in every heart.

Review today's lesson. Pray and ask God to identify one or more statements or Scriptures that He wants you to understand, learn, or practice. Underline it (them). Then respond to the following:

What was the most meaningful statement or Scripture you read today?

_____

_____

Reword the statement or Scripture into a prayer of response to God.

_____

_____

_____

What does God want you to do in response to today's study?

_____

_____

SUMMARY STATEMENTS

- Koinonia with God is an experience of His presence.
- Koinonia with God is the basic element of salvation and eternal life.
- I must love God with my total being.
- I must submit to God's sovereign rule.
- Koinonia is possible only if a church is made up of individuals who are willing to submit to the lordship of Christ in the body of Christ.

ESSENTIALS OF KOINONIA, PART 2

Only a personal encounter with the living Christ will result in an effectively functioning Koinonia.

Yesterday you learned that Koinonia with God requires that you love God with your total being and that you submit to His sovereign rule in your life. Many people, things, and influences in your life and in your church can threaten your fellowship with God if you allow them to distract you from loving Him and following Him. Today, I want you to look at two more essentials of Koinonia and the possible threats to your fellowship with God.

Experience God

3. We must experience God in a real and personal way. Your Koinonia with God is based on your personal experience with Him. No substitutes will do. You cannot rely on the personal experience of your spouse, your parents, your pastor, your Sunday School teacher, or your fellow church members. Your Koinonia with God must be *real* and *personal*.

The threat to Koinonia comes when you allow anyone or anything to make you a spectator rather than an active participant in relationship to God. You must encounter God firsthand; or you will become passive, apathetic, or just drop out all together. You must continually encounter God firsthand or your fellowship with God will grow cold. You will quit caring about the concerns of God for His church, for the Kingdom, or for the lost world.

What are some things that happen in churches that can tempt a person to become more of a spectator than an active participant?

_____

_____

_____

_____

What is one way in which you have substituted a "spectator religion" for a personal and real experience of God?

_____

Although organizations and programs are designed to promote outreach, growth, and ministry, they can lead to shallow relationships and indifference. If a church is not careful, it may be helping people experience a program and miss a personal encounter with the living Christ. Well organized programs, plans, methods, and Bible studies are valuable but they must not take the place of the creative experience of the personal guidance of the Holy Spirit. This does not mean that churches should not be organized. But they must be careful that the organization encourages personal experiences with God.

Spiritual truths and realities that already have been experienced by others must not be taught just for the sake of knowledge. Instead, persons must be led to experiences where God reveals the same spiritual truth or reality in a personal way to the individual believer. Secondhand experiences will not do.

Agencies of a denomination, for instance, have a place in doing God's will in ways that individual churches cannot accomplish alone. Yet individuals and churches must not allow the work of the denomination to become a substitute for their personal involvement in God's work. This can lead to social and spiritual indifference rather than responsible involvement and participation. Only a personal encounter with the living Christ will result in an effectively functioning Koinonia.

What are some things your denomination is able to do that most churches could not do alone?

_____

_____

In what way could reliance on these good things, if misused, become a hindrance to a real and personal encounter with God?

_____

_____

This is not an "either/or" situation. It is a "both/and" situation. Denominations, programs, methods, prepared study materials, and so forth are helpful tools for churches. But, they must not become substitutes for personal encounters with God. Each individual needs to experience the presence of the Lord at work in his or her life. Individuals experience Koinonia when they follow God's leadership and are empowered by the Holy Spirit to accomplish God's purposes.

When programs and ministries become ends instead of means, activity for activity's sake, or just superficial signs of success, then Koinonia is in grave danger of being obscured and lost. Churches must not just concern themselves with numerical results. They must look carefully at the motive and inner spirit of their work. Are lives being transformed? Are broken people finding spiritual and emotional healing? Are people personally encountering a living Christ at work in the midst of the church? If not, something is wrong with the personal relationships of members to God.

What is a third essential of Koinonia?

1. We must love God with our total beings.
2. We must submit to God's sovereign rule.
3. _____

What are some things in a church that can take the place of a real and personal encounter with God?

_____

_____

_____

What is one thing in your past that you have allowed to take the place of a personal experience with God? (One person might say, "I gave money to the church, but I avoided getting personally involved in God's work through my church. I never

experienced a sense of personal involvement in what God was doing through my church.")

_____

_____

4. We must trust completely in God. You must depend on the Holy Spirit to do the things only God can do. You must trust in God alone.

Trust God

Once when Israel was faced with trouble, they turned to Egypt for help rather than to the Lord. God said to them:

> "Woe to those who go down to Egypt for help, who rely on horses, who trust in the multitude of their chariots and in the great strength of their horsemen, but do not look to the Holy One of Israel, or seek help from the Lord" (Isa. 31:1).

What are some things or people in which a church may be tempted to place their trust? (For instance, a church may trust in some wealthy givers who provide financial stability rather than trust in the God who provides through His people.)

_____

_____

_____

Placing your trust in anything other than God breaks your fellowship with Him. Trusting in any of the following things to accomplish God's work instead of trusting in God will break fellowship with Him:
- yourself, your abilities, your resources
- other people, their abilities, their resources
- programs or methods
- manipulation or coercion
- pressure tactics or guilt
- deceit
- and others

God provides people, relationships, resources, methods, and programs to be used by a church. However, a church that yields to the temptation to trust in these rather than the Lord, will displease Him. Your church may be tempted to trust in yourselves; your pastor; a well-organized Bible study program; a denominational agency; a bank; an outreach method; the government; or other organizations, people, or things. When you depend on any of these rather than God to accomplish His work in a church, fellowship with God and other believers is broken. Sometimes leaders try to use pressure tactics to get members to do God's will. That, too, denies God's power to guide His people Himself. Then when conflict arises, leaders may depend on a manual on handling church conflict instead of leading people back to trusting in God and loving Him alone.

The Holy Spirit manifests Himself through believers and empowers them to accomplish God-sized tasks. God grows His church. The Holy Spirit produces unity. Christ brings forth the spiritual fruit. You and your church must depend on God to accomplish His purposes in His ways through you. Completely depend on God.

Yes, He will call on you to join Him. Yes, He will ask you to do some things through which He will work. Often He will lead you to a program or method to help you organize and function to accomplish what He purposes. He will call on you to use your money, resources, skills, and abilities. But, in everything you must depend on God's guidance, provision, gifts, and power if you hope to bear lasting fruit. Without Him, you can do *nothing* (John 15:5). His presence creates and maintains fellowship, and He bears lasting spiritual fruit through an obedient and trusting people.

"I am the vine; you are the branches. If a man remains in me and I in him, he will bear much fruit; apart from me you can do nothing."
—John 15:5

What is the fourth essential of Koinonia?

1. We must love God with our total beings.
2. We must submit to God's sovereign rule.
3. We must experience God in a real and personal way.
4. _____

Name one thing you have been tempted to place your trust in rather than in God.

_____

_____

Once again take time to pray. Pray through today's lesson. Ask God to identify ways you have missed experiencing Him by substituting religious practices for personal encounters with Him. Ask Him to reveal any ways you are trusting in other people or other things rather than in the Lord your Provider.

Pray also for your church and ways the church may unknowingly be encouraging people to substitute religion for personal experiences with God. Pray that your church will always trust only in the Lord and Him alone.

Review today's lesson. Pray and ask God to identify one or more statements or Scriptures that He wants you to understand, learn, or practice. Underline it (them). Then respond to the following:

What was the most meaningful statement or Scripture you read today?

_____

_____

Reword the statement or Scripture into a prayer of response to God.

_____

_____

_____

What does God want you to do in response to today's study?

_____

_____

Practice quoting or writing your Scripture memory verses.

SUMMARY STATEMENTS

- I must experience God in a real and personal way.
- I must trust completely in God.

DAY 4

HELPING EACH OTHER

We must help each other learn to obey everything Christ commanded.

Christians need each other. That is why God places us in a church—the body of Christ. As we experience God at work in the body of believers, we know God in ways we would not know Him apart from the body. Christ dwells in every believer (John 17:23, 26; Col. 1:27), and believers are in Christ (John 17:21; 2 Cor. 5:17). We need to help each other continue in right fellowship with God and with each other.

Because the living Christ is in every believer, which of the following is true? Check one.
 ❏ 1. I cannot experience God as He works in and through other believers.
 ❏ 2. I can experience God as He works in and through other believers.

Outside the body you do not have access to all the parts of the body that are necessary to help you become a complete person.

You can experience God through relationships with other believers as He works in and through their lives. God can speak to me through you. He can speak through any member of the church at any time He chooses. That is why we need each other. Since we were created to function as a body, we cannot be healthy apart from an intimate relationship with other believers. Outside the body you do not have access to all the parts of the body that are necessary to help you become a complete person. Fellowship with the body of Christ is an important part of fellowship with God.

Helping Each Other in Discipleship

In Jesus' commission to His church He said, "Go and make disciples of all nations . . . teaching them to obey everything I have commanded you" (Matt. 28:19-20). Jesus didn't say "teach them what I commanded." He said, "teach them to obey everything I have commanded." What an assignment! Our role as a church in the life of a new believer is not complete until we help him or her learn to *obey everything* Christ commanded.

A person could *learn* what Christ commanded by reading the Bible. Certainly he needs to do that. But learning to *obey* everything is a different matter. God knew that new believers would have a hard time practicing and obeying everything. That is why He puts believers into a body of Christ. Learning to follow Christ is a life-long process. You do not learn to follow Him all by yourself.

Paul said to Timothy, "The things you have heard me say in the presence of many witnesses entrust to reliable men who will also be qualified to teach others" (2 Tim. 2:2). Paul taught in a group setting. His relationship with Timothy was not primarily one-on-one discipleship training. Paul taught in the context of the body.

No one can become the kind of complete believer he ought to be outside the functioning body of a New Testament church. Why? Because God has set the discipling process in a body. A person who is saved is called out and added to a spiritual body where Christ is the Head. A person is only one part of the body, and he absolutely needs every other part of the body to help him function properly.

No one can become the kind of complete believer he ought to be outside the functioning body of a New Testament church.

Read the following list. Check the reasons why learning to follow Christ within the body of Christ is better than trying to grow into maturity by yourself. Check all that you believe are good reasons for group discipleship training.

❏ 1. When I get discouraged, others in the body can encourage me to go on.
❏ 2. Closely observing a godly Christian's life challenges me to want to live close to the Lord too.
❏ 3. I can best learn how to live as a Christian when I see someone else giving me an example to follow.
❏ 4. When I stray from truth or yield to false teaching, God can correct me through His Word, the Holy Spirit, and the church.
❏ 5. When I fall into sin, Christian brothers and sisters can lovingly correct me and call me to repent and return to the Lord.
❏ 6. When God gives spiritual understanding to a fellow believer, I can learn that same truth as the person shares it and the Holy Spirit affirms it.
❏ 7. I can come to know God's will for my role in the body of Christ through the affirmation of other members in the body.
❏ 8. I get excited when I experience God working through me to touch deeply the life of another believer.
❏ 9. I feel fulfilled when God uses me in a way that builds up the body and helps others grow toward maturity.

List any other reasons you can think of that explain why learning to follow Christ in a body of believers is better than trying to follow Him alone.

_____

_____

Describe one way your *Experiencing God* small group has helped you grow spiritually that would not have happened if you had tried to study this book by yourself.

_____

_____

If a friend of yours wanted to study this course, what reasons would you give him or her for participating in the small-group study rather than trying to do the study alone?

_____

_____

"It was he who gave some to be apostles, some to be prophets, some to be evangelists, and some to be pastors and teachers, to prepare God's people for works of service, so that the body of Christ may be built up until we all reach unity in the faith and in the knowledge of the Son of God and become mature, attaining to the whole measure of the fullness of Christ."

—Ephesians 4:11-13

God wants every believer to grow into maturity and become like Christ. Any ministry, spiritual gift, or equipping of service that God gives to a believer is for the body of Christ (Eph. 4:11-13). Apart from the body, a gift or a ministry is out of context. But, when all parts of the body function where God puts them in the body, the whole body grows up in love to experience the fullness of Christ.

> **Your Scripture memory verses for this week tell some ways we can help each other. What does Hebrews 10:24-25 say? Write them below:**
>
> _____
> _____
> _____
> _____
> _____
>
> **What is one way you can "spur" other believers on toward loving God, each other, and the lost world?**
>
> _____
>
> **What is one way you can "spur" other believers on toward good deeds?**
>
> _____
>
> **What are two ways you can "encourage" other believers as you meet together for worship, study, and fellowship?**
>
> _____
> _____

Experiencing God is only one of many LIFE—Lay Institute For Equipping—courses designed to equip the laity in discipleship, leadership, and ministry. Two courses are especially helpful to a believer in the very basic disciplines of his or her walk with the Lord.

> **Read the following descriptions. Pray about whether God would have you continue your growth in discipleship by studying one of these other LIFE courses.**

MasterLife: Discipleship Training by Avery T. Willis, Jr. is considered the core curriculum for LIFE. MasterLife helps you lay a strong foundation in your life as you learn to abide in Christ. It teaches the disciplines of Living in the Word, Praying in Faith, Fellowshiping with Believers, and Witnessing to the World. Then it guides you to allow God to work through you in ministry to others. MasterLife is being used in over 115 countries of the world, in 50 or more languages, and by people in over 30 different denominations. If your church does not have a certified MasterLife leader, or if you need information about basic English or other language editions, write to the Adult Discipleship and Family Department address given later in this unit.

Disciple's Prayer Life: Walking in Fellowship with God by T. W. Hunt and Catherine Walker teaches you to develop an effective prayer life based on the principles used in the prayers of the Bible. It gives you very practical helps to deepen your fellowship with God as you pray. PrayerLife will inspire you to develop and practice a life of praying with and for others. Helps for a personal and a church ministry of intercessory prayer also are provided. PrayerLife does not require a certified leader.

> **Do you sense God wants you involved in one of these LIFE courses? If so, draw a star in the margin beside the description and write yourself a note. Now read about two other courses that may be helpful to you.**

BibleGuide to Discipleship and Doctrine by Avery T. Willis, Jr. teaches you 13 Bible study methods to use in studying doctrine and applying the teaching of Scripture to life in Christian discipline and ministry. The practical study and application helps in the Disciple's Study Bible (required for the course) make this a foundational study for a lifetime of following Jesus Christ as your Life Guide.

MasterDesign: Your Calling as a Christian by Tommy Lea and Curtis Vaughn guides you through an inductive Bible study of the Book of Ephesians. This study teaches you how to study the Bible in order to dig out biblical truths for yourself and apply them to your life. It also helps you understand the teachings of Ephesians for the church and for your own calling as a Christian.

Other LIFE courses provide training in leadership skills, Bible study and ministry skills, lay counseling, commitment counseling during invitations, parenting, and marriage enrichment. For more information about LIFE courses or other Adult Discipleship Training resources write to: Adult Discipleship and Family Department, 127 Ninth Avenue, North, MSN 151, Nashville, TN 37234.

Helping Each Other in Worship

You have learned that one essential of Koinonia with God is that we must experience God in a real and personal way. To continue in this fellowship with God, your worship of Him must be real and personal encounters with Him.

Read the following passages on the worship of the New Testament churches. Underline the things they did in their worship services.

> **Acts 2:42, 46-47**—"They devoted themselves to the apostles' teaching and to the fellowship, to the breaking of bread and to prayer. Every day they continued to meet together in the temple courts. They broke bread in their homes and ate together with glad and sincere hearts, praising God and enjoying the favor of all the people. And the Lord added to their number daily those who were being saved."

> **Ephesians 5:19-20**—"Speak to one another with psalms, hymns and spiritual songs. Sing and make music in your heart to the Lord, always giving thanks to God the Father for everything, in the name of our Lord Jesus Christ."

> **1 Corinthians 14:26, 29-33**—"When you come together, everyone has a hymn, or a word of instruction, a revelation, a tongue or an interpretation. All of these must be done for the strengthening of the church. Two or three prophets should speak, and the others should weigh carefully what is said. And if a revelation comes to someone who is sitting down, the first speaker should stop. For you can all prophesy in turn so that everyone may be instructed and encouraged. The spirits of prophets are subject to the control of prophets. For God is not a God of disorder but of peace."

Since the New Testament church functioned as a Koinonia of the Spirit, no member of the early churches had an exclusive monopoly on any of the gifts given to the church. On the contrary, when the congregation assembled for worship, each member was a potential contributor to the service. The primary requirement was that each contribution help build up the life of the total Christian community.

If worship experiences are going to improve your fellowship with God, they must lead you to experience Him in real and personal ways. When worship services encourage passive response, when they encourage you to be a spectator rather than a participant, when they focus on people and programs rather than God, they may lead to coldness, apathy, doubt, conflict, and a host of other problems.

In your opinion, which of the following best describes your personal experiences in most worship services of your church? Check one.

❏ 1. I sense God's presence. I sense God instructs me. I rejoice with others at what God is doing in our midst. I am encouraged to live like Christ during the coming week.

❏ 2. I sometimes experience God doing things in my life and in our church. Most of the time I go home feeling about like I did when I came.

❏ 3. I seldom experience God doing anything in our worship service. They seem to be cold and mere ritual.

Other: _____

_____

Prior to worship, how much time do you normally spend preparing your heart?

_____

If you sense that you are not experiencing worship the way you should, ask God to guide your prayers for the worship leaders and for your own preparation and participation. How does God want you to pray for the worship leaders of your church?

_____

_____

What do you sense you ought to do to better prepare yourself for worship?

_____

Helping Each Other Obey

A little girl wouldn't obey

Once I visited in the home of a couple that had a three-year-old child. When the parents said, "Come here," the little girl would run the opposite way. The parents and grandparents would just say, "Isn't that cute."

One day the little girl was playing in the front yard. The gate was open, and she ran out between two parked cars. The mother, seeing a car coming down the street, shouted to the little girl, "Come here!" The little girl laughed and walked straight out in front of the oncoming car and was killed. That was the very first funeral I ever had to conduct.

If you see your children doing something wrong do you ever correct them or punish them? If you love them, you do. Hebrews 12:6 describes God's discipline as love. Correction, discipline, and punishment can be expressions of perfect love. We must help each other learn to obey everything Christ commanded.

If you see a Christian brother or sister doing something that is going to hurt him or her, which of the following would be an expression of God-like love? Check your response.
- ❏ 1. I would never say anything in the way of correction that might offend him.
- ❏ 2. I want to be open-minded, so I would tolerate her wrong behavior.
- ❏ 3. I would give a subtle hint and hope that he gets the message.
- ❏ 4. I would go to her privately and share my concern for her well being, and I would share a Scripture that gives a word of correction.
- ❏ 5. I would go straight to the church and suggest we kick him out of the church.

Many modern day churches have shied away from discipline in the church. One reason is that sometimes church discipline was abused in years past. Churches used discipline in frivolous or vindictive ways that did not demonstrate a loving and caring spirit (like #5 above). As a pastor, I determined I would not get upset because people were spiritually sick. I just saw that as the reason God put me there. I set about to love them back to health. I have never found God's people unresponsive when correction comes as a genuine demonstration of love.

"The Lord disciplines those he loves, and he punishes everyone he accepts as a son."
—Hebrews 12:6

Loving discipline

When God disciplines His children, He is demonstrating perfect love for them (Heb. 12:6). If we love our brothers and sisters we will discipline them in a loving manner to help them return to fellowship with God. This is a way we can help each other, but it must be done only out of a spirit of love. The Bible gives us some guidelines about loving discipline:

> "If your brother sins against you, go and show him his fault, just between the two of you. If he listens to you, you have won your brother over. But if he will not listen, take one or two others along, so that 'every matter may be established by the testimony of two or three witnesses.' If he refuses to listen to them, tell it to the church; and if he refuses to listen even to the church, treat him as you would a pagan or a tax collector" (Matt. 18:15-17).

In Matthew 18:15-17 Jesus gave four stages for trying to restore a wayward brother. What are the four stages?

_____

_____

_____

Do you remember the instructions of 1 Corinthians 13 about godly love? Love will be patient and kind. Some who have strayed may require much loving before they return. Loving discipline requires that you first approach a person privately. Any discipline should only come at God's direction. Loving discipline will call for much fervent prayer. Do not be hasty in moving to stages two, three, or four. You, too, are a sinner saved by God's grace. Someday you may need the loving correction of a Christian friend. Treat others as you would want to be treated. In so doing you may win the lasting friendship of your Christian brother or sister.

☀ **Review today's lesson. Pray and ask God to identify one or more statements or Scriptures that He wants you to understand, learn, or practice. Underline it (them). Then respond to the following:**

What was the most meaningful statement or Scripture you read today?

_____

_____

Reword the statement or Scripture into a prayer of response to God.

_____

_____

_____

_____

What does God want you to do in response to today's study?

_____

_____

_____

SUMMARY STATEMENTS

- Christians need each other.
- We must help each other learn to obey everything Christ commanded.
- Worship of God must be real and personal encounters with Him.

YOUR SPIRITUAL INVENTORY

What God has begun in your life He Himself will bring to perfect completion!

"He who began a good work in you will carry it on to completion until the day of Christ Jesus."
—Philippians 1:6

Review

Several months ago we began this journey together. My prayer has been that you would come to know God more intimately as you experienced Him at work in and through your life. Today, I want you to briefly review the past 12 units and identify what God has been doing in your life. Then, I want you to spend time with the Lord taking a spiritual inventory of your present walk with Him. If God has been working in your life through these studies, He has been preparing you for more intimate fellowship with Himself and for assignments in His kingdom. I hope you have come to this time with a deep sense of God's presence and activity in your life. What God has begun in your life He Himself will bring to perfect completion! (Phil. 1:6)

☀ **A. Using the hints below, in your own words write the seven realities of experiencing God.**

1. God's work— _____

2. Love relationship— _____

_____

3. God invites— _____

_____

4. God speaks— _____

_____

_____

5. Crisis of belief— _____

_____

6. Major adjustments— _____

_____

7. Obey Him— _____

_____

B. Which of these realities has been the most meaningful to you and why?

_____

_____

C. Review your 12 memory verses. Which one has been the most meaningful to you and why?

_____

_____

D. Briefly review some of your end of the day responses. Which statement or Scripture has God used to touch your life most deeply?

_____

_____

E. How did God use that statement or Scripture in your life?

_____

_____

F. Describe your most meaningful experience of God during your study of *Experiencing God*.

_____

_____

G. What name of God has become the most meaningful to you and how?

_____

_____

Spiritual checkup

Why

Pray and ask the Holy Spirit to guide your thoughts as you respond to the following.

H. Which of the following best describes how you feel about your love relationship with God? Check one or more.

❑ 1. Grows sweeter every day   ❑ 6. Needs a tune-up
❑ 2. A roller coaster ride   ❑ 7. Cold
❑ 3. Bubbling over with joy   ❑ 8. Solid as a rock
❑ 4. Lukewarm   ❑ 9. Deep and wide
❑ 5. A tree planted by the water

Other: _____

I. Which of the following best describes how you feel about your relationship with your church, the body of Christ? Check one or more.

❏ 1. Ready for a marathon
❏ 2. In training
❏ 3. Out of shape
❏ 4. Recuperating at home
❏ 5. In for tests

❏ 6. In the progressive care unit
❏ 7. Satisfactory condition
❏ 8. Critical condition
❏ 9. In intensive care
Other: _____

J. What is your greatest spiritual challenge?

_____

_____

K. What would be the most meaningful thing your small group could pray about for your spiritual growth and walk with the Lord?

_____

_____

L. What do you sense God would have you do next to continue your training as a disciple of Jesus Christ?

_____

_____

M. What, if any, specific assignment(s) do you sense God has called you to join Him in doing?

_____

_____

N. How are you praying for your church and her relationship to Christ?

Others

_____

_____

O. What does God want you to do to help others in their walk with the Lord? Check any that you sense God leading you to do or fill in the blank.
❏ 1. Bear witness to what God has done and is doing in my life.
❏ 2. Help a group I already work with to know and experience God this way.
❏ 3. Offer to lead a group study of *Experiencing God: Knowing and Doing the Will of God.*
❏ 4. Encourage others to participate in a study of *Experiencing God.*
❏ 5. Lead a group study of *MasterLife, Disciple's Prayer Life, DecisionTime, MasterDesign, BibleGuide,* or other LIFE course.
❏ 6. Lead a group in some other training course in Christian discipleship.

Other: _____

Take some time to pray. Thank God for what He has done and what He is doing . . .

- in your life
- in your family
- in your small group

- in your church
- in your denomination
- in the world

God has been so gracious to allow me to join Him as He has been working in your life. I thank God and praise Him for the many wonderful things He has done in our day. Now...

I pray that out of his glorious riches he may strengthen you with power through his Spirit in your inner being, so that Christ may dwell in your hearts through faith. And I pray that you, being rooted and established in love, may have power, together with all the saints, to grasp how wide and long and high and deep is the love of Christ, and to know this love that surpasses knowledge —that you may be filled to the measure of all the fullness of God.

Now to him who is able to do immeasurably more than all we ask or imagine, according to his power that is at work within us, to him be glory in the church and in Christ Jesus throughout all generations, for ever and ever! Amen.

APPENDIX A: NAMES, TITLES, AND DESCRIPTIONS OF GOD

The following are names, titles, and descriptions of God found in the New International Version of the Bible.

FATHER

a faithful God who does no wrong
a forgiving God
a fortress of salvation
a glorious crown
a jealous and avenging God
a Master in heaven
a refuge for his people
a refuge for the needy in his distress
a refuge for the oppressed
a refuge for the poor
a sanctuary
a shade from the heat
a shelter from the storm
a source of strength
a stronghold in times of trouble
an ever present help in trouble
architect and builder
builder of everything
commander of the Lord's army
Creator of heaven and earth
defender of widows
eternal King
Father
Father of compassion
Father of our spirits
Father of the heavenly lights
father to the fatherless
God
God Almighty (El Sabaoth)
God Almighty (El Shaddai)
God and Father of our Lord Jesus Christ
God Most High
God my Maker
God my Rock
God my Savior
God my stronghold
God of Abraham, Isaac, and Jacob
God of all comfort
God of all mankind
God of glory
God of gods
God of grace
God of hope
God of love and peace
God of peace
God of retribution
God of the living
God of the spirits of all mankind
God of truth
God our Father
God our strength
God over all the kingdoms of the earth
God the Father
God who avenges me

God who gives endurance and
    encouragement
God who relents from sending calamity
great and awesome God
great and powerful God
great, mighty and awesome God
he who blots out your transgressions
he who comforts you
he who forms the hearts of all
he who raised Christ from the dead
he who reveals his thoughts to man
Helper of the fatherless
him who is able to do immeasurably more
    than all we ask or imagine
him who is able to keep you from falling
him who is ready to judge the living and
    the dead
Holy Father
Holy One
Holy One among you
I AM
I AM WHO I AM
Jealous
Judge of all the earth
King of glory
King of heaven
living and true God
Lord (Adonai)
Lord Almighty
Lord God Almighty
Lord is Peace
Lord (Jehovah)
Lord Most High
Lord my Banner
Lord my Rock
Lord of all the earth
Lord of heaven and earth
Lord of kings
Lord our God
Lord our Maker
Lord our shield
Lord who heals you
Lord who is there
Lord who makes you holy
Lord who strikes the blow
Lord will Provide
love
Maker of all things
Maker of heaven and earth
Most High
my advocate
my Comforter in sorrow
my confidence
my help
my helper
my hiding place
my hope
my light
my mighty rock
my refuge in the day of disaster
my refuge in times of trouble

my song
my strong deliverer
my support
One to be feared
only wise God
our dwelling place
our judge
our lawgiver
our leader
our Mighty One
Our Redeemer
our refuge and strength
Righteous Father
righteous judge
Rock of our salvation
Shepherd
Sovereign Lord
the Almighty
the compassionate and gracious God
the Eternal God
the consuming fire
the everlasting God
the exalted God
the faithful God
the gardener (husbandman)
the glorious Father
the Glory of Israel
the God who saves me
the God who sees me
the great King above all gods
the just and mighty One
the living Father
the Majestic Glory
the Majesty in heaven
the one who sustains me
the only God
the potter
the rock in whom I take refuge
the spring of living water
the strength of my heart
the true God
you who hear prayer
you who judge righteously and test the
    heart and mind
you who keep your covenant of love with
    your servants
you who love the people
your glory
your praise
your very great reward

JESUS

a banner for the peoples
a Nazarene
all
Alpha and Omega
Ancient of Days
Anointed One
apostle and high priest

author and perfecter of our faith
author of life
author of their salvation
blessed and only Ruler
Branch of the Lord
bread of God
bread of life
bridegroom
chief cornerstone
Chief Shepherd
chosen and precious cornerstone
Christ Jesus my Lord
Christ Jesus our hope
Christ of God
consolation of Israel
covenant for the people
crown of splendor
eternal life
Faithful and True
faithful and true witness
first to rise from the dead
firstborn from among the dead
firstborn over all creation
firstfruits of those that have fallen asleep
fragrant offering and sacrifice to God
friend of tax collectors and "sinners"
God of all the earth
God over all
God's Son
great high priest
great light
great Shepherd of the sheep
guarantee of a better covenant
he who comes down from heaven and
    gives life to the world
he who searches hearts and minds
head of every man
head of the body, the church
head of the church
head over every power and authority
heir of all things
him who died and came to life again
him who loves us and has freed us from
    our sins
his one and only son
Holy and Righteous One
Holy One of God
holy servant Jesus
hope of Israel
horn of salvation
image of the invisible God
Immanuel (God with us)
indescribable gift
Jesus
Jesus Christ
Jesus Christ our Lord
Jesus Christ our Savior
Jesus of Nazareth
judge of the living and the dead
KING OF KINGS
King of the ages
Lamb of God
light for revelation to the Gentiles
light of life
light of men

light of the world
living bread that came down from heaven
Lord and Savior Jesus Christ
Lord (Kurios)
Lord of glory
LORD OF LORDS
Lord of peace
Lord of the harvest
Lord of the Sabbath
Lord (Rabboni)
man accredited by God
man of sorrows
Master
Mediator of a new covenant
merciful and faithful high priest
messenger of the covenant
Messiah
morning star
my friend
my intercessor
one who makes men holy
one who speaks to the Father in our
    defense
one who will arise to rule over the nations
our glorious Lord Jesus Christ
our God and Savior Jesus Christ
our only Sovereign and Lord
our Passover lamb
our peace
our righteousness, holiness, and
    redemption
Physician
Prince and Savior
Prince of Peace
Prince of princes
Prince of the hosts
ransom for all men
refiner and purifier
resurrection and the life
righteous Judge
righteous man
Righteous One
Rock eternal (rock of ages)
ruler of God's creation
ruler of the kings of the earth
Savior of the world
second man
Shepherd and Overseer of your souls
Son of Man
Son of the Blessed One
Son of the living God
Son of the Most High God
source of eternal salvation
sure foundation
Teacher
the Amen
the atoning sacrifice for our sins
the Beginning and the End
the bright Morning Star
the exact representation of his being
the First and the Last
the gate (door)
the good shepherd
the Head

the last Adam
the life
the Living One
the living Stone
the Lord Our Righteousness
the man from heaven
the man Jesus Christ
the most holy
the One and Only
the only God our Savior
the radiance of God's glory
the rising of the sun (Dayspring)
the stone the builders rejected
the testimony given in its proper time
the true light
the true vine
the truth
the way
the Word (logos)
true bread from heaven
wisdom from God
witness to the peoples
Wonderful Counselor
Word of God
Word of life
your life
your salvation

HOLY SPIRIT

a deposit (earnest)
another Counselor
breath of the Almighty
Holy One
Holy Spirit
Holy Spirit of God
seal
Spirit of Christ
Spirit of counsel and of power
spirit of faith
spirit of fire
Spirit of glory
Spirit of God
spirit of grace and supplication
Spirit of his Son
Spirit of holiness
Spirit of Jesus Christ
spirit of judgment
spirit of justice
Spirit of knowledge and of the fear of
    the Lord
Spirit of life
Spirit of our God
Spirit of sonship (adoption)
Spirit of the living God
Spirit of the Lord
Spirit of the Sovereign Lord
Spirit of truth
Spirit of wisdom and of understanding
Spirit of wisdom and revelation
the gift
the promised Holy Spirit
the same gift
Voice of the Almighty
Voice of the Lord

GROUP COVENANT

Experiencing God

I,_____

covenant with my Experiencing God group to do the following:

1. Complete the study of the Experiencing God workbook each week before the group session.

2. Pray regularly for my fellow group members.

3. Participate in all group sessions unless urgent circumstances beyond my control prevent my attendance. When unable to attend, I will make up the session at the earliest possible time with the group leader or group member assigned.

4. Participate openly and honestly in the group sessions.

5. Keep confidential any personal matters shared by others in the group.

6. Be patient with my Christian brothers and sisters and my church as God works in us all to make us what He wants us to be. I will trust God to convince others of His will. I will not try to manipulate or pressure others to do what I think is best. I will simply bear witness of what I sense God may be saying to us and watch to see how the Spirit uses that witness.

7. Pray at least weekly for my pastor and my church.

Others: _____

_____

_____

_____

_____

_____

Signed: _____ Date: _____

Experiencing God Group Members

_____   _____

_____   _____

_____   _____

The Church Study Course is a Southern Baptist educational system consisting of short courses for adults and youth. More than 500 courses are available in 23 subject areas. Credit is awarded for each course completed. These credits may be applied to one or more of over 125 diploma plans in the recognition system. Diplomas are available for most leadership positions as well as general diplomas for all Christians. These diplomas are the certification that a person has completed from 5 to 8 prescribed courses.

Complete details about the Church Study Course system, courses available, and diplomas offered may be found in a current copy of the Church Study Course Catalog. Study course materials are available from Baptist Book Stores.

The Church Study Course system is sponsored by the Sunday School Board, Woman's Missionary Union, and Brotherhood Commission of the Southern Baptist Convention.

Each course is designed for a minimum of 21/2 hours of combined home and small-group study for a total of 15 hours. An Experiencing God Diploma is awarded for completion of the six courses included in this book. Experiencing God: Knowing and Doing the Will of God is the text for the following six courses in the subject area Christian Growth and Service:

03279 Experiencing God: Introduction (Units 1-2)

03280 Experiencing God: Love Relationship (Units 3-4)

03281 Experiencing God: God Speaks (Units 5-6)

03282 Experiencing God: Major Adjustments (Units 7-8)

03283 Experiencing God: The Church (Units 9-10)

03284 Experiencing God: Kingdom People (Units 11-12)

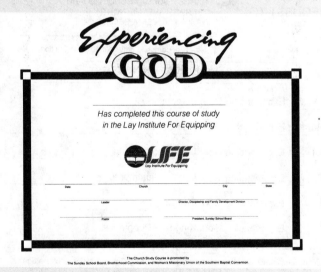

How to Request Credit for These Courses

Credit for these courses may be obtained only through a combination of individual and group study. Read the entire book and complete the learning activities as you read. Attend a group study session for each unit. If you are unable to attend one or more group sessions, make arrangements with the group leader to complete any make-up work he or she may assign.

A request for credit may be made on Form 725 "Church Study Course Enrollment/Credit Request" and sent to the Church Study Course Awards Office, Baptist Sunday School Board, 127 Ninth Avenue, North, Nashville, Tennessee 37234. The form on the following page may be used to request credit. You may photocopy the form if you prefer. A record of your awards will be maintained by the Awards Office. As you remain active in requesting course credits, a copy of your transcript will periodically be sent to your church for distribution to you.

Diploma Completion Record

Check the boxes on the left as you complete the learning activities for the units indicated. Check the boxes on the right for the units you have attended the small group sessions. If you miss a group session, check with your leader to find out what you need to do to make up the work.

Learning Activities	Course Number		Group Sessions
☐	03279	Units 1-2	☐
☐	03280	Units 3-4	☐
☐	03281	Units 5-6	☐
☐	03282	Units 7-8	☐
☐	03283	Units 9-10	☐
☐	03284	Units 11-12	☐

OPTIONAL HELPS FOR *EXPERIENCING GOD*

Experiencing God Video Cassettes (Item 8483-80) — Provides an introductory overview and 12 sessions that involves participants in a study of the Bible to learn how to know God better, how to know when God is speaking, and how to adjust one's life and ministry to God's revelation of His will, plus special helps for leaders. The 15-minute overview may be used to promote participation in the course. Features co-authors Henry Blackaby and Claude King with a live audience.

Experiencing God Audiotapes (Item 5160-43) — Taped live at a Nashville workshop, these audiotapes provide 12 45-minute messages by Henry Blackaby relating directly to the 12 units in the course. In addition, Henry answers questions commonly asked by conferees, with a special emphasis on spiritual leadership. The audiotapes serve as a supplemental resource for personal enrichment. This audiotape series makes it possible for you to listen to Henry in your home or car. The vinyl cassette album includes 12 messages on six C-90 audiotapes .

Pronouncing Bible Names by W. Murray Severance (Item 4691-08) – Pronounce all 3492 proper names in the Bible with confidence, plus names of places, weights and measures, leaders, and more.

Order from the Customer Service Center,
127 Ninth Avenue North, Nashville, Tennessee 37234

Or call 1-800-458-2772.

**CHURCH STUDY COURSE
ENROLLMENT/CREDIT REQUEST**
FORM - 725 (Rev.1/93)

**MAIL THIS
REQUEST TO** ▶

CHURCH STUDY COURSE RESOURCES SECTION
BAPTIST SUNDAY SCHOOL BOARD
127 NINTH AVENUE, NORTH
NASHVILLE, TENNESSEE 37234

Is this the first course taken since 1983? ☐ **YES** If yes, or not sure complete all of Section 1. ☐ **No** If no, complete only bold boxes in Section 1.

SECTION 1 - STUDENT I.D.	SECTION 3 - COURSE CREDIT REQUEST		

SECTION 1 - STUDENT I.D.

Social Security Number | | | – | | | – | | | |

Personal CSC Number* | | | – | | | – | | | |

☐ Mr ☐ Miss ☐ Mrs. ☐   **DATE OF BIRTH** ▶   Month | Day | Year

STUDENT

Name (First, MI, Last)

Street, Route, or P.O.Box

City, State   Zip Code

CHURCH

Church Name

Mailing Address

City, State   Zip Code

SECTION 3 - COURSE CREDIT REQUEST

Course No.	Title (Use exact title)
1. 03-279	Experiencing God: Introduction
2. 03-280	Experiencing God: God Speaks
3. 03-281	Experiencing God: Love Relationship
4. 03-282	Experiencing God: Major Adjustments
5. 03-283	Experiencing God: The Church
6. 03-284	Experiencing God: Kingdom People

SECTION 4 - DIPLOMA/CERTIFICATE ENROLLMENT

Enter exact diploma/certificate title from current Church Study Course catalog. Indicate age group/or area if appropriate. Do not enroll again with each course. When all requirements have been met, the diploma/certificate will be mailed to your church. Enrollment in Christian Development Diplomas is automatic. No charge will be made for enrollment or diplomas/certificates.

SECTION 2 CHANGE REQUEST ONLY (Current Inf. in Section 1)

☐ Former Name

☐ Former Address   Zip Code

☐ Former Church   Zip Code

Title of Diploma/Certificate	Age group or area
Title of Diploma/Certificate	Age group or area
Signature of Pastor, Teacher, or Other Church Leader	Date

*CSC # not required for new students. Others please give CSC # when using SS # for the first time. Then, only one ID # is required. SS# and date of birth requested but not required.